MIXED HERITAGE IN THE FAMILY

# MIXED HERITAGE IN THE FAMILY

## RACIAL IDENTITY, SPOUSAL CHOICE, AND CHILD-REARING

### Carolyn A. Liebler and Miri Song

*Russell Sage Foundation*   NEW YORK

THE RUSSELL SAGE FOUNDATION

The Russell Sage Foundation, one of the oldest of America's general purpose foundations, was established in 1907 by Mrs. Margaret Olivia Sage for "the improvement of social and living conditions in the United States." The foundation seeks to fulfill this mandate by fostering the development and dissemination of knowledge about the country's political, social, and economic problems. While the foundation endeavors to assure the accuracy and objectivity of each book it publishes, the conclusions and interpretations in Russell Sage Foundation publications are those of the authors and not of the foundation, its trustees, or its staff. Publication by Russell Sage, therefore, does not imply foundation endorsement.

ROR: https://ror.org/02yh9se80
DOI: https://doi.org/10.7758/edyf5459

Library of Congress Cataloging in Publication Control Numbers:
2024044600 (print) | LCCN 2024044601 (ebook)
ISBN 9780871545411 (paperback) | ISBN 9781610449359 (ebook)

The paper used in this publication meets the minimum requirements of American National Standard for Information Sciences—Permanence of Paper for Printed Library Materials. ANSI Z39.48-1992.

Text design by Matthew T. Avery. Front matter DOI: https://doi.org/10.7758/edyf5459.7042

RUSSELL SAGE FOUNDATION
112 East 64th Street
New York, New York 10065
10 9 8 7 6 5 4 3 2 1

# CONTENTS

# ILLUSTRATIONS

## Figures

# Tables

# ABOUT THE AUTHORS

CAROLYN A. LIEBLER is a professor of sociology at the University of Minnesota.

MIRI SONG is visiting professor of social policy at the London School of Economics and Political Science and emeritus professor of sociology at the University of Kent.

# ACKNOWLEDGMENTS

We would first like to thank the participants who generously entrusted us with their life stories. We are extremely grateful to them. This project was made possible by a Russell Sage Foundation Presidential Grant (no. 4443). We appreciate and acknowledge Christopher Levesque for his work on developing the RESCI measure (funded in part by the Minnesota Population Center, National Institutes of Health Award no. P2CHD041023). The CUNY Graduate Center Arc Fellowship enabled Miri to pursue the Russell Sage grant with Carolyn. Our thanks to Phil Kasinitz for his friendship and help at CUNY. We have unquestionably produced a more incisive and readable book because of the thoughtful and comprehensive reviews undertaken by three expert reviewers (thank you!) and by Suzanne Nichols of Russell Sage. Many academic colleagues have been a great source of inspiration and wisdom during the writing of this book: In the United States, Jenifer Bratter, Ann Morning, Wendy Roth, and Paul Spickard were particularly helpful, as were many colleagues at the University of Minnesota. On the other side of the pond, Miri thanks Maurice Crul, Rebecca King-O'Riain, Frans Lelie, Dan Rodriguez-Garcia, and Patrick Simon for their friendship and scholarly interchange. A special thanks to John Solomos, whose generosity and wisdom is hugely appreciated. Miri also thanks her many colleagues at the University of Kent, especially Caroline Chatwin, Dawn Lyon, Vince Miller, and Carolyn Pedwell for their encouragement and great company along the way. Carolyn would like to thank her children, Miles Liebren and Avery Liebren, for their solidarity and support as well as her parents and ancestors for their love and guidance. Miri extends her thanks to Charlie Song-Smith, Theo Song-Smith, and Murray Smith, for their interest, love, and support. Miri also thanks her siblings Vivian Song, Paul Song, and Joe Song, and especially her parents Moon-Won Song, and Yung-Hee Song, for their love and encouragement.

# CHAPTER ONE

# IDENTITY, SPOUSE CHOICE, AND CHILD-REARING AMONG MIXED-HERITAGE GROUPS

People have always mixed across racial and ethnic lines.[1] Nevertheless, the persistent increase in the proportion of people who have acknowledged having mixed heritage has engendered important theoretical questions about their social positioning in racially stratified societies such as the United States. The American racial hierarchy has historically placed White people at the top and Black people at the bottom.[2] How might this hierarchy shift with the increase in the number (and visibility) of people who have both White and non-White heritage? Our research delves into the experiences of three such mixed-heritage groups through three important aspects of their personal lives: identity, spouse choice, and child-rearing. The many themes and complexities we have found reveal that there is no single answer to this question.

In the 2010 US census, 2.9 percent of the population was reported as being of two or more races.[3] Although this was an increase from the share of multiracial persons in the 2000 census, it did not reflect the potential share of this population estimated by some researchers. Jennifer Lee and Frank Bean have predicted that one in five Americans could self-identify as multiracial by 2050.[4] The 2020 census results reported 10.2 percent of the US population as multiple-race, though the Census Bureau cautioned against comparing this percentage to the 2010 percentage because it used a new coding strategy for race and Latino-origin responses.[5]

The growth in the number of people with mixed racial heritage raises questions about how we measure and count the multiracial population.

https://doi.org/10.7758/edyf5459.7855

The answer to "who is multiracial?" is far from obvious.[6] How far back in a person's family tree should we go in determining who "counts"? Most extant studies of multiracial people have focused on the offspring of parents who are deemed to be of distinct (single) races, such as a Black parent and a White parent.[7] But this definition of multiracial status obscures the racial mixture that goes further back in many family trees.[8] It also ignores the likelihood that some racial and ethnic ancestries are embraced and transmitted from one generation to the next, while others are forgotten, suppressed, or disregarded.[9] The choice to racially identify with a heritage racial group can depend on a sense of linked fates, a connection to a racially meaningful place, or a wide variety of other factors.[10]

Given the centuries of interracial coupling in the United States, the potential size of the multiracial population is even larger than the 33.8 million seen in the 2020 census results. A person's racial identification can change over their lifetime, and many multiracial people sometimes self-report as single race.[11] In our research, we use the terms "mixed heritage" and "mixed racial heritage" for a person who has ancestors in any generation from more than one socially defined race group, regardless of how the person racially identifies. We use the terms "multiracial" and "biracial" for a mixed-heritage person who reports more than one race group and/or identifies with more than one race group. The racial and ethnic identity choices of people with a mixed racial heritage are fundamental to self-presentation and often drive their other choices, such as who to marry or how to raise children. These decisions and impacts are the focus of our research.

As interracial unions and multiracial people are becoming more ordinary in the United States, racially mixed people have been regarded by some as a bellwether of race relations in the country. The increase in interracial unions and the number of people identifying as multiracial has engendered much debate about whether this growth is evidence that we have entered a postracial era in which racial identities do not impact daily life. For most scholars of race, the response has been a resounding no. While the crisscrossing of historically drawn racial boundaries is undeniable, scholars find that race continues to shape and structure the lives of people in the United States today.[12] The experiences of those in minoritized groups, such as Asian, Black, and

American Indian people, are distinct from each other and also divergent from the experiences of White Americans. How do people of both White and minoritized racial heritages navigate racial boundaries as they raise their families?

More specifically, in this book we ask: *How do a mixed-heritage person's identity choices link to their choice of spouse and the racial identification of their children? Do these choices vary across different mixed-heritage groups? Is there meaningful variation by location in the United States?*

Our project breaks new ground by being the first to combine and integrate the study of three aspects of life—identity, spouse choice, and child-rearing—for people of mixed racial heritage. Asking these three questions allows us to show how complicated racial identification can be, and how it can be expressed in an individual's choice of partner or in how they raise their children. The central contribution of *Mixed Heritage in the Family* is ushering in a new generation—a version 2.0— of "mixed-race studies" (to paraphrase Jayne Ifekwunigwe).[13] It does so by pushing beyond the focus on the individual that has characterized this body of research since the early work by psychologist Maria Root on "the multiracial experience."[14] We investigate multiraciality within a broader social context, interweaving analyses of racial identification, choice of spousal race, and children's racial identification and upbringing. We invite other researchers to consider how the impact of multiracial identification radiates further outward through social networks, via other ties like friendship, neighborhood acquaintances, or workplace collaboration.[15]

To extend our understanding of how identities intertwine with family choices, we take a mixed-methods approach. We use data from the US Census Bureau spanning 1980 through 2019 to gain a big-picture understanding of recent patterns in self-identification, spouse choice, and child identification in the United States. To investigate the impact of racial context on these social processes, we developed an innovative measure, the Racial/Ethnic Spatial Context Indicator (RESCI), that summarizes a wide variety of county characteristics. We used in-depth interviews with sixty-eight mixed-heritage adults about their identity, spouse choice, and parenting to provide nuance and insight into the patterns seen in the Census Bureau data.

Our focus on families in the mixed-heritage population opens an important and understudied area of social research—the intergenerational transmission of racial identities. We investigate whether and how mixed-heritage people, having chosen partners and become parents, transmit, along with their chosen partners, culturally and racially informed perspectives and practices to their children.

All too often, monolithic pronouncements are made about what the growth of the mixed-race population portends for the American racial landscape. Another contribution of this book is showing that there is no singular impact on the US racial hierarchy of the growth in the share of multiracial people and families because there is simply too much variation and diversity among this population, not only in distinctive ethnic and racial backgrounds but in generations and regional locations. We dive into the nuances and complexities of racial categories, as well as their limits, even in the context of being able to "mark one or more" races. Will the United States be defined by a White/non-White divide or a Black/non-Black divide? Will "multiracial" become its own identity? Will growth in the multiracial population blur racial categories and eventually make race less salient?[16]

In fact, these questions may be more difficult to answer than is commonly assumed. Our findings caution against superficial predictions about race relations based on looking simply at how mixed-heritage people identify themselves on government and other official forms. We show that mixed-heritage people's choices about their identities, spouses, and socialization of their children need to be examined in relation to each other, as these choices can influence each other. For example, the racial identity of their spouse can influence the racial identity of a mixed-heritage person, just as a person's racial identity (and the salience of their race more generally) is likely to shape their choice of spouse.

We also innovate by focusing on three types of mixed-heritage people—Black-White, Asian-White, and American Indian/Alaska Native–White (shortened to Native-White). The experiences of these three mixed-heritage groups are not usually compared.[17] We are particularly interested in the intersection of minoritized and White experiences within individuals and families because of their varied histories and social meanings. We aim to contribute to the literature focused on the question of whether people of mixed heritage "lean" more toward one race than another.[18] We show that mixed-heritage people are no monolith; the increase in the size of the multiracial population does not have straightforward consequences for US race relations. At the same time, we show that there are also important areas of convergence among disparate mixed-heritage populations in the United States.

This study's critical consideration of what it means to be a person of mixed racial heritage in the United States today has implications for policymakers, researchers, and social theory. Leveraging both census data and in-depth interviews, we illustrate national social patterns and then dive into an investigation of them using results from our interviews. Throughout the book, we weave together results from these very different sources to triangulate, deepen, and broaden our understanding of the life decisions and family choices of people of mixed racial heritage. Research that uses only quantitative data misses the nuance that comes from interviews, while research that relies solely on interviews is limited by small and nonrandom samples.

Our research explores the variable salience of racial backgrounds within this population—whether and how specific racial ancestries over several generations may become largely symbolic, may continue to mark or disadvantage a person or family, or may be embraced as a touchstone and birthright. The differential impact and intergenerational transmission of racial identification and experiences is important to policymakers aiming to address past and current racism. We inform other researchers about the highly heterogeneous population represented in US race data. The continued increase of people in the US population with racially mixed heritage raises important questions for social theories of race that consider the impact of growing numbers—and greater visibility—of people of mixed racial heritage on the American racial order.

## Integrating Questions About Identity, Spouse Choice, and Child-Rearing Within Families

There is now a very substantial body of research, both quantitative and qualitative going back several decades, about the racial identities and lived experiences of mixed-heritage people in the United States. But most of this research has not considered the key life transitions of multiracial people and how these transitions shape—and are shaped by—their identity. Such life transitions include coming of age and beginning to identify in particular ways, choosing romantic partners, including a spouse, and becoming parents—three life areas that have been generally studied separately by sociologists but that we bring together in this study.

## IDENTITY AND IDENTIFICATION AMONG MIXED-HERITAGE PEOPLE

Given the significant population of adolescents and adults in the United States who have mixed racial heritage, researchers have focused on how they racially identify themselves.[19] The 2015 Pew survey "Multiracial in America," the first large-scale survey of mixed-heritage people to investigate the racial ancestries of this population, was an important contribution to our knowledge about this population. Rather than relying solely upon a respondent's self-reported race, the Pew survey enumerated the mixed-heritage population on the basis of the reported ancestries of parents and grandparents, thus adding generational depth to our understanding of this population.[20] Consistent with this consideration of generational depth, we do not rely on one isolated measure of racial identity or identification.

Despite the burgeoning literature on how mixed-heritage people in the United States report their race (or races), it is important to remember that there can be a significant gap between people who know about multiracial ancestry in their family trees and those who actually self-identify with multiple races.[21] People make a range of choices about which parts of their family tree they will recognize and pass on to younger generations.[22]

Furthermore, a reported race can be understood in many possible ways, and its meaning to the individual should not be assumed to be obvious. Scholars increasingly observe that there are multiple dimensions of race, not a singular meaning or experience attached to it.[23] These multiple dimensions of race—for example, how a person racially identifies on a survey, how they describe themselves to family and friends, and how others see them racially—do not always match.[24] Qualitative studies have shown that physical appearance, parental upbringing (and cultural exposure more generally), and experiences of racial marginalization or prejudice can shape individuals' identity.[25]

A growing body of sociological research shows that ethnic and racial identity development is fluid.[26] Moreover, studies have found that people can vary in how they report their race over time, according to age, gender, and factors such as spatial context, parental race, and how others see them.[27] These studies show that, for example, over time, some individuals change their response from monoracial to multiracial, and then change their response from multiracial to monoracial.[28] Not only may an individual's identifications differ according to context, but self-identity and self-identification may continue to evolve over the life course.[29] Qualitative (and quantitative) studies of mixed people and families have increasingly examined the belief that ethnic and racial identities are relatively stable once individuals have gone through adolescence. Moreover, how others classify a person's race varies depending on the local size and history of each racialized group.[30] Thus, researchers now acknowledge that racialized context must be considered when studying racial identities.[31] Gender, contested racial options, and racial appearance may also influence how mixed-heritage people identify themselves.

*Gender*

Does the gender of a mixed-heritage individual have any bearing on their racial identification, spouse selection, or how they identify and raise their children? Some prior studies have suggested that mixed-heritage women are more likely than mixed-heritage men to identify as multiracial.[32] Women engage more heavily in kin work and kin documentation and are thus more likely to be knowledgeable about their ancestry.[33] Other studies, however, suggest that there are no clearly patterned gender differences in how mixed-heritage people self-identify.[34] Indeed, some prior research has found very similar rates of change in race responses for males and females.[35] Cautioning against the view that multiracial self-identification is a predominantly female tendency, Janet Xu and her colleagues consider the impact of the generational locus of multiracial ancestry.[36] They find that while first-generation multiracial women are more likely to be *aware* of multiracial ancestry, men are more likely to self-identify as multiracial if they are second- or higher-generation multiracial. Our analysis finds no strong gender pattern in how mixed-heritage people racially identify in the national data. Our qualitative data do show more subtle influences of gender, but like most other researchers, we collected interview data that are skewed toward the experiences of women; relatively few men participated in our study.[37] There is still little research on the identities and experiences of mixed-heritage men.[38]

### Contested Racial Options

Given the rise in mixed-heritage people identifying with multiple races, one central theme has garnered tremendous interest: expanded and less restrictive racial options. We are living through times when there is significant debate about the basis of ethnic and racial group membership. Analysts like Rogers Brubaker have argued that there is more recognition for subjective feelings about one's racial identity and belonging.[39] Ann Morning has argued that, in the twenty-first century, it is more "socially plausible" for individuals to claim racial membership based on various criteria, such as genetic or emotive bases for membership. As Paul Spickard has observed, "shape shifting" can occur throughout one's lifetime.[40]

Mixed-heritage people's assertions of group membership are not necessarily validated by others, who may contest their identities and question their group membership; monoracial people of color—those without known mixed heritage—are especially likely to do so. Many scholars have pointed to the constraints that operate around how mixed-heritage people identify themselves.[41] Constraints on identity options include physical appearance, cultural knowledge, and immersion in a BIPOC (Black, Indigenous, and People of Color) culture and/or network, among others. Mixed-heritage people can be confronted with microaggressive questioning of their racial identity, leading them to resort to 'racial elevator speeches' aimed at meeting the expectations of others.[42]

This enlarged scope for autonomy, choice, and self-transformation has provoked anxieties about fraudulent identity claims and broader debates about ethnic and racial authenticity.[43] Such debates extend to how multiracial people should be defined. For example, tribal citizenship rules based on so-called blood quantum are seen as a "necessary evil" to ensure that only "real" tribal members are included.[44]

### Racial Appearance

Having a darker skin tone and experiencing racial discrimination can influence how mixed-heritage people identify.[45] Although mixed-heritage people's identities can be influenced by how others see them racially, they can also resist these racial assignments and choose not to identify according to the perceptions of others. People of mixed heritage who are seen as White could resist a White identity and identify as multiracial, especially if they feel emotionally connected to multiple heritages.[46] In her study of college students on the West Coast, Lauren Davenport found that "aversion to adopting a White identity, despite having a prototypically White appearance, was a recurring finding among participants across biracial subgroups."[47]

Racial visibility has been central to our understandings of stigmatized racially minoritized status.[48] Social scientists have tended to assume that a person's race is readily apparent to the observer, such that people can identify their racial in-groups and out-groups without much difficulty.[49] In other words, racial visibility—that is, an unambiguously non-White appearance—is an assumed characteristic of BIPOC status and does not require further reflection.

But exactly who is deemed a BIPOC person has become less clear in the contemporary United States than in the past.[50] Also defying the neat theoretical binary of White and non-White is the presence of large numbers of "hidden" racially mixed people with generationally distant mixed-racial heritage (such as those enumerated in the 2015 Pew survey), who may look either racially ambiguous or White to others. Black-White people have more consistently been seen as Black, while Asian-White people are seen more variably.[51] Native-White people are often defined within the community based on their legal status.[52] They can struggle to be seen as legitimately Native if they lack legal status or a stereotypically Native phenotype.[53] Our findings with three mixed-heritage groups suggest that there is more variety in how mixed-heritage people are racially perceived than is typically acknowledged in extant research—especially for mixed-heritage people *without* Black heritage.

## INTERRACIAL MARRIAGE AS IT RELATES TO MIXED-HERITAGE IDENTITY

A number of studies, many of them with a demographic focus, look at homogamy and exogamy in marriage partner choices.[54] Others have looked at "binational" marriages.[55] In general, most studies on race and partner choices have been presented separately from studies on identity, and they treat each spouse's race as given rather than as a point of negotiation both internally and within the partnership. Cross-group comparisons are more commonly offered in these analyses, but mixed methods are generally not employed. Miri Song's qualitative study of multiracial people's White and non-White spouses, and the implications of their spousal choices, is one of the few to explore the link between the identities and spousal choices of people of mixed racial heritage.[56]

Among people of all race groups in the United States there is a powerful and persistent pattern of choosing same-race marriages. Given the relatively small sizes of BIPOC populations in many parts of the country, the prevalence of same-race marriages among BIPOC people is striking. One research team noted: "If race did not matter in assortative mating, exogamy would be the norm for all racial minorities."[57] However, because race group population sizes vary, racial context is an important factor in any understanding of the racialized marriage market.

Even as race continues to matter in shaping marriage patterns, interracial unions have grown considerably more common since 1967, when the US Supreme Court nullified all race restrictions on marriage.[58] When anti-miscegenation laws were overturned that year at the national level, 3 percent of all newlyweds were married to someone of a different race or ethnicity. By 2015, the share of new interracial marriages had grown to 17 percent.[59]

Scholars have long regarded intermarriage as an important indicator of assimilation into the "mainstream" society. The extent of a BIPOC group's intermarriage with White people has been seen by some as the ultimate sign of a group's integration into the so-called mainstream.[60] However, other scholars have warned of seeing growing rates of interracial unions as a straightforward marker of diminishing racial boundaries.[61] Other researchers have questioned whether a non-White partner would necessarily be assimilated into the (mainly White) "mainstream" by marrying a White person, which is implied by this interpretation.[62] Kimberly DaCosta critiques researchers who depict interracial families as sites where racial differences meet and melt away and warns against conflating the experience of parents in these families with that of the children.[63] Others have challenged the related idea that interracial unions with White people are devoid of racism.[64] Dan Rodríguez-García and his coauthors argue that the relationship between intermarriage and integration is multidirectional or segmented.[65] Jessica Vasquez-Tokos has criticized the characterizations of intermarriage in the assimilation literature, which tends to presume that the non-White partner, not the White partner, does all of the adapting and changing within a marriage.[66] Instead, for example, she argues, "intermarriage [with Latinos] disrupts non-Latino whites' white habitus." Intermarriage with a White person does not necessarily result in the "whitening" of the Latino spouse.[67]

Past research and theorizing about intermarriage and assimilation are not easily applied to mixed-heritage people because understandings of intermarriage are premised upon membership in a *single* racial or ethnic grouping.[68] As such, there are no conventions for characterizing the unions of mixed-heritage people, who may or may not share some racial overlap with their spouse.[69] Although relatively little is known about the dating or marriage choices of mixed-heritage people in the United States, one study found that multiracial people are more comfortable than White or monoracial BIPOC people with entering into interracial relationships.[70] According to the 2015 Pew survey, when "they do wed, mixed-race Americans are more likely than other adults to marry someone who also is multiracial."[71] But researchers are not clear about what would constitute endogamous or exogamous spouse choices for the unions of mixed-heritage people, or about how to characterize such unions.[72] Our research has shown that spousal choice is indicative of a mixed-heritage person's racial identity, but we also find that the spouses shape each other's racial identity.

## THE RACIAL SOCIALIZATION AND IDENTIFICATION OF CHILDREN OF MIXED-HERITAGE PARENTS

Another line of research investigates the reported races of children of interracial marriage. Quantitative studies predict the way a child will be described by their parent.[73] Overall, these studies found that the racial context of the family's location was a powerful predictor of how the child would be racially identified, as was the parents' apparent cultural connections to the racialized groups. Black-White couples were more likely to identify their children with their non-White race than were Asian-White, Native-White, and Latino-White couples, who racially identified their children in more varied ways.

The racial identification of children of interracial marriages is often treated as a proxy for their assumed racial socialization, although this is neither explicitly stated nor empirically substantiated.[74] Some qualitative studies have focused on the raising of Black-White children, but very few have compared the parenting of disparate types of mixed-heritage children.[75] We build on Miri Song's research on how multiracial people in Britain identify and raise their children, and whether they wish to transmit their non-White ancestry to them.[76]

In comparison with most studies, which investigate the children of the interracial unions of monoracial individuals, our research explores what happens when mixed-heritage people raise their children. We examine how a mixed-heritage parent's identification and upbringing of their children is influenced by not only their own experiences (as racially mixed individuals), but by the racial and ethnic backgrounds of the other parent.

In sum, while we know a great deal about how multiracial people identify racially, and what this may signify, we know very little about how choosing a spouse and becoming a parent relate to the identities, cultural attachments, and practices of mixed-heritage people. After all, finding a life partner and becoming a parent are major life transitions.[77] This broader perspective, in which racial identification, choice of spouse, and the identification and socialization of children are all examined in relation to each other, extends existing knowledge and theory about this heterogeneous population. Our focus on generational change in the mixed-heritage population opens up an important and understudied area of social research. We break new ground by investigating whether and how a new cohort of mixed-heritage people who have become parents transmit, along with their chosen partners, particular culturally and racially informed perspectives and practices to their children.

In the remainder of this chapter, we first describe two ways in which our research contributes to and extends the theoretical and empirical understanding of mixed-heritage people and their families. We then provide a preview of our results. We conclude with an outline of the chapters of the book.

## Comparing Three Mixed-Heritage Populations

The possibility and prevalence of interracial unions, as well as the treatment of their offspring, were shaped by historical circumstances; policies, laws, and other institutions consolidated particular social rules for categorizing mixed-ancestry individuals by race, and changing political and economic conditions fostered certain types of interracial union at some times and not others.

—JANET XU ET AL., "Gender, Generation, and Multiracial Identification in the United States" (2021), 1610

An important contribution of this book is its comparative exploration of mixed-heritage groups that are not usually compared: Native-White, Black-White, and Asian-White people. Only a few other researchers have previously compared mixed-heritage groups. Hephzibah Strmc-Pawl, for instance, has made a comparative study of Black-White and Asian-White people, and Lauren Davenport focuses on Latino-White, Asian-White, and Black-White college students in a mixed-methods study.[78]

According to the 2015 Pew survey on multiracial Americans, three-quarters of the multiracial population can be found in just four mixed categories: Native-White, Black-White, Asian-White, and White–some other race (Latino for the most part). In fact, most mixed-heritage people have some White ancestry. American Indian, Asian, Black, and White people have long-standing and distinct histories in the United States.[79] Michael Omi and Howard Winant have described the experiences of Native American, Black, Mexican, and Asian people in the United States as the distinct trajectories of "genocide, slavery, colonization, and exclusion," respectively.[80]

The specifics of these histories vary across time and place. In his study of the historical origins of White supremacy in late nineteenth-century California, Tomás Almaguer points to the differential treatment of "uncivilized" American Indians, "half-civilized" Mexicans, and "heathen" Chinese against a backdrop of tussles over land ownership, labor market position, and concerns about enslaved Black people in a "free" state.[81] Almaguer unequivocally argues that "California Indians, for example, were singled out as the complete antithesis of white Californians and were summarily relegated to the very bottom of the racial hierarchy."[82] His study of California speaks to the importance of place as well as the historical specificity of different places and their societal treatment of racial and ethnic "others": Late nineteenth-century California, for example, differed in its treatment of non-White peoples from the slave-owning South, with its racial fault lines and class struggles.

Many African Americans still suffer the continuing injuries of the slavery and Jim Crow eras, which impacted the generational transmission of disadvantage. American Indians and Alaska Natives who are members of tribal nations have a unique relationship with the federal government. The relationship has been rife with genocidal policies such as war, mandatory boarding schools, and excessive out-adoption.[83] Hundreds of treaties reserved lands for tribal use, leaving pockets of sovereign homelands scattered in mostly rural areas.[84] Although fewer than half of Native people live on tribal lands, many live nearby and visit often.[85] By comparison, the vast bulk of Asian Americans came to the United States as immigrants—especially after 1965—as "voluntary migrants."[86] Asian Americans have tended to be characterized as "model minorities."[87] They constitute a highly diverse population, however, and some Asian ethnic groups are far more socioeconomically successful than others.[88] Moreover, Asian Americans have not escaped racial hatred and discrimination in the United States, most recently during the COVID era.[89]

Mixed-heritage Asian-White and Native-White people, however, are said to be characterized by flexible racial identities, especially in comparison with Black-White people.[90] They also are regarded as "tilting" toward their White ancestry rather than their Asian or American Indian ancestry.[91] We engage with this argument throughout the book.

Because of the variation in histories, the family trees of people of mixed heritage vary across groups. Interracial unions between White and American Indian people and between White and Black people were not uncommon centuries ago, while most interracial Asian-White unions are more recent. This difference creates group-level variation in personal connection to single-race ancestors, within-group discussions of what it means to be "mixed," and varying societal pressures to identify in one way versus another.[92]

Janet Xu and her colleagues have observed that different groups of racially mixed people are subject to disparate "racial classification regimes" governed by society.[93] Blackness is on one end of this spectrum and is seen as a dominant ancestry in a person of mixed racial heritage (the "one-drop rule" of hypodescent), while Indigeneity has been "treated as vanishing, overpowered, and rendered invisible when combined with other racial heritage."[94] For example, while the 1930 census institutionalized hypodescent for all people of interracial parentage, enumerators were given discretion when it came to American Indians and instructed to distinguish them as either "full blood" or "mixed blood."[95] Native-White people could also be categorized as White, depending on community acceptance.

Black and Native American racial classification regimes are based on longer histories in the United States compared to relatively more recent Asian and Latino histories in the United States (and their related classification regimes), and these differences are likely to influence both the awareness of multiracial ancestry and the tendency to self-identify as multiracial.[96] The 2015 Pew study found that while "biracial adults with White and American Indian backgrounds" comprise half of the multiracial population in the United States, many of them self-report as White and are the least likely to consider themselves multiracial.[97] Recently, Sarah Iverson and her colleagues have argued that while mixed people have historically been believed to identify on the basis of these classification regimes, there is growing evidence that mixed people are characterized by a "co-descent" regime.[98] In a co-descent regime, mixed individuals do not identify solely in relation to one racial ancestry but instead align themselves along a range of their parental races. In fact, a growing number of Black-White mixed people in the United States are now asserting multiracial identities.[99]

A binary emphasis on part-Black mixed-heritage people versus those without Black ancestry reveals some important patterns of experience but obscures some convergence and commonalities across disparate types of mixed people. Grace Kao and her colleagues argue that we need to move "beyond thinking about the black-white color line in understanding race relations in the United States."[100] In this book, we move beyond the traditional focus on Black-White biracial individuals. In all aspects of our study, we focus on people with three types of mixed-heritage backgrounds: Native-White, Asian-White, and Black-White.

### Is Growth in the Mixed-Heritage Population Expanding the "White" Category?

Another way in which our research extends the collective understanding of race in US society is by critically examining claims about the expanding boundaries of who is included in the socially defined White category. As they consider the social and political implications of the growing numbers of Americans of mixed racial heritage, some leading researchers have pointed to the expansion of Whiteness.[101] For example, Lee and Bean argue: "Based on patterns of multiracial identification, Asians and Latinos may be the next in line to be white, with multiracial Asian-whites and Latino-whites at the head of the queue."[102]

Debate about the impact of racially mixed people on the American racial hierarchy has emerged at a time when many scholars of race are pointing to the primacy of a Black/non-Black divide in society that is supplanting the White/non-White framework, which emphasized commonalities among different racially minoritized groups.[103] Central to this debate are questions about the status of part-White mixed-heritage people in relation to White and monoracial BIPOC groups in the United States.[104] In comparison with mixed-heritage Black-White people, Asian-White and Latino-White people are socioeconomically more privileged.[105] Less is known about Native-White people, or about any of these groups' social affiliations and lived experiences.

Individuals from mixed majority-minority backgrounds *without Black ancestry* are characterized as possessing an array of ethnic options.[106] They are also increasingly seen as central to the "expansion of the American mainstream"—a mainstream that does not include only White Americans, as in the past.[107] "For adults who are part white and part American Indian, Asian, or Latino," observe Richard Alba and his coauthors, "these identities 'tilt white,' reflecting a sense of affinity with whites. They do not generally perceive racial barriers to their participation in mainstream settings. They tend to have white friends, live in neighborhoods with many white neighbors and to marry whites."[108] Such mixed-heritage people are described as "deracialized" or "White enough" and seen as largely accepted into an expanding American mainstream.[109]

Other scholars of race have similarly argued that part-White mixed-heritage people, such as Asian-White, Native-White, and Latino-White people, are effectively honorary Whites who benefit from their non-Blackness.[110] In fact, some scholars have gone as far as to suggest that their racial backgrounds do not heavily shape the experiences of many non-Black mixed-heritage young Americans, or their interactions with others. According to Richard Alba, "For those in the mainstream, ethno-racial origins carry much diminished weight in determining life chances, social affiliations, and even identities. This reduced role of origins can be characterized as *decategorization*, which also entails interactions with others that are not fundamentally colored by ethno-racial categories."[111]

Our research shows that it is premature to suggest that "decategorization" is underway for all non-Black mixed-heritage people in the contemporary United States. The huge diversity among mixed-heritage people—both across and within disparate mixed-heritage groupings—makes it extremely difficult to generalize about them. Our results indicate that Whiteness may have expanded for some individuals, but that this hypothesis is far from universally supported. In comparison with *non*-Black mixed-heritage people, many scholars characterize individuals from mixed majority-minority backgrounds *with Black ancestry* as not experiencing "decategorization," since they continue to face race at every turn.[112] Notably, Black-White is the fastest-growing multiple-race subgroup reported to the Census Bureau, growing 238 percent over the fifteen years from 2000 to 2015.[113] Our research (and the 2015 Pew survey) has found that the majority of mixed-heritage Black-White individuals, as well as the majority of mixed-heritage Asian-White individuals, reported both groups as their races rather than foregrounding a single race. This finding complicates the claim that Black-White mixed-heritage people have a fundamentally and universally distinct experience; their experiences require more nuanced consideration. In her study of college students, Davenport found that "black-white biracials are also the least likely to singularly identify with their minority race. This contradicts black-whites' traditional adherence to the one-drop rule and indicates that it no longer drives their identification. . . . Rather, black-white biracials are making a point of defining themselves as both white and black—and simultaneously neither white nor black."[114]

Prior to our work, research on the lived experiences of different mixed-heritage people has been relatively limited. For example, prior research has not shown how people from various mixed-heritage groups decide to fill out survey questions about race, or how survey choices translate to how people live their lives—and perhaps in ways that are not straightforward. Also, most research on intermarriage focuses on single-race individuals, producing little evidence about people who identify multiracially. While some people of mixed heritage choose White partners, many others do not.[115] What happens when mixed-heritage people partner with White people has been an empirically open question, as there is very little data on their parenting, social networks, and day-to-day lives. Even mixed-heritage people with a White spouse may vary from each other in their ethnic leanings and attachments.[116] It is also possible that their White spouses are committed to cultivating non-White heritages and affiliations.[117] Experiences are likely to vary depending on the particular combination of heritages in these unions, whose dynamics and practices are also shaped by racial/ethnic spatial contexts.[118]

Furthermore, people within the same mixed-heritage group—even within the same family—can have a variety of racial appearances.[119] For example, while some Asian-White individuals may look White to others, others are seen as Asian, and still others as racially mixed or racially ambiguous.[120] Richard Alba observes that one "unknown is the impact of phenotype on the ethno-racial orientation of mixed individuals. . . . The evidence that Asian-whites, for example, are often comfortable in milieus with many whites can hide the very different experiences and self-understandings of a minority within this group."[121]

There is a great deal of phenotypical variation among people with the same racially mixed background.[122] In our research, we address phenotype (as reported by participants) as well as the influence of racial appearance on others' social treatment of participants. Our research shows that others' perception of a person's racial phenotype can influence every part of their experience. The studies suggesting that non-Black mixed-heritage people "lean White" have largely assumed that most of these individuals appear White, but we find that this is not a safe assumption.[123] Importantly, an individual's White appearance, though an important predictor of their social treatment and of why they may choose a White identification, does not always determine a White identity.[124] As Mary Campbell wrote, "It is time to reconsider the idea that black identification is straightforward and unambiguous, while other racial identities are fluid and contextual."[125]

Our research examines the empirical evidence for the purported differences in the ethnic attachments and leanings of Black-White people from those of Asian-White and Native-White people. We would expect that some mixed-heritage people's attachments and practices are not easily characterized in relation to the binary of White or BIPOC "sides."[126]

Our study contributes to a fuller and more nuanced understanding of the diversity of the mixed-heritage population in different parts of the United States. In our in-depth interviews, we explore the particular practices and concerns in relation to their spouses and children reported by parents of various mixed heritages.

## Preview of Our Results

*Reporting multiple races:* We find that the most common way to report Black-White and Asian-White mixed racial heritage in modern Census Bureau data is to report multiple races. Native-White people of mixed heritage, on the other hand, even when allowed to report multiple races, tend to report a single race, while reporting the other race in the ancestry question. Though most of our interview participants reported biracial identities, many emphasized being attached to their non-White ancestry much more than to their White European ancestry. How biracial identities translated in terms of their attachments to their Black, Native, Asian, and White backgrounds varied considerably both within and across the three mixed-heritage groups.

*Reported race predicts spouse's race:* In both the Census Bureau and interview data, we find that the way a mixed-heritage person reports their race is closely tied to their spouse's race. For example, the only group in our study with a substantial proportion of biracially identified spouses are people who are biracially identified themselves. Also, people of mixed heritage who identify as racially White (with BIPOC ancestry) commonly marry other single-race White people. However, our interviews reveal that participants with White spouses (and the spouses themselves) varied in their attachment to and interest in their BIPOC heritage, as well as in their racial consciousness.

*Reported race, spouse's race, and children's race and upbringing:* We find that the way a person of mixed heritage racially identifies and raises their children is strongly related to how they racially identify and whom they chose to marry. This congruence can be seen in the census data and interviews, both of which highlight similarities between how the child's races are reported and how their parents report their own races. However, the interviews show that the racial background of the other parent is far more revealing about the racial upbringing of children than the specific way the child is racially identified on a form.

*Questioning a trend toward "whitening"*: Some researchers have concluded that race is becoming less salient for mixed people with Asian and Native heritage, while those with Black heritage continue to be racially stigmatized and socially excluded. A key insight of our research is that race is *not* becoming less salient for many mixed-heritage Asian-White and Native-White people. For example, many of our Native-White and Asian-White participants valued and wanted to cultivate ties with their minority ancestry, though they felt subject to unwritten rules about racial and ethnic authenticity that could prevent them from being fully seen as Native or Asian. Other researchers' presumptions about "whitening" and the idea that race no longer matters obscure these dynamics and overlook variations in the racial appearance of mixed-heritage people that bring nuance to their experiences.

## Overview of the Book

*Chapter 2: "Looking from Two Angles and Considering Context"*: In this research, we take a close-up view of experiences using in-depth interviews as well as a bird's-eye view using data from the US Census Bureau (1980 to 2019). Although using mixed methods requires twice as much data collection and analysis work, it is worthwhile: We are able to synthesize a fuller and more nuanced set of results than would be possible using just one method. Mixed-methods research carries the promise of counterbalancing the shortcomings of one method with the strength of the other, yet this promise can be realized only if the different data sources are considered simultaneously, as we do throughout the book. To include racial context in our analyses, we created a measure that summarizes the racial/ethnic context of interview participants as well as of Census Bureau respondents: the Racial/Ethnic Spatial Context Indicator. RESCI is designed to correspond with important variation in cultural context in distinct parts of the United States, as local cultures shape the treatment and experiences of mixed-heritage people.

*Chapter 3: "How Do Mixed-Heritage People Identify Themselves?"*: In chapter 3, we explore the possible meanings of mixed-heritage people's race responses, as well as how and why they come to identify themselves in particular ways. We use Census Bureau data to illustrate variations in patterns of racial identification over time, across types of places, and across three groups of mixed-heritage people. Because the interview participants were recruited based on known parental ancestries, not on their stated racial identifications, we are able to map out the different ways in which individuals with substantially similar mixed ancestries describe their racial identity in Census Bureau data and experience it in life. The majority of our interview participants, across all three mixed-heritage groups, reported a biracial identity, but how this identity affected their attachment to their Black, Native, Asian, or White backgrounds varied considerably both within and across the groups. Despite observing some notable differences between the mixed-heritage groups, we are able to discern several prominent themes running throughout our interviews, across all three groups: (1) the impact of racial phenotype, (2) the nature of the cultural and/or racial experience to which people were exposed while growing up, and (3) contestations around ethnic and racial authenticity and membership. The influence of these key factors on our mixed-heritage participants' sense of self and their feelings about their family background varied even among those who gave the same race and ancestry responses in the preinterview surveys.

*Chapter 4: "Choosing a Spouse: The Implications of Racial Overlap":* Almost all existing research on intermarriage is based on the interracial unions of single-race (monoracial) individuals. In this chapter, we examine the spousal choices of mixed-heritage people and what those choices may reveal about their racial identities and lived experiences. One way to more fully investigate the impact of racial identification on the lives of mixed-heritage people is to look at their marriage choice. In this chapter, we ask: How do mixed-heritage people who are married make sense of their identity in relation to their spouse's race? And how does the racial overlap (or non-overlap) impact or reflect the relative salience of race in their relationship? To answer these questions, we rely on census data for an overview and our interviews for further context and deeper understanding.

In both types of data, we find that a mixed-heritage person's decision about how to report their race is closely related to their spouse's race. Those in all three mixed-heritage groups who reported being biracial chose a spouse from a variety of race groups. Biracially identified people with White heritage in all three mixed-heritage groups—including biracially identified Black-White people—quite commonly chose a White spouse. Interviews revealed that participants with a White spouse (and the spouses themselves) varied in terms of their attachment to and interest in their BIPOC heritage, as well as in their racial consciousness.

*Chapter 5: "How Do Mixed-Heritage People Identify and Raise Their Children?":* Prior research on parents in interracial unions has tended to assume that their racial identification of their children is a reliable proxy for how they raise and socialize their children, but this assumption requires investigation. We use Census Bureau data to show patterns in the racial identification of children across parent race/ancestry and identification choices. We then use our interview data to explore what mixed-heritage parents' identifications of their children mean in practice.

We find that how a person of mixed heritage racially identifies and raises their children is strongly related to how they themselves racially identify, as well as to their choice of spouse. This congruence of parent and child racial identification can be seen in the census data and interviews, both of which highlight similarities between how the child's race is reported and how their mixed-heritage parent reports their own race and that of their spouse. Based on both the census data and the interviews, we find that the racial background of the other parent is far more revealing about the racial upbringing of children than the specific racial identity they give to their children on a form. How parents racially identify their children—especially those who identify their children biracially—does not necessarily reveal much about the child's upbringing. Participants' identification of their children as solely White or solely BIPOC is fairly predictive of their racial socialization. But in the vast majority of interview cases, there is significant variation in the upbringing of children identified biracially and in parents' commitment to fostering ethnic distinctiveness.

*Chapter 6: "Conclusions":* In the concluding chapter, we review our main findings and relate them to our theoretical conclusions. We discuss the policy implications of our results, consider the limitations of our research, and highlight promising directions for future work. In particular, we consider what the increase in the number of mixed-heritage people portends for the racial landscape of contemporary US society.

*Appendixes:* Appendix A shows the text of our preinterview survey. Appendix B provides the interview guide that we used for our participant interviews. Details about the Census Bureau questions on race and ancestry are given in appendix C. Appendix D summarizes the characteristics of our sixty-eight interview participants, and appendix E gives more details about the development of the RESCI measure.

# CHAPTER TWO

# LOOKING FROM TWO ANGLES AND CONSIDERING CONTEXT

We aim to understand mixed-heritage people's identities, spouse choices, and racial identification of their children by comparing three groups of people of mixed racial heritage and considering racialized context. We approach this vast set of topics from two angles: in-depth interviews and analysis of data from the US Census Bureau. Although applying and integrating multiple methods to study social processes involves significantly more analysis and synthesis than using a single method, we feel it is an important approach that counterbalances the shortcomings of one method with the strengths of the other.

Local racial and ethnic context influences racialized experiences like the ones we study, so we also developed a measure that indicates five possible racial/ethnic contexts in which participants might live. We call this new measure the Racial/Ethnic Spatial Context Indicator (RESCI).

This chapter provides an overview of the Census Bureau data, the interview data, and the RESCI measure that we use together in the remainder of the book.

## US Census Bureau Data

US Census Bureau data hold information about the three groups we are studying: mixed-heritage people of Black-White, Native-White, or Asian-White background. Our quantitative analysis covers the period 1980 through 2019 using the public-use versions of the US decennial census long forms from 1980, 1990, and 2000, as well as the American

https://doi.org/10.7758/edyf5459.1189

Community Survey (ACS) five-year samples from 2006 to 2010 and from 2015 to 2019, accessed through IPUMS.[1] The ACS is the US Census Bureau's replacement for the census long form and became nationally representative starting in 2006 (except in 2020). The 2010 and 2020 decennial censuses do not include the ancestry question and thus cannot be used for this research. ACS samples after 2019 cannot be used because the Census Bureau significantly changed the way it codes race responses. To maximize the number of people in the smaller groups, we show all years of data combined; our investigation of individual samples did not show substantially different results than we share here. Throughout the book, all Census Bureau data were weighted to represent the US population of the time.

We present census results for mixed-heritage individuals whose race response was reported on the form, excluding those whose race was assigned by the Census Bureau during post-processing. We label this "self-identification" for simplicity, but in fact we do not know who filled out the census form. When a household does not respond, proxy respondents (for example, neighbors) often give a simplified answer.[2] Unfortunately, the public data do not indicate which records are from proxy responses. The data are also muddied by information about people in group quarters (for example, jails or hospitals) because their race information is usually drawn from records and not asked specifically for the census.[3] However, family relationships are not recorded in most group quarters in the census or ACS, and so very few people living in group quarters are included in our analyses.

It is unlikely that children completed the census form themselves; others usually report information about them on their behalf. How parents report their children's race on a form could be seen as *aspirational*, especially if the children are too young to articulate a sense of their racial self. As Steven Holloway and colleagues observe, parents' identifications of their children are meaningful acts that "reflect, if only imperfectly, their understanding of who their children are racially, as well as who they may want their children to become racially."[4] Importantly, as noted by other researchers working with census data, census data do not tell us *why* parents identify their children in the ways they do, or how these identifications relate to the parents' own identities and their parenting concerns.[5] Our interview participants' responses fill in these important gaps.

## CENSUS DATA ON THE RACE AND ANCESTRY
## OF PEOPLE OF MIXED RACIAL HERITAGE

People can report having multiple race groups in their background on a census form in two ways: as mixed ancestry, and as mixed race. Starting in 1980, respondents could report mixed ancestry by giving an answer in the ancestry question that indicated a different race group than their answer to the race question. Mixed race could be reported beginning in 2000; multiple-race responses on the race question were invited in the instruction to "mark one or more boxes" and reported in the public-use data from 2000 to the present.

The ancestry question introduced in 1980 asks: "What is this person's ancestry or ethnic origin?" (such as Italian or Jamaican). The Census Bureau provides only the first two responses to this open-ended question in the public-use data.[6] See appendix A for more about the census questions on ancestry and race.

The census has asked about race every year since its inception in 1790, with changes each year in the instructions or categories. Census respondents in 1980 and 1990 were instructed to choose a single race, and so the only way to report a mixed racial heritage was to report one race group in the race question and another in the ancestry question. The invitation to "mark one or more" races, introduced in the 2000 census, introduced a second option for reporting a mixed racial heritage. Our analyses focus on people who reported a mixed racial heritage in one of these two ways, and we subdivide them into those who reported (1) Native, Black, or Asian race with White ancestry, (2) White race with Native, Black, or Asian ancestry, or (3) both White and Native/Black/ Asian races.

Translating identity to a survey form and translating survey responses to categories are imperfect processes, so both methods of identifying people of mixed heritage in census data (through answers to the ancestry versus race question and through multiple answers to the race question) exclude some people of mixed heritage. For example, people can choose not to report their mixed heritage in these questions, presumed links between ancestry responses and race groups may be faulty, or the form may be filled out by someone who does not know of (or prioritize) the person's mixed heritage.

We focus on people with only two racialized groups in their heritage because people with an additional group (Pacific Islander, Latino, or multiple minoritized groups) may (or may not) experience identity and family dynamics that differ from those we study. Similarly, the experiences of people of mixed heritage who do not have a White background is probably different from that of the people we include in this study. Our focus in this work is specifically on the intersection of White and non-White identities and experiences. We hope our work can launch and support research on these other important mixed-heritage groups.

Note that a person can change their answer to any question, including race or ancestry, from year to year (or moment to moment), as circumstances change.[7] We consider the census race and ancestry data to be point-in-time indicators of a person's current identification.

## SPOUSES OF PEOPLE OF MIXED HERITAGE

Mixed-heritage people marry spouses from all racial backgrounds. For simplicity, we have coded spouses' race responses into four categories (coded separately for each of the mixed-heritage groups). For example, the spouse race categories for the Black-White analysis are: (1) non-Latino White; (2) White and Black (and no other races, but a Latino response is allowed); (3) Black (including Latino Black); and (4) everyone else.

To maximize the chances that both parents are biologically related to the child whose race response is being studied, we have included only married coresident couples in our spouse analyses and further restricted to heterosexual couples for the analyses of children's identification. Unfortunately, this limitation leaves out many family types. Our analyses are not truly representative of the partnerships and experiences of mixed-heritage people in the United States, and we hope our work can be the basis of future research on more diverse family types.

## THE CHILDREN OF PEOPLE OF MIXED HERITAGE

Census data allow us to study how mixed-heritage people and their spouses identify their children's race and ancestry. We use the word "child" in this work to mean a coresident person ages zero to nineteen who was reported as "child of Person 1" on the census or ACS.[8] Because the mixed-heritage person is either "Person 1" or their spouse, we assume that the child's response was probably given by a parent. Unfortunately, we are not able to study non-coresident children using census data, and we exclude other family configurations, such as multi-family households for which the mixed-heritage person is not listed as Person 1 or Person 1's spouse.[9]

Summarizing children's race and ancestry responses is complex. We use six categories (coded separately for each mixed-heritage group), three of which match the mixed-heritage parent categories. For the Native-White group, for example, these categories are: (1) White race and no mention of Native ancestry, (2) White race with Native ancestry, (3) Native and White races and no other races, (4) Native race with White ancestry, (5) Native race and no mention of White ancestry, and (6) everyone else.[10] Some parent-child race combinations are not common; if there are fewer than sixty children with a parent-child race combination in the unweighted data, we do not show it in the results.

## In-depth Interviews

To gain a deeper understanding of how individuals of varied racial heritages view their race and ancestry, and how their reported race relates to their racial identity, choice of spouse, and children's socialization, we conducted sixty-eight in-depth interviews with US adults in 2018, 2019, and 2020. To be invited into the study, a person had to be a non-Latino adult with Native-White, Black-White, or Asian-White mixed heritage, have a biological child or children, and have ever been married to the other biological parent of their children. We required that participants were married or had been married for two reasons: Marriage was a better match to the quantitative analysis, and marriage indicated a level of choice and commitment that was not necessarily present in other relationships (though it might have been).

We relied on a variety of social media and word-of-mouth methods for recruiting participants. We avoided recruitment channels that specifically catered to mixed-heritage people and families, such as websites for mixed-heritage people.

As a screening tool and source of information to be probed in the interview, we sent an online preinterview survey to our respondents (shown in appendix B) in which we asked the 2010 census race question (which instructs respondents to "mark one or more" among fifteen race categories) and the open-ended ACS ancestry question ("What is your ancestry or ethnic origin?").[11] Potential participants were asked these census-worded questions on race, ancestry, and Latino origin in relation to themselves, their child(ren), their spouse, and their birth parents. Their choice of race(s) and ancestry to report was a subject of study and not used as an additional screening tool except to ensure that they had a Native-White, Asian-White, or Black-White heritage.

We found that many participants provided significant detail in their ancestry responses in the preinterview survey, especially those with White and Asian ancestries. Tribal origin was also usually reported in the ancestry question by those who were Native-White. The interviews showed, however, that reporting ancestry detail was not tightly correlated with identity; for example, few of our respondents showed interest in their White ancestral heritage, though many reported it.[12]

Almost all interviews were conducted in person or by video call, but a few were conducted by telephone. Miri Song, a Korean American woman living in England, conducted more than fifty of the interviews, and Carolyn Liebler, a White American woman living in the United States, conducted the remainder. After the interview, each participant was mailed a $20 Visa gift card in thanks for their time.

In each interview, we discussed participants' responses to the race and ancestry questions in the context of a broader conversation about identity and family-related choices. We asked participants about why they identified in particular ways and how they were seen, racially, by others. We also asked people about their upbringing, about how they met and chose their spouse, and finally, about how they identified and raised their children. The complete interview schedule is shown in appendix C.

Among our sixty-eight interview participants were twenty-one Native-White people, twenty-seven Asian-White people, and twenty Black-White people of mixed racial heritage and varied racial identities. Our participants included twenty-five men and forty-three women. They ranged in age from twenty-six to sixty-four, with most in their thirties and forties. While most of the participants were college-educated, middle-class professionals (and/or living in middle-class households), about half of our participants had grown up in working-class households where economic resources and associated cultural and human capital were limited. To our knowledge, all participants were in heterosexual unions when they were married to the other parent of their biological children. Participants lived in forty-two counties in twenty states, with Minnesota and California overrepresented. Appendix D summarizes our participants' characteristics.

On the preinterview survey race question, all twenty-seven of our Asian-White interview respondents reported having both White and an Asian race. Of the twenty Black-White respondents, nineteen reported both races and one reported solely Black. Fifteen of the twenty-one Native-White respondents reported both races on the preinterview survey, five reported as solely American Indian/Alaska Native race (with a specific tribal affiliation and White ancestry), and one reported White race with Native ancestry.

Results in chapter 3 will show that this distribution is not nationally representative of people with mixed racial heritage; our participants were much more likely than the general population to report multiple races, perhaps in part because many of them were highly educated.[13] It is possible that some people who primarily "felt" White were uncomfortable about reporting a solely White race in the context of a study recruiting mixed-heritage people. As we discuss in chapter 3, census data also show that Native-White mixed-heritage people choose one race more often than people in the other mixed-heritage groups. Because of how normative biracial reporting is becoming, a mixed-heritage interviewee's choice of only one race, we found when talking to them, tended to be pointed and meaningful. At the same time, given how common it was to report two races, a range of disparate perspectives and experiences were associated with biracial reporting across all three mixed-heritage groups.

All interviews were recorded, transcribed, and subsequently analyzed using traditional coding methods based on thematic strands drawn from repeated audio and written analyses of the interviews. All names and tribes reported here have been changed for confidentiality. All participants identified as either male or female, and we cite the age (at the time of the interview) and sex of each respondent to provide context.

## The Racial/Ethnic Spatial Context Indicator (RESCI) in Census Bureau Data

The experiences we are studying are known to vary by racial context.[14] Context clearly matters in the formation of racial identity and the salience and meanings of race. Contexts can also be associated with differing regimes of multiracial classification—the historical laws, norms, beliefs, and practices concerning racial classification associated with specific areas.[15]

In fact, a varied and significant body of literature has shown the importance of place for various outcomes related to race. For instance, racial segregation in American cities and towns has been linked with differential patterns in unemployment and poverty, attitudes toward local public services, and differential educational outcomes in schools, among many other aspects of life.[16] The ethnic and racial composition of neighborhoods and the concentration of specific migrant groups, such as Haitians and Cubans in disparate parts of Florida, have fundamentally shaped ethnic groups' life chances and trajectories.[17] Studies of Native Americans have shown just how fundamental specific places (and their associated histories and relationships to tribal communities) have been in shaping Native identities and how children's races are reported.[18] The racial/ethnic context can heighten or diminish intergroup boundaries and social rules, impacting identity and identification.[19] It can also change whether others "see" a person's race—an important validation for identity—and affect the pool of potential marriage partners.[20]

Prior researchers have often used a simple measure to capture "context," such as the percentage of a county's population who report each single race group. We have developed a new measure rather than using this type of simple measure for several reasons. First, the simple measure focuses on one race group at a time, yet our study is about people from three mixed-heritage groups; thus, we need to focus on those from all the component race groups (Asian, Black, Native, and White), including those who identify with multiple races. Second, it is obvious in any consideration of why context might matter that contemporary racial composition is an overly simplistic measure that ignores historical laws, the economic and political context, and other factors that structurally constrain experiences of race. Third, Native people in particular are not well served by a simple measure that ignores the relative location of tribal governments and tribally controlled lands. Fourth, a categorical measure of context can be presented more easily in charts and when summarizing interview participants' racialized locations.

In order to include racial context while working with the census data, we developed—in collaboration with Christopher Levesque of the University of Minnesota and Kenyon College—a measure that we term the Racial/Ethnic Spatial Context Indicator. In this mixed-methods study, we also discuss the contexts of our interview participants in terms of RESCI. In developing and using RESCI, we aim to capture

**Figure 2.1** *Counties in 2010, by Racial/Ethnic Spatial Context*

RESCI
1
2
3
4
5

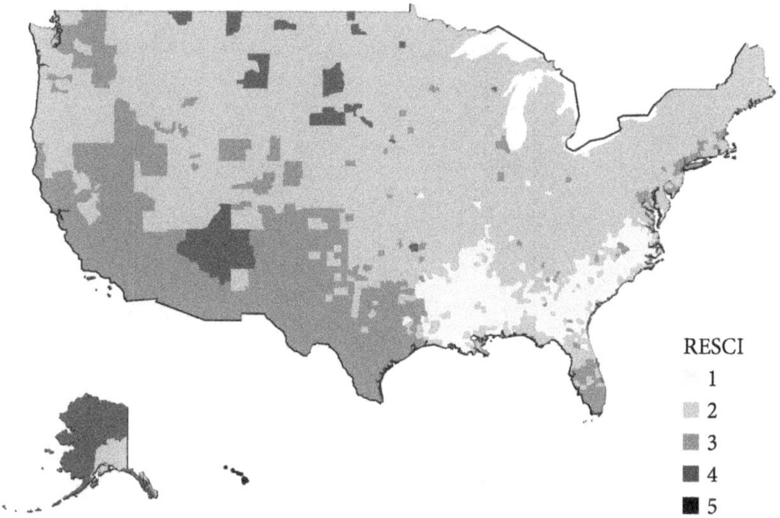

*Source:* Authors' calculations, with special thanks to Christopher Levesque.

characteristics of the place-specific cultures that influence how race is perceived and made meaningful in different locations. For each US county, we gathered information on twenty-eight historical and contemporary dimensions relevant to the component racial groups—its historical events and laws, current demographic and economic factors, racial/ethnic composition—in 1980, 1990, 2000, and 2010 (347,200 spatial context data points). These measures and other information about RESCI are listed and discussed in appendix E. In combination, the measures present a general portrait of each location. We used statistical tools (principal components analysis and cluster analysis) to identify patterns in these county characteristics and assign each county-year to one of five types of racial/ethnic spatial contexts.

## RESULTS OF THE RESCI ANALYSIS

Figure 2.1 shows the location of the 2010 counties, by RESCI cluster, and table 2.1 provides a statistical description of each. Note that RESCI category 5 is difficult to see on the map because it consists only of Hawaii and San Francisco.

**Table 2.1** *Characteristics of Five Racial/Ethnic Spatial Contexts in 2010*

| | RESCI 1 | RESCI 2 | RESCI 3 | RESCI 4 | RESCI 5 |
|---|---|---|---|---|---|
| *Percentage of Counties with Each Characteristic* | | | | | |
| In a former Confederate slave state | 96.5 | 20.5 | 54.1 | 0.0 | 0.0 |
| In a former non-Confederate slave state | 1.5 | 11.7 | 0.6 | 0.0 | 0.0 |
| Area had a reservation in 1875 | 0.4 | 16.5 | 15.6 | 64.4 | 0.0 |
| Area had a reservation in 1930 | 0.0 | 4.9 | 10.6 | 42.2 | 0.0 |
| Was ever in Mexico | 1.5 | 4.6 | 71.9 | 15.6 | 16.7 |
| Had any race riots in the 1960s or 1970s | 11.0 | 2.9 | 6.2 | 0.0 | 0.0 |
| Had a high Asian-born population in 1970 | 0.1 | 0.1 | 0.2 | 0.2 | 8.8 |
| *Average in Counties within this Racial/Ethnic Spatial Context* | | | | | |
| Percentage non-Latino single-race White | 55.2 | 89.3 | 56.2 | 31.4 | 30.2 |
| Percentage non-Latino single-race Black | 38.1 | 3.3 | 6.2 | 0.6 | 1.5 |
| Percentage non-Latino single-race American Indian/Alaska Native | 0.6 | 1.2 | 1.0 | 57.0 | 0.2 |
| Percentage non-Latino single-race Asian or Pacific Islander | 0.8 | 0.8 | 2.8 | 2.1 | 41.9 |
| Percentage of Hispanic/Latino origins | 4.0 | 3.9 | 32.2 | 4.7 | 9.2 |
| Percentage of marriages that are interracial marriages | 3.8 | 4.5 | 6.7 | 12.0 | 32.4 |

| | | | | | |
|---|---|---|---|---|---|
| Percentage who spoke Spanish at home | 3.2 | 2.8 | 23.9 | 2.9 | 3.4 |
| Percentage who spoke another non-English language at home | 1.9 | 2.4 | 4.7 | 21.5 | 22.8 |
| Percentage of population born outside the United States | 3.1 | 3.0 | 13.6 | 3.6 | 18.7 |
| Number of hate groups in 2010 | 5.8 | 4.2 | 8.4 | 0.8 | 1.5 |
| Percentage of votes for the senate Democrat candidate | 49.5 | 41.0 | 41.3 | 45.2 | 75.5 |
| Percentage whose income was at or below poverty level | 21.4 | 13.7 | 15.1 | 22.3 | 10.0 |
| Mean of median per capita household income (in 2010 dollars) | $36,191 | $45,040 | $48,627 | $40,915 | $60,787 |
| Percentage of householders who rent (versus own) their home | 31.3 | 25.7 | 32.5 | 37.9 | 54.1 |
| Percentage of homes occupied (versus vacant) | 85.0 | 83.4 | 84.4 | 76.5 | 80.2 |
| Income difference between non-Latino White residents and others | $6,275 | $2,059 | $7,119 | $13,116 | $16,108 |
| Percentage of households with a householder, spouse, and child | 15.9 | 19.2 | 21.3 | 18.4 | 14.5 |
| Percentage of children living with nonrelatives | 3.9 | 1.9 | 3.0 | 7.0 | 3.4 |
| Percentage of children living with a single mother | 9.6 | 5.4 | 6.8 | 10.5 | 4.3 |
| Percentage of householders age sixty-five and older | 27.4 | 29.1 | 27.0 | 22.8 | 29.1 |
| Percentage of tracts considered urban | 42.3 | 36.7 | 63.3 | 16.5 | 72.3 |
| Mean county population | 81,954 | 59,437 | 291,513 | 19,111 | 360,923 |
| # counties in the cluster in 2010 | 458 | 2,153 | 481 | 45 | 6 |

*Source:* Authors' calculations.

The five types of places identified by RESCI are likely to be different in terms of their "racial schema," which can include the racial categories and terms used in each place, and which people are associated with such categories.[21] For example, the Deep South (most of which is in RESCI 1) is a different kind of place to be Asian than San Francisco (which is in RESCI 5).

RESCI 1 includes many counties with large Black populations and a history of slavery. In these counties, median household incomes are lower and there is relatively little economic difference between non-Latino White residents and racialized minorities. Eleven percent of the counties in RESCI 1 experienced at least one race-related "riot" in the 1960s and 1970s. Three of our participants lived in a RESCI 1 county. Examples of RESCI 1 places are Atlanta, Georgia, Detroit, Michigan, and Tallahassee, Florida.

RESCI 2 contains the most counties and covers the largest area. In 2010, an average of 89 percent of the residents were single-race non-Latino White, and the income gap between that group and racialized minorities was the lowest of any RESCI area. Some areas of RESCI 2 are in former slave states and/or present (and former) American Indian reservations. Nineteen of our participants lived in a RESCI 2 county, examples of which are Fort Collins, Colorado, Clemson, South Carolina, and Duluth, Minnesota.

RESCI 3 counties are mostly in densely populated areas of the US Southwest and West that have a high proportion of foreign-born people and large Latino populations. (In 2010, an average of 32 percent of the population in these counties identified as Latino.) These areas have substantially higher median household income than RESCI 1 areas. Forty-one of our participants lived in a RESCI 3 county. Examples of RESCI 3 places are Minneapolis, New York City, Los Angeles, Houston, and Seattle.

RESCI 4 areas have sparse populations (an average county population of less than twenty thousand people), and, on average, 57 percent of people in these counties are American Indian or Alaska Native, compared to 2 percent nationally. The median household income is relatively low, while the income difference between White- and non-White-headed households is more than double that of RESCI 1 areas. Two of our participants lived in a RESCI 4 county. Although many reservations are not in RESCI 4 areas (many are in RESCI 2 areas), examples of RESCI 4 places are the Hopi Reservation in Arizona and the Rosebud Reservation in South Dakota.

RESCI 5 includes only the six counties of Hawaii and San Francisco. In these heavily urban areas, a high proportion of marriages are between people whose race responses are not identical, and, on average, 41.9 percent of the 2010 county population was single-race Asian or single-race Pacific Islander. The income gap between White and racially minoritized people is highest in RESCI 5. Three of our participants lived in a RESCI 5 county.

Overall, the RESCI measure provides a simple but effective way to separate the United States into areas with distinct racial/ethnic contexts. The RESCI measure is not a fine-grained measure, given that the entire country is categorized into only five groups, but as shown by our results in chapters 3, 4, and 5, interview participants' experiences and census data patterns do in fact vary in meaningful ways depending on their RESCI location.

In sum, our mixed-methods study, utilizing national data from the US Census Bureau from 1980 to 2019 in concert with results from sixty-eight in-depth interviews, allows us to address the limitations of each method while leveraging their strengths to better understand the experiences of people with mixed racial heritage.

# CHAPTER THREE

# HOW DO MIXED-HERITAGE PEOPLE IDENTIFY THEMSELVES?

What motivates mixed-heritage people to identify themselves in a certain way rather than other potential ways? In this chapter, we use Census Bureau data spanning thirty-nine years to illustrate ways in which patterns of racial identification have varied over time, across type of place (in terms of RESCI), and across the three groups of mixed-heritage people who are the focus of this study—Asian-White, Black-White, and Native-White people. The majority of the chapter takes a closer look at each of the mixed-heritage groups, drawing on both the census and interview data, to make sense of how and why mixed-heritage people racially identify themselves in particular ways. The census data provide a broader context, while the interview results reveal aspects of racial identity that are obscured in purely numerical data, such as ambivalent feelings about or attachments to their White and BIPOC backgrounds.

The interview results show that mixed-heritage people can vary considerably in their life experiences and the reported salience of their races. Despite some notable differences between the mixed-heritage groups, we elaborate on several prominent factors that arose throughout our interviews with people from all three groups: (1) racial phenotype (and how others see them), (2) the nature of the cultural and/or racial exposure they experienced while growing up, and (3) contestations around ethnic and racial authenticity and membership. How these key factors influenced our mixed-heritage participants' sense of self and how they felt about their family background varied even among people who gave the same race and ancestry responses in the preinterview surveys. We find that identity choices by people of mixed racial heritage

https://doi.org/10.7758/edyf5459.8037

**Figure 3.1** *Percentage of Native-White, Asian-White, and Black-White Mixed-Heritage People Who Gave Each Race/Ancestry Response, 1980–2019*

|  | Native-White Heritage | | | Asian-White Heritage | | | Black-White Heritage | | |
|---|---|---|---|---|---|---|---|---|---|
| Race(s) | Native | Both | White | Asian | Both | White | Black | Both | White |
| Ancestry | White | | Native | White | | Asian | White | | Black |
| 1980 | | | 95 | 32 | | 68 | | | 95 |
| 1990 | | | 95 | 26 | | 74 | | 87 | 13 |
| 2000 | 19 | | 78 | 7 | 62 | 30 | 39 | 49 | 12 |
| 2006–2010 | 15 | | 83 | 7 | 62 | 31 | 45 | 46 | 9 |
| 2015–2019 | 21 | | 76 | | 75 | 20 | 33 | 60 | 7 |
| 1980–2019 | 12 | | 85 | 10 | 58 | 33 | 52 | 40 | 8 |

■ Native, Asian, or Black single race, with White heritage reported as ancestry
▨ Both races reported
☐ White single race, with Native, Asian, or Black heritage reported as ancestry

*Source:* Authors' calculations.

across all three groups are not distinct along gender lines. Many factors and experiences, typically built up over a lifetime, shape how people report their race, as revealed when our interviews touched on the multi-layered and "messy" aspects of their lives.

## Racial Identification Responses Differ Across Groups

A broad overview of relatively common—and relatively uncommon—ways in which people of mixed racial heritage have been identifying can be gleaned from Census Bureau data. Figure 3.1 shows cross-group variation graphically, as well as numerically, using data from 1980 to 2019. For example, in 1980 people could reveal their mixed heritage only by reporting different aspects of their background in the ancestry question versus the race question. Of those who reported having Native-White mixed heritage this way, almost all (95 percent) reported White race and Native ancestry, while 5 percent reported Native race and White ancestry. This proportion is the inverse of the pattern for people of Black-White mixed heritage in 1980, when only 5 percent reported White race with Black ancestry. Although this result may not

be surprising to Americans, it is notable as an indicator of the pronounced racial boundaries at the time in the United States. We might
conclude that in 1980 a person could successfully make a social claim
to being a White person if they had Native (or Asian) heritage, but that
this was not usually an option for people with Black heritage. The racial
identity claims of Asian-White people in 1980 and 1990 show that neither
way of expressing mixed racial heritage (Asian race with White ancestry
or White race with Asian ancestry) was seen as always appropriate;
the social rules seem to have been less rigid for Asian-White than for
Native-White and Black-White mixed-heritage people.[1]

In 2000, when the race question added the instruction to "mark
one or more boxes," the three groups continued to show different patterns. Asian-White mixed-heritage people immediately used the new
option, perhaps revealing that this had been the socially appropriate
identification strategy even before it became an option on the census.
Black-White mixed-heritage people also embraced the multiple-race
response option immediately, despite their history of being told that,
legally, they were to self-define as Black (according to the so-called
one-drop rule). It is believed that most of the African American population has multiracial heritage, with at least three-quarters having some
White heritage, and one-quarter having some Native heritage.[2] In the
most recent Census Bureau data (2015 to 2019), 60 percent of people
who reported both Black and White in the race and/or ancestry question did so by reporting both Black and White as races. In the most
recent data, only a relatively small proportion reported Black race and
White ancestry—a striking departure from the recent past (1990).

American Indians and Alaska Natives are often not included in
national conversations about race and racial minority groups and usually
remain invisible in media and academic discourses. In this context, it
may not be surprising that Native-White people have not been making
the same self-identification choices as Asian-White and Black-White
people. Instead, only a relatively small proportion of people reporting
Native-White mixed heritage have been reporting two races. Most are
still reporting White race with Native ancestry, though some report two
races. It is plausible that many have wholly single-race Native relatives
who are several generations in the past. This generational gap may be
seen as especially important, given that Native people have been told
by the US government (and sometimes their own tribal governments

and other Native people) that they are not "real Indians" unless they have a certain lineage or "blood quantum." Generational distance is also important to consider in the context of the many decades of assimilation programs that aimed to stop Native people from passing Native identities to their descendants. The racialization of Native people treats them as a relatively harmless historical group that can be in a White person's ancestry without disqualifying them from Whiteness, as evidenced in the large number of people reporting White race and Native ancestry.[3] Given the persistent trope of the "vanishing Indian," many people with Native heritage who did not feel able to legitimize their claims to be racially American Indian or Alaska Native have relegated this identity to "ancestry" status.[4]

Although American Indian/Alaska Native is defined by the US government as a race group and is functionally a race group in many ways, Native identity contains an important legal-political dimension.[5] Tribal citizenship is based on enrollment criteria determined by sovereign tribal nations and does not necessarily require a predominantly Native family tree. Many enrolled tribal citizens have mixed racial heritage but a singular Native identity; their enrollment status strongly influences their racial identity.[6] The relationship between the dimensions of belonging and racial identity are particularly complex for Native people, as we show in results throughout this book. Although we use the term "race" to describe the American Indian/Alaska Native category, we acknowledge the layers of complexity and meaning added by tribal sovereignty, blood quantum and related documentation issues, varied tribal citizenship rules, and the like.

Black Americans and Asian Americans have also faced pressures related to identity erasure and racial denigration, albeit in very different ways. For example, enslaved Black people were often separated from others who spoke the same non-English language. Many enslaved people experienced the "social death" of losing a communal memory and a meaningful heritage.[7] The United States has a long history of anti-Asian treatment—as exemplified by the 1882 Chinese Exclusion Act barring all Chinese laborers and the "yellow peril" panics of the nineteenth century—stemming from perceptions of the enduring foreignness and otherness of Asian Americans.[8] Such attributions of foreigner status and racial hostility came to the fore with the mass internment of Japanese Americans during the Second World War, when they were deemed to be enemies of the state.

**Figure 3.2** *Percentage of Native-White, Asian-White, and Black-White Mixed-Heritage People Who Gave Each Race/Ancestry Response, by Sex, 1980–2019*

| | Native-White Heritage | | | Asian-White Heritage | | | Black-White Heritage | | |
|---|---|---|---|---|---|---|---|---|---|
| Race(s) | Native | Both | White | Asian | Both | White | Black | Both | White |
| Ancestry | White | | Native | White | | Asian | White | | Black |
| Male | 12 | | 84 | 9 | 58 | 33 | 51 | 41 | 8 |
| Female | 11 | | 85 | 10 | 57 | 33 | 52 | 40 | 8 |
| Total | 12 | | 85 | 10 | 58 | 33 | 52 | 40 | 8 |

■ Native, Asian, or Black single race, with White heritage reported as ancestry
▨ Both races reported
□ White single race, with Native, Asian, or Black heritage reported as ancestry

*Source:* Authors' calculations.

Claire Jean Kim has argued that Asian and Black Americans are racially "triangulated" in relation to White Americans in contrasting ways: Black people are seen as racially inferior but also as "real" Americans, while Asians, though not seen as racially inferior (at least not to the same degree), are never seen as bona-fide Americans.[9] People with Asian heritage were first counted in the US census in 1870, under the category "Chinese." The 1870 Naturalization Act expanded citizenship to individuals with African heritage, but it continued to exclude other non-White groups from becoming citizens.[10] Davenport explains: "The greater racial ambiguity of non-black minorities in the eyes of the law meant that whiteness was theoretically more plausible for these individuals. But the adoption of ethnically exclusionary naturalization policies pointedly clarified Asians' non-whiteness." Thus, Davenport points out, these policies could be "used to justify their lesser treatment."[11]

Yet Asian Americans have historically been depicted as a "model minority" that defies racial barriers via hard work and determination—a narrative that has been problematized.[12] Anti-Asian racism and violence rose significantly in the COVID era as they were blamed for what Donald Trump called "kung flu" and "the China virus."[13]

As we see in figure 3.2, the identity choices made by people of mixed racial heritage are not distinct along gender lines. Specifically, women were not more likely to report multiple races than men. We also did not find gendered patterns in identity choice in our discussions with interview participants.

In the remainder of the chapter, we use census and interview results to dive more fully into these topics as we explore mixed-heritage people's identity choices and the constraints they feel. We illuminate how racial identifications link to lived experiences, especially for people who identify as biracial. Most of our interview participants named multiple races on the preinterview survey. We discuss three key themes arising across all three mixed-heritage groups—racial phenotype, exposure, and challenges to racial authenticity and group membership—as well as other themes, such as specific groups' concerns about racism, marginalization, and historical trauma. We also discuss participants' reported ancestries from the preinterview surveys. Across all three mixed-heritage groups, our participants' ancestry responses suggest that, when given the opportunity, mixed-heritage individuals report both of their parents' ethnic and racial ancestries, if they know them (and even when they are uncertain).[14] We also find that most mixed-heritage individuals report that their Asian, Native, or Black ancestry is more personally meaningful than their White European ancestry.

## RACIAL IDENTIFICATION AMONG PEOPLE WITH NATIVE-WHITE MIXED HERITAGE

Native-White interaction over the past five centuries has often included significant efforts to assimilate Native people into White culture—for example, through boarding schools and relocation programs. Assimilation pressures were applied during most of the centuries-long history of interracial unions between American Indians and White people. Forty-seven-year-old Ron, who reported his race as American Indian (Fond du Lac Ojibwe) and lived in RESCI 2, described the impact of assimilation policies on the way his Native grandparents raised his father:

> My grandparents downplayed being Native American to my dad. In that sense . . . they lived outside the reservation. It was almost like they didn't want anything to do with being Native. Almost wanted to be White people. That Native people were messed up, backwards. My grandma grew up . . . she was a fluent Ojibwe speaker, and she lost

her language in part because of the boarding school movement. My dad moved off the reservation when [he] was a teenager. [His grandparents] never encouraged my dad to learn the language or participate in culture.

The impact of historical trauma can be seen in the racial identification patterns of Native people in the past four decades of census data. Assimilationist policies like sending Native children to boarding school aimed to limit the connection of people with Native ancestors to their Native culture, traditions, and community, with the charge to "Kill the Indian, Save the Man."[15] The experience of being assimilated can limit a person's internal willingness and interpersonal ability to claim American Indian/Alaska Native as a race, though an increasing number of families have overcome this barrier. Given the historical context of genocide and attempts at cultural erasure, it is not easy for many younger Americans with Native ancestry to connect with their Native relatives. Yet some of our participants had made concerted efforts to do so, while drawing comparisons with the experiences of their Native parents.

Like Ron, whose Native father and grandfather had distanced themselves from their Native ancestry, the father of thirty-seven-year-old Tara had had traumatic experiences as a Native person. During his childhood, he had been sent far away to live with a Mormon family. Tara, a woman who lived in RESCI 3, compared her next-generation experience of her heritage to what she knew of her father's Native heritage, which he had buried. Although she had grown up in an area populated by many Native people, she had not really contemplated the painful history of many tribes, or even her Native father's experiences.

> When I got to college and learned about the history of boarding schools . . . I became very angry. . . . Sometimes I wish I hadn't studied American Indian Studies because . . . I would have just been living my best life, being ignorant (*laughs*). I had a lot of mental health issues, and I attribute it to that, because I was so upset about what happened to Natives.

Yet Tara regarded her Native background very positively, knowing that she had benefited from that background, which had enabled her to get a college scholarship: "I say that everything that was bad that happened to my father was because he was Native, and then just one generation later, I think every opportunity I've had is because I was Native."

In fact, almost all of our sixty-eight interviewees reported that they were much more interested in their Native, Black, or Asian ancestry than in their White European ancestry.[16] Reflecting a kind of historical inversion, many Native-White participants, unlike their older Native relatives, were keen to assert their Native background. But for many, doing so was not easy or uncontroversial.

As a result of this historical treatment of Native people, a great many people have had very limited exposure to Native cultural practices, people, tribes, and communities, and they have only genealogical knowledge of their Native family members.[17] This fact alone could account for the high proportion of people with Native heritage reporting a White race (and Native ancestry), even after 2000, when multiple races could be reported.

The trope of American Indians as historical and vanished, as opposed to a currently thriving group, supports the common construction of American Indian as primarily an ancestry group. At the same time, the social construction of the White group (and the Black group, though Native-Black biracial people are not included in our study) has allowed people to claim Native ancestry while still identifying racially as only White (or Black), as depicted in the 1959 painting *A Family Tree* by the celebrated American painter Norman Rockwell (figure 3.3). In this image, an American boy imagines his idealized family tree, including an Indigenous great-grandmother (wearing braids near the center of the image) whose ancestors are not pictured and who partnered with the son of a Confederate soldier.

The national results reported in figure 3.1 show that most people of Native-White mixed heritage report Native as an ancestry rather than as a race. Before 2000, an overwhelming 95 percent of mixed-heritage Native-White people reported White race only, and even after 2000 almost 80 percent still reported White as their only race. This reflects the violent history of assimilation programs for American Indians, centuries of high levels of interracial unions between Native and White people, and a White "racial boundary" that celebrates Native ancestry as one of the more exciting "ethnic options."[18] In their education, income, and residence patterns, people who report White race and Native ancestry in the census data have been shown to be relatively similar to others who identify as racially White.[19] However, spatial context—the history and culture of their specific area—matters for how Native-White people racially identify themselves across the country.[20]

The identity choices of mixed-heritage Native-White people vary considerably depending on the type of place where they live (using the

**Figure 3.3** A Family Tree *by Norman Rockwell, 1959*

*Source:* Artwork courtesy of the Norman Rockwell Family Agency.

RESCI measure of type of place). As noted in chapter 2, RESCI 4 and RESCI 2 areas, both today and in the past, feature American Indian and Alaska Native tribal lands and have significantly more Native people per capita than the rest of the nation. Alex, who was thirty-eight, lived on a large reservation. Residing in an area like that was significant to Alex because his surroundings enabled him to cultivate his interest in and ties to his American Indian heritage, even though his father had not exposed him to many Native practices in his childhood and adolescence. Figure 3.4 shows that in RESCI 4 areas the proportion of people of mixed Native-White heritage who identify as racially American Indian/Alaska Native is many times higher than in other types of areas.

**Figure 3.4** *Percentage of Native-White Mixed-Heritage People Who Gave Each Race/Ancestry Response, by Racial/Ethnic Spatial Context, 1980–2019*

| | Native Race, White Ancestry | Both Races Reported | White Race, Native Ancestry |
|---|---|---|---|

**RESCI 1: E.g., Atlanta, Georgia, Detroit, Michigan, and Tallahassee, Florida**

| | Native Race, White Ancestry | Both Races Reported | White Race, Native Ancestry |
|---|---|---|---|
| 1980 | | | 97 |
| 1990 | | | 97 |
| 2000 | | 13 | 85 |
| 2006–2010 | | 9 | 90 |
| 2015–2019 | | 14 | 85 |
| 1980–2019 | | 6 | 92 |

**RESCI 2: E.g., Fort Collins, Colorado, Clemson, South Carolina, and Duluth, Minnesota**

| | Native Race, White Ancestry | Both Races Reported | White Race, Native Ancestry |
|---|---|---|---|
| 1980 | | | 95 |
| 1990 | | | 95 |
| 2000 | | 18 | 79 |
| 2006–2010 | | 15 | 83 |
| 2015–2019 | | 19 | 78 |
| 1980–2019 | | 11 | 85 |

**RESCI 3: E.g., Minneapolis, New York City, Los Angeles, Houston, and Seattle**

| | Native Race, White Ancestry | Both Races Reported | White Race, Native Ancestry |
|---|---|---|---|
| 1980 | 7 | | 93 |
| 1990 | 6 | | 94 |
| 2000 | | 23 | 73 |
| 2006–2010 | | 19 | 78 |
| 2015–2019 | | 28 | 68 |
| 1980–2019 | | 17 | 79 |

**RESCI 4: E.g., Hopi reservation, Arizona, and Rosebud reservation, South Dakota**

| | Native Race, White Ancestry | Both Races Reported | White Race, Native Ancestry |
|---|---|---|---|
| 1980 | 42 | | 58 |
| 1990 | 41 | | 59 |
| 2000 | 18 | 54 | 28 |
| 2006–2010 | 13 | 47 | 40 |
| 2015–2019 | 19 | 55 | 26 |
| 1980–2019 | 23 | 39 | 37 |

**RESCI 5: Hawaii and San Francisco**

| | Native Race, White Ancestry | Both Races Reported | White Race, Native Ancestry |
|---|---|---|---|
| 1980 | 10 | | 90 |
| 1990 | 12 | | 88 |
| 2000 | | 51 | 44 |
| 2006–2010 | | 46 | 49 |
| 2015–2019 | | 54 | 41 |
| 1980–2019 | 7 | 33 | 60 |

*Source:* Authors' calculations.

*Note:* Maps show the Racial/Ethnic Spatial Context Indicator (RESCI) for PUMAs as of 2010, but decade-specific RESCI geography was used to calculate results.

This singular identification as Native could be seen as making a political claim related to tribal sovereignty or as evidence of a "legal identity"— that is, an identity based on tribal enrollment that is separate from racial and ethnic identities.[21]

Both RESCI 4 (primarily Native tribal lands) and RESCI 5 (Hawaii and San Francisco) have a large share of Native-White people reporting both White and Native races. The two areas are not contextually similar, and people may have different reasons for reporting both races. For example, RESCI 5 has very high rates of multiple-race reporting for all groups in our study, so the high rates among Native-White people could be reflecting a broader acceptance and insistence that claiming heritage groups as race groups is appropriate. In RESCI 4, people's connection to the lands and communities may support Native identity, while "blood quantum" regulations highlight both Native and non-Native heritage.

Despite historical pressures to let go of tribal identities, almost all of our Native-White interview participants answered the ancestry question with specific tribal information about their Native side, as well as about their White European countries of origin. For instance, two respondents, who reported two races, described their ancestry as "Swedish, Polish, Belgian, German, Native American (likely some Mexican/Spanish descent, unsure)" (forty-three-year-old woman) and "Italian, German, French, Leech Lake and White Earth Ojibwe" (thirty-seven-year-old woman). Even those participants who said that they did not feel a strong connection to their Native heritage knew of, and reported, their tribal ancestry. In the 2010 census, 37 percent of multiple-race Native people did not report a tribal affiliation, so knowledge of such an affiliation may indicate a bias in our sample toward people with an interest in or special knowledge of their tribal heritage.[22]

Two decades ago, Carolyn Liebler interviewed people of Native mixed heritage to understand the factors that impact identity.[23] She found that connection to a homeland (such as a reservation) and identity validation by someone who is seen as a "real" Indigenous person were particularly important for mixed-heritage Native people who claimed American Indian/Alaska Native race as an identity. As in that earlier study, we find in the present study that many mixed-heritage Native-White people who are exposed to and have a relationship with their Native relatives, or who have experience on tribal lands, report

Native as their race (see RESCI 4 results in figure 3.4). As discussed earlier, Ron reported only an American Indian race and tribe, but he also said that, despite his Native grandparents' distancing from their Native ancestry, he grew up with a lot of exposure to his Native culture and people:

> I didn't grow up on the reservation, but I spent a lot of time on the rez growing up, especially during the wild rice season. I spent a lot of time with my father on the rez as well—with my father, hunting—when I was a kid. There was just a big influence of Native American culture in my family when I was growing up. In Native cultures you often have large families living together. I remember my uncles living with my grandma. I also remember my grandma had these silver canisters for commodities. We talked about reservation life a lot when I was a kid.

Ron reported that he did not have positive feelings about being Indigenous until he became interested in his heritage during college: "So today I'm proud of being a member of a federally recognized tribe. But it wasn't always the case." Choosing solely "American Indian/Alaska Native" on the latest census form, he demonstrated a clear commitment to cultivating his ties with his tribe and his Native culture.[24] Despite feeling that he looked White, Ron knew that being enrolled as a tribal member helped to ensure that other Native people saw him as Native.

Like Ron, Devon, age forty-three and a resident of a RESCI 2 area, chose only Native for her race and was very clear about why she did so. In the community with Native people where she grew up, she had much more exposure to and appreciation of her maternal Native heritage than her paternal European heritage. Like the other Native-White participants who reported only Native race on the preinterview survey (five out of twenty-one), Devon pointed to the importance of asserting her American Indian heritage to fight against statistical erasure:

> I put Menominee because it's a political status for me; so in order for the United States government to recognize American Indians we need to identify ourselves, even though we may be multiracial . . . in order for us to be counted as American Indian and not as Caucasian or any other race. My mother always drilled it into me that even though I am half White that I need to identify on those forms as American Indian so that way we can be counted.

Like most of the participants in this study, Devon showed no interest in or attachment to her White European ancestry, though she did report it on the form:

> [My father] just said, "Why do you act more Native than French?" and so we had a conversation about how I'm identified in society just by the way that I look and the way that I appear, and then I said I feel like because I do know my language and I do know my culture that I feel more attached to my Menominee side. I said none of my [paternal, French] side of the family ever taught me French language or French foods or any of that; they were pretty well assimilated, and so I identified as being Native.

Devon's strong identification as Native was also reflected in her day-to-day life and choice of partner, topics we discuss in other chapters. Her self-described "Native" appearance, in addition to her exposure to her mother's Native culture, enabled her to assert her Native identity. But many mixed-heritage people identify as Native with White ancestry but are seen as White by others.[25]

Sam, age fifty-two, reported his race as solely American Indian because his Native heritage was extremely important to him. Sam lived in a rural, White-dominated RESCI 2 area and did not live in or near an American Indian community. However, he was enrolled in his tribe (in another state) and maintained active ties with his tribal community, including visits to the reservation several times a year. However, living far away from an area with a sizable Native population made his efforts to maintain his Native ties more challenging. Sam also acknowledged that not all American Indians or people in the wider population saw him as "really" Native. When asked about how others saw him, Sam said that he looked White to others. But he refuted the belief that specific criteria can determine who is authentically Native:

> Yeah, so you're touching on . . . who's really Indian? How do you . . . how long is your hair? Do you speak the language? Do you live on the reservation, or did you grow up on the reservation? Do you live off reservation? All these things sort of contribute to one's Indian-ness. And that's so wrong, because being Native or being Indian is, it's in your soul. It's not something you can decide to do or not do.

Even as reporting their race solely as American Indian tended to reveal their concrete and meaningful connection to that heritage, some Native-White participants still felt conflicted about their ties with their Native family and communities. Sam spoke, for example, of how difficult it was to have ongoing contact with his Native extended family:

> A lot of my extended family are what we . . . term "historical trauma." And I see it. I see that historical trauma being played out in that whole Native side of my family. There's a lot of poverty. We have uncles die of heart disease before the age of fifty years old. There is just a lot of suffering that goes along with that historical trauma.

Moreover, that historical trauma is largely forgotten by others, as pointed out by forty-seven-year-old Susie, who identified as Native and grew up immersed in an American Indian community (in RESCI 2): "I hate the fact that . . . Native people have been so disenfranchised over the years. . . . But I think people have become accustomed to forgetting us as a people—that it's okay to discriminate against us and it's never brought up in the news."

Susie's strong sense of being Native derived not only from awareness of this historical trauma but also from her heightened awareness of feeling racially denigrated by the White people she encountered in her day-to-day life. She perceived White people's contempt for her, she said, based on her Native appearance. She was therefore very careful to dress in a professional way for any meetings with teachers or officials of any kind. She recalled a meeting she attended with her daughter's teachers to discuss the bullying of her daughter (who, Susie said, looked unquestionably Native) by some White children: "I had to think about it before I went in because I had to dress up, because I didn't want them to judge me because I'm already Native, and if I went in there in jeans and a sweatshirt, I would be judged." Her inability to trust White people—based, Susie said, on a lifetime of negative interactions—reinforced her sense of being Native. Even though she acknowledged that she had White ancestry, her lived experience was that of a Native person, and this was how she reported her race on the form.

In comparison with those who reported only Native race, fifteen (of twenty-one) participants who reported both American Indian and White races varied considerably in their attachment to and interest in their Native background. As with participants who identified as solely Native, meaningful contact and relationships with older Native relatives (such as grandparents) was often critical for their cultural and social exposure to Native people and culture and thus fundamental for developing an attachment to their Native heritage.

Gabriella, who was forty and lived in a RESCI 2 area, identified as both Native and White. She talked about how important her paternal grandmother (with whom they lived when she was young) had been in fostering her sense of being a Native person when she was growing up: "Culturally, I was raised Lakota [Rosebud] on my father's side, and we go home—my extended family is mostly in Mission [on the reservation in South Dakota]." Gabriella's grandmother, who raised Gabriella and her siblings during the first years of their lives, "really shaped that connection to the reservation." Her grandmother worked at the Indian technical school in a Southwestern city with many Native people. "So she was forever getting invited to other pueblos and knew students and faculties. And she told us: 'Wherever you are, go find the other Native people and you'll be taken care of.' She said, 'Go make community wherever you are.' She was very intertribal."

Unsurprisingly, participants who lived on a reservation had a lot of exposure to other Native people, practices, and sensibility, and that exposure reinforced their sense of being Indigenous. Cathy, age forty-one, lived and worked on the reservation (in a RESCI 4 area, which has many Native homelands) where she had grown up. Like Gabriella, Cathy was raised by her grandmother, who had reinforced her sense of being Native. "I'm eleven/sixteenths blood quantum. My grandma said to me, 'Cathy, you should always know your blood quantum.'... And I thought... why? But I always remembered it.... I think that it was so that when I had children, they'd also be eligible for membership. The reality is that ... membership is the key to benefits."

In the preinterview survey, Cathy reported both her White and Native races (and tribal affiliation—Ho-Chunk). In the interview, however, she said: "I don't really think of myself as a mixed person, even though I have some European DNA." According to Cathy, she "looked" Native, with her long dark hair, coloring, and presentation. Cathy also felt deeply Native:

There's a way of living that's Native.... When my daughter wants to invite someone over, I always ask if they are American Indian or White, because then I'd have to adjust things in the house if they were White or feel that we would have to act a different way.... Whereas if they were American Indian, I'd know the guest would just understand how we lived. . . . It's like people who have placement of our children, they say, "We can give them everything they need," but they really can't [if they aren't Native].

Not all Native-White people, however, had access to such ties or recollected positive relationships with their American Indian relatives. Forty-four-year-old Aaron, who lived in a RESCI 3 area, marked both Native and White on his preinterview survey, but he did not feel a strong attachment to his American Indian heritage. Moreover, he lacked tribal membership, although both of his parents were Native: "When I fill in forms, I think I'm slightly over half, but nobody qualifies as full blood anymore. I've got quite a bit in me, but not enough for any one tribe."

Aaron was born on his father's reservation but moved away around age five, when his parents divorced.

I didn't feel very accepted by my father's side of the family. Got a lot of flak for being White—acting White. The classic accusations of being an apple—red on the outside, white on the inside. At various family events everyone was nice to me, but I always felt on the outside. It was clear that I was . . . on the outside looking in. I was never really invited to the events, and I didn't really participate in that stuff, and I just wasn't . . .

After leaving the reservation, Aaron lived in mostly White towns and had very little contact with his father's Native relatives or with other Native people. Aaron reported that he was often seen by others as White, but he had no interest in his maternal Dutch heritage. Unfortunately, his efforts to connect with other Native people were rebuffed: "I would sometimes meet other students who were Native, and I would tell them that I had family in White Earth [a reservation] to establish a connection, but there was no real camaraderie."

As articulated by Aaron ("being an apple"), many of our interviews with Native-White participants brought up their experiences of having their Indianness challenged, or their views on criteria for tribal membership, such as blood quantum rules.[26] These discussions often touched on questions about racial authenticity and the basis of tribal membership.

Nina, age forty, lived in an urban RESCI 3 area that had significant numbers of Native people. She identified as Native and White and reported both races on the preinterview survey, but she did not qualify for tribal enrollment, though her father was a tribal member. Nina reported that she was usually seen as White. She felt a strong connection with her Native ancestry but was careful about making claims to *being* Native. Although she was disappointed that she didn't have tribal membership—especially since she was more active in the Native community than her father—she also understood why some people supported the idea of linking blood quantum with being "really" Native: "I wish I had had more access to it [tribal enrollment], but it's important to me just in the sense of . . . kind of understanding that it's like a culture that's about to disappear, right, and unless people maintain that through some way, through maintaining the language and maintaining the cultural practices and traditions, it's just going to be gone." Although Nina felt constrained in her ability to engage with her Native ancestry, she made genuine efforts to do so by taking advantage of her geographical proximity to Native communities to attend language tables and powwows.

Alex reported both races and, because he was highly motivated to learn more about his Native heritage, had made the major commitment of living on his reservation, as mentioned earlier. He grew up in a predominantly White town in a Southwestern RESCI 3 area (what he called "a bubble") surrounded by Native people and reservations. His Navajo father, who had been enrolled in one of the infamous Indian boarding schools growing up, had not raised Alex with much exposure to his Native heritage, although Alex did visit his grandparents regularly on the reservation growing up. Alex was proud of being Navajo, but he said that people could see that he was half White, and he did not feel accepted as "one of them." However, Alex reported, he had always wanted to be "more Navajo":

> I never felt like I really fit in at school. I was proud of being Navajo, and I wanted to be more Navajo, I did. I didn't understand all the jokes, some things said in the language, I wanted to be more Navajo. I remember one of our White teachers was invited to a butchering, and I was thinking, "I've never been to a butchering and I'm half Navajo!" It kind of made me feel bad.

His desire to more fully embody his Navajo identity impacted a number of life decisions that Alex made (see chapter 4)—including his decision to move onto the reservation—that involved both exploration and commitment to learning about his Navajo heritage. Thus, while his childhood exposure to his Native heritage had been limited, he had had enough contact with his Navajo grandparents, and was close enough geographically to Navajo people, to make this transition possible. Liebler identified such factors as particularly likely to lead to identification as racially Native, as was the case for Alex.[27]

Given that some people with little knowledge of or attachment to their Native ancestry are derided as opportunistically claiming a Native identity, some Native-White participants were wary about doing so.[28] But some Native-White participants, undeterred by others' skepticism, were determined to claim their Native identity and ancestry. For example, Sandy, sixty-four years old and living in a RESCI 2 area, reported both Native and White races and said that she did not know anything about her American Indian ancestry while growing up. When she turned thirty, she found out that her paternal grandmother, who had died when her father was only eight years old, was American Indian. Sandy's cousin had been looking into their family tree and discovered this information. Up until that point, she had had no idea that one of her father's parents was American Indian (his father was German American):

> As she [my cousin] was doing this, she found out about this Indian stuff. So I went to talk to my dad, and I said, "Why didn't you ever tell me that we have Native in us?" And he was very quiet, and then he finally said, "Do you know how much torture we went through growing up out in the country when people would find out that my mother was Indian?" He said, "We were ridiculed," and I mean . . . he said it was awful. "We were always taught to be ashamed."

Once his mother died, Sandy's father had no further contact with her side of the family, and that heritage was effectively buried. Such a discovery in one's family history may not be that uncommon, especially today, when the widespread popularity of genetic ancestry tests, which can provide clues, has enabled some people to make genealogical discoveries and claim ethnic and racial identities that were previously unknown to them.[29] Sandy cheerfully reported that, even though she looked White and some White and Native people scoffed at her identification as someone with American Indian heritage, she "paid them no attention."

Other mixed-heritage Native-White participants, especially those who looked White and had limited exposure to Native communities, regarded the assertion of a Native identity with trepidation and wariness. Although forty-year-old Dawn, who lived in a RESCI 3 area, had an Ojibwe grandmother, she had had little contact with or knowledge of her grandmother, or any other Native people, while growing up. Her part-Native father had distanced himself from his Native heritage. When younger, she had identified as Native, but she started identifying herself as White when she realized that strangers saw her as a White person. Dawn seemed uneasy, even fearful, of potential pushback if she said that she had Native heritage:

> It's like, where do you walk that line between reclaiming something that is without being like this cultural appropriator, this Cherokee princess fakeness about it, I don't know. So, in your worldview anyone who's not involved can't say they have this heritage. . . . Where do people like me, I'm not being disingenuous, I'm not trying to claim something I'm not. I'm also not necessarily going to go enroll in . . . is there a space for us in a way?

Despite her misgivings about claiming to be part–American Indian, Dawn wavered about her racial self-identification:

> So, I was at an antiracism conference two or three years ago now, and this woman who was Dakota was speaking . . . and she said, "We need to reclaim our identities because this is White supremacy. We've erased a people, and the people still exist, but we've erased it." And she's like, "It's something we can reclaim, and even just saying, 'I'm Ojibwe,' or 'I'm a Dakota,' even if you're not connected, is reclaiming that space." And I just thought that was a really powerful way of thinking about it, and like, I haven't gone out and like, "I'm Ojibwe," but maybe my dad isn't right about that. Maybe there's a space for reclaiming that or, like, redefining what it means.

Although Dawn did not feel that she could legitimately claim to be part–American Indian, other participants (whose claims to being American Indian could be refuted by others) were highly motivated to do so. But a number of factors—racial appearance, cultural exposure, and rules around tribal membership (and group membership more generally)—made it difficult for participants to claim a link to their Native heritage that was seen as "authentic."

Dawn's experience may be common, though she was our only participant to report White race and Native ancestry on the preinterview survey. The Census Bureau data show that among people with Native-White mixed heritage, reporting Native as only an ancestry (see figures 3.1 and 3.4) is the most common response, especially in areas dominated by White, Black, and Latino worldviews (RESCIs 1, 2, and 3).

## RACIAL IDENTIFICATION AMONG PEOPLE
## WITH BLACK-WHITE MIXED HERITAGE

The national-level census results illustrate a pattern for mixed-heritage Black-White people that is distinct from the patterns for Native-White and Asian-White people. In the context of violent domination and enslavement (as well as consensual unions), Black-White interracial unions have a centuries-old history in the United States. For many people of Black and White heritage, the generational locus of "mixing" is a period long ago when the social and legal definitions of the "Black" and "White" categories pushed Black-White individuals to be both legally and self-defined as Black and the Black community accepted them as Black. Historically, Black-White people of mixed heritage have often been treated as single-race Black.[30]

The nonconsensual nature of some Black-White unions impacts how mixed heritage is discussed and experienced.[31] Reflecting the long and complex social and legal history of Black-White relations in the United States, the census results in figure 3.1 show that in 1980 and 1990 very few Black-White people reported White race with Black ancestry; instead, mixed-heritage Black-White people overwhelmingly reported Black race with White ancestry. White women married to Black men led the "multiracial" social movement of the 1990s.[32] Their efforts were instrumental in changing the federal definition of race so that multiple race responses would be recorded in data as of 1997.[33] Nonpublic census data reflect this, showing that multiple-race responses were not uncommon for first-generation Black-White children in the 1980 and 1990 censuses, before the federal definition of race allowed multiple-race responses.[34]

In many ways, the multiracial social movement was a success. In recent years, the one-drop rule of Black blood—by which a person with African heritage was legally and socially defined as Black—has been

less culturally dominant or legally enforced.[35] The rise of biracial identification among Black-White mixed-heritage people marks a significant
change in how Black-White people identify themselves.[36] Prior qualitative research has shown that first-generation, multiracial Black-White
people (those with single-race parents) often have complex internal
identities that do not respond easily to a single-response instruction.[37]
In 2000 and later, fewer than half of mixed-heritage Black-White people
reported Black race with White ancestry in the census data, and about
as many reported *both* Black and White as races (figure 3.1).

We show geographic patterns in the race/ancestry reports of Black-
White people, as shown in Census Bureau data, in figure 3.5. In RESCI
1 areas—which, like Atlanta, Georgia, have a long and present history
of larger Black populations—98 percent of people who indicated that
they had both Black and White heritage on the 1980 census reported
this as Black race and White ancestry. Twenty years later, in 2000,
when multiple-race responses were first allowed in federal data collection efforts, that number dropped to 52 percent as a plurality of Black-
White people in RESCI 1 reported both as races (40 percent). In the
most recent data in RESCI 1, 48 percent of people of Black and White
heritage reported both to the Census Bureau as races, and 48 percent
reported Black race with White ancestry. Compared to RESCI 1, biracial
Black-White responses have been even more common in recent decades
in more rural, heavily White areas (69 percent in RESCI 2) and in
San Francisco and Hawaii (66 percent in RESCI 5). These patterns
provide evidence that the racial/ethnic context (for example, the social
acceptance of identifying as multiracial) is related to patterns of racial
self-identification.

Few Black-White mixed-heritage people reported a single-race White
identity between 1980 and 2019. Mirroring this pattern, none of our
twenty Black-White participants identified as White race with Black
ancestry. In fact, as we show in a subsequent chapter on how mixed-
heritage people identify their children, it is rare for Black-White people,
even those with a White spouse, to report their children as single-race
White. However, our interview participants shared that not choosing
White for their race did not necessarily mean that they felt no affinity
with their Whiteness.

In our interviews, only one of our twenty Black-White participants
identified solely as Black. Sixty-year-old Yetta, who lived in RESCI 2,

**Figure 3.5** *Percentage of Black-White Mixed-Heritage People Who Gave Each Race/Ancestry Response, by Racial/Ethnic Spatial Context, 1980–2019*

| | Black Race, White Ancestry | Both Races Reported | White Race, Black Ancestry |
|---|---|---|---|

**RESCI 1: E.g., Atlanta, Georgia, Detroit, Michigan, and Tallahassee, Florida**

| | Black Race, White Ancestry | Both Races Reported | White Race, Black Ancestry |
|---|---|---|---|
| 1980 | | 98 | |
| 1990 | | 91 | 9 |
| 2000 | 52 | 40 | 8 |
| 2006–2010 | 61 | 34 | |
| 2015–2019 | 48 | 48 | |
| 1980–2019 | 73 | 23 | |

**RESCI 2: E.g., Fort Collins, Colorado, Clemson, South Carolina, and Duluth, Minnesota**

| | Black Race, White Ancestry | Both Races Reported | White Race, Black Ancestry |
|---|---|---|---|
| 1980 | | 90 | 10 |
| 1990 | | 85 | 15 |
| 2000 | 32 | 57 | 11 |
| 2006–2010 | 36 | 57 | 8 |
| 2015–2019 | 25 | 69 | 6 |
| 1980–2019 | 41 | 51 | 8 |

**RESCI 3: E.g., Minneapolis, New York City, Los Angeles, Houston, and Seattle**

| | Black Race, White Ancestry | Both Races Reported | White Race, Black Ancestry |
|---|---|---|---|
| 1980 | | 94 | |
| 1990 | | 85 | 15 |
| 2000 | 41 | 44 | 15 |
| 2006–2010 | 48 | 40 | 13 |
| 2015–2019 | 37 | 55 | 9 |
| 1980–2019 | 50 | 39 | 11 |

**RESCI 4: E.g., Hopi reservation, Arizona, and Rosebud reservation, South Dakota**

| | Black Race, White Ancestry | Both Races Reported | White Race, Black Ancestry |
|---|---|---|---|
| 1980 | | | |
| 1990 | | | |
| 2000 | | | |
| 2006–2010 | | | |
| 2015–2019 | | | |
| 1980–2019 | | | |

**RESCI 5: Hawaii and San Francisco**

| | Black Race, White Ancestry | Both Races Reported | White Race, Black Ancestry |
|---|---|---|---|
| 1980 | | 87 | 13 |
| 1990 | | 88 | 12 |
| 2000 | 43 | 42 | 15 |
| 2006–2010 | 33 | 54 | 14 |
| 2015–2019 | 23 | 66 | 11 |
| 1980–2019 | 48 | 39 | 13 |

*Source:* Authors' calculations.

*Note:* Maps show the Racial/Ethnic Spatial Context Indicator (RESCI) for PUMAs as of 2010, but decade-specific RESCI geography was used to calculate results. The graph for RESCI 4 is not shown because the underlying sample is very small.

was the oldest of our Black-White respondents; by the time multiple-race reporting was possible or more common, she was already middle-aged. When asked why she identified as Black, Yetta referred to the convention of identifying as "just Black" when she was growing up (in RESCI 3). But she also spoke of her White mother being disowned by her family:

> I grew up in a Black environment is what I can say. So, when my parents married, you know, a thousand years ago, it wasn't as popular or as accepted as it is now, and when my mother got married, her family said, you're dead to me. So, I never knew . . . she had one sister actually, who stayed in touch over the years, but I never knew any of her family, so we grew up in what started out as . . . I would say probably sixty-forty integrated neighborhood, but then over the years it became White flight, and it became a predominantly Black neighborhood.

Yetta explained ruefully that, because her White mother had been disowned by her family, she'd always been curious about the White side of her family and was frustrated by her lack of access to her Italian American heritage. In comparison with Native-White participants, who expressed concerns about other Native people challenging their racial authenticity as Native, Black-White participants like Yetta felt constrained in their ability to claim a connection to their White European ancestry—especially given that, as many of them reported, their racial appearance immediately ruled out their acceptance as part-European people. Yet, as discussed later, Black-White participants could also encounter social rejection for not being authentically Black.

Despite the fact that nineteen of the twenty Black-White participants in our study identified as biracial, a smaller proportion of them provided specific ancestry information in the preinterview surveys, especially about their Black ancestry. For example, a few Black-White participants simply wrote "African American," or "don't know," in their ancestry responses. Most of them did, however, provide details of ancestry from both sides of their families, albeit more details about their White ancestry. For instance, Mallory, age forty-four and a RESCI 3 resident, identified biracially as Black and White and described her ancestry as "Creole, Native American, Irish Catholic, Scottish." Another participant, thirty-year-old Kendra from a RESCI 3 area, identified as both White and Black and reported her ancestry as such: "My dad is African American.

My mom is English, Irish, and German, but her family has been in the US for generations." But greater knowledge of their White ancestry did not lead these participants to value it more than their Black ancestry or to identify with it more often. Although they lived in different areas in RESCI 3, Mallory and Kendra both felt able to assert their mixedness and their racial and ethnic multiplicity in urban settings where cosmopolitanism seemed both normal and valued.

Although nineteen participants reported both Black and White race on the preinterview survey, many reported feeling a strong attachment to their Black background. Furthermore, despite having a biracial background in common, these participants varied significantly in how they related to their White and Black races and in the salience of their racial background in their lived experience. For example, Mallory, who grew up in a predominantly White town in the Northeast, now lived in a diverse metropolitan area. She grew up with a Black father and White mother who were both professional working parents. Although her mixed family definitely "stood out" in her town, she described a happy family life that enabled her to feel positive about both her Black and White sides. When asked about how she thought about being racially mixed, she said:

> It's very important. It's one of the primary ways I identify myself. It's how I think about myself. . . . I think my parents encouraged me to develop my own sense of identity, but I think they probably encouraged me to . . . to look at myself as being both and to be proud of . . . to be proud of myself and to say that, "Oh, I have this interesting background."

In reporting that she identified as *both* "Black" and "mixed," Mallory noted that "Blackness is vast," meaning that there was no one way of being Black, especially in combination with other backgrounds.[38]

While Mallory enthusiastically embraced both her White and Black ancestries and family members from both "sides," many of the other biracially reporting Black-White participants revealed that they felt closer to either their White or Black side, and some had changed their racial identification over time, especially with a change in geographical context. It was not uncommon for exposure to their Black and White families and social worlds to be skewed, as happened with a number of Black-White participants who had grown up with only their White mother.[39] Corey, who was twenty-eight, grew up with her White mother and her White extended family in a town on the West Coast (RESCI 2), and she had virtually no contact with her Black father. Corey reported that her mother had raised her to see herself as biracial. Growing up, she had not felt accepted or comfortable with the other Black students in her school. She did not feel culturally connected to other Black people, reporting that, when she met some Black people who had been adopted by White families, she felt that her own experiences were very similar to theirs.

However, after Corey moved away from home to attend college in a large and diverse metropolitan area, her Blackness became more salient to her and her sense of self. Her exposure to Black people and Blackness in this new setting engendered a different way of seeing herself racially.[40] As she entered higher education, she realized that the fact that she had a White mother did not register in most of her interactions with other people, especially other White people. Although she acknowledged her White ancestry and family in her interview and reported both Black and White races for herself in the preinterview survey, Corey now saw herself as a Black woman.

Thirty-two-year-old Wendy, who lived in RESCI 2, also grew up with a White mother and had a good relationship with her White family. She reported growing up "poor" in a college town. Unlike Corey, Wendy felt comfortable in her surroundings, and she connected to different racial groups in her school. Like Corey, Wendy saw herself as biracial when she was growing up:

> I think being Black was always a part of me. In high school I was part of the Black student union and things like that. But being biracial was the identity I most often shared. . . . I was raised in the house by my White mother and my father wasn't in the house, so . . . and I had a close relationship with the White part of my family. So being biracial made sense to me.

Wendy's mother was "racially conscious," and because they lived in an area with many other Black people, her mother provided Wendy with some exposure to Black people:

> I appreciate that my mom—she tried to instill a positive racial iden-
> tity in us. Not always in an explicit way. But she would take me to her

friends to get my hair braided. Things like that. And because of her own networks, we were around a lot of Black people. So, she herself was like the "black sheep" of the family, though. They were more conservative and White.

When Wendy moved out of the house and moved to the South, she met many more Black people, including her Black husband. She now identified primarily as a Black woman, even though she still saw herself as "biracial."

Darrell, age twenty-eight, was also raised solely by his White mother, in what he described as a working-class household. They lived on the outskirts of a city with a substantial Black population (in RESCI 3). Although Darrell acknowledged having a mixed heritage, he said that his mother raised him as a Black boy, knowing that he would be racially targeted:

> One day in [his heavily White Midwestern state] was particularly bad. My brother and I were walking home from school, and they were shouting racial slurs at us. We had bad experiences at school, and my mom was like, "Hey, y'all, this is what you're gonna have to deal with. Black boys in America, it's something you're gonna have to deal with a lot." She was very clear with us about that kind of stuff.

So, while Darrell reported that he was both Black and White in the preinterview survey, he clearly identified primarily as a Black man, and his lived experience was that of a Black man who was subject to racial stigma.[41] Like Darrell, some of the Black-White men we interviewed, though few in number (we had more women in our interview study), were especially vocal about the negative depiction and treatment of Black men in society.

Illustrating the diverse range of experiences among biracially reporting Black-White people, some participants, especially those who had grown up in predominantly White places, were more relaxed around White people and in predominantly White settings. Forty-four-year-old Max, from a RESCI 3 area, was raised by his White mother and had very limited contact with his Black father growing up. He reported that, although they "did not have much money," he grew up in mostly affluent White towns in the Northeast where he had little contact with Black people, and he felt very comfortable in most White settings. In fact, Max had won a scholarship to attend an elite private school in the Northeast. He grew up feeling that he was neither White nor Black, and he now felt comfortable thinking of himself as a mixed Black-White person.

> I don't think about it [my race] too much. It depends on the situation. I feel a bit out of place more in relation to poor neighborhoods, such as a poor Black neighborhood or poor White neighborhood. It was interesting to go to Atlanta, where there were so many Black people, and many of them were professional and middle-class, which hadn't been my experience, and I felt very comfortable with that.

In comparison with the participants who had grown up with their White mother and had little contact with their Black father, some Black-White participants grew up with both of their parents but little exposure to their other Black family members; thus, these participants felt a relative lack of attachment to that part of their family tree. Blair, who was forty-six, lived in RESCI 3 and identified as White and Black, reported that his African American father had effectively steered him away from his Black heritage (as did the parents of some Native-White participants in an attempt to distance them from traumatic experiences):

> Like, my dad is very, I don't know if you know . . . very class kind of conscious, but certainly oriented toward class, and I don't know if he recognized, like, I don't know, some of the stuff just seemed like he'd always tend to favor the dominant culture, and maybe it was just to make sure that I could fit in. I don't know.

Growing up, Blair had little contact with other Black families or people, including his father's side of the family. In addition to recalling how "class conscious" his father was, Blair himself mentioned several times during the interview being most comfortable with "the dominant culture." When asked if there was a race with which he most identified, he replied: "Yeah, I mean, I guess like I said, I'm most comfortable . . . [with] the White dominant society."

Saskia, who was twenty-six and lived in a RESCI 2 area, grew up in a predominantly White town with both parents and reported that she was biracial. She did not believe, however, that her race was central to her sense of self. Saskia also revealed that her faith and Christian network were more important to her than her race: "Um, I prefer to identify as mixed. I don't like using race as an identifier, because I feel like there's so much more to a person than . . . within being mixed. What I wanted most of all was a cultural heritage than a racial heritage, so I found that I gravitate more toward strong cultures." Furthermore, Saskia had had more contact with her White mother's family, because she believed that her Black father's family had disapproved of her White mother:

> There were times with us that we were looked at as not fully a part of the [Black] family because we were different. My dad's light skinned, and I was told that he was made fun of [in his family] for being light skinned. Most of his family were darker. Nothing was said to our face, but there was this sense of discomfort.

Thus, despite how normative it is becoming for mixed-heritage Black-White people to identify biracially in Census Bureau data, participants' feelings about and attachments to their White and Black backgrounds varied. Significantly for our understanding of the impact of racial identity on life choices, Saskia and Blair, both of whom seemed more comfortable with their White family and with White people generally, both had a White spouse. We focus on spouse choice in relation to personal identity in chapter 4.

A common theme emerging from the remarks of some of our Black-White participants (especially those who had grown up in predominantly White areas) was their experience of diverging from prescribed scripts of behavior for Black people, and they spoke about the impact of their awareness of such rules on their lives. Jessica, a thirty-six-year-old who identified as a mixed, Black-White woman and lived in RESCI 3, spoke of the difficulty of behaving in ways that were not coded as "Black."[42] "In junior high, it was a good experience overall, but I was made fun of for acting White, talking White. I was kind of wacky. I played ice hockey (not typical for Black kids), I liked country music, rap music. So, I was made fun of." Jessica was very clear about the behaviors and musical preferences that were considered White or Black, and she knew that she displayed "White" behaviors and tastes; as such, she was seen as "wacky" by her school classmates.

In fact, not all of the Black-White participants, especially some light-skinned female respondents, felt accepted by other Black people. For example, although Helen, age forty-two, lived in a highly diverse

RESCI 3 metropolitan area and identified as both White and Black, she described a lifetime of rejection and hostility from Black people, especially other Black women.[43] "If I were mixed, but with darker skin, like Barack Obama, I would have been accepted. Mixed with lighter skin, I'm automatically in the White box."

When they first met, Helen's African American manager at work told her, "You don't look Black," to which Helen retorted: "In my family, we were snow to crow." According to Helen, she was one of the lightest skinned among her siblings.[44] Over time, her sense of rejection by other Black people appeared to make her quite wary around other Black people, even though she still identified as a mixed-race woman and reported both races in the preinterview survey.

> Because of how I talk, how I sound, and the color of my skin. The Black girls didn't look like me because I looked White. . . . I can laugh about it because it's been forty-two years of it, but I'm very sensitive to it. . . . I went to a national work event for African Americans, and as soon as I walked in the room, all eyes were on me. . . . What's she doing here? When they see me up close or when they see pictures of my children, I might get a bit more acceptance, but . . .

Thus, for a Black-White person—especially a Black-White woman—with a White appearance, asserting Black group membership was often difficult. Interestingly, Native-White individuals who did not see themselves as looking stereotypically "Native" were still acknowledged, in certain Native contexts, as Native people, especially if they were tribally enrolled.

Although none of our Black-White mixed-heritage people identified as racially single-race White, some did want validation of a White ethnicity that was meaningful to them. However, our participants' experiences show that it remains very difficult for a Black-White person—especially those who do not look White—to have their White European ancestry validated. Thirty-seven-year-old Adriana, from a RESCI 3 locale, identified herself as White and Black, but she longed for validation of her (mother's) Italian American ancestry. Adriana's ancestry response was "Italian, Bajan, African American," but her Italian ancestry was not recognized by others. She reported that other people usually saw her as either Black or Latina. When she started working at her job in a large public-sector organization, an older Italian American colleague had been surprised when Adriana told him that she had an Italian grandmother

> Well, one of [my colleagues], he just retired. His daughter's name is Adriana, so when I met him, he said, "Well, I'll never forget your name because my daughter's name is [also] Adriana. She was named after my mother, an old Italian lady." And I said, "Me too, well, I was named after my grandmother Adriana, another old Italian lady." He was clearly surprised. And people tend to assume I have a Latino background . . . people come into the precinct and assume I speak Spanish. So, he was definitely surprised.

Adriana did not usually have an opportunity to divulge her Italian ancestry, because she knew that her racial assignment as Black (or Latina) was the dominant way she was seen: "Well, it's the way the world sees me. Personally, I can feel like, oh, I've got all this going on. I know that. But the outside world, no one is looking and saying, 'Her grandmother is Italian.'"

As famously documented by Mary Waters, in comparison with White Americans, who are able to claim a variety of European ethnic ancestry options, racialized individuals who do not look White cannot assert their claims (as in Adriana's claim to Italian ethnicity) without encountering significant skepticism.[45] Not only did Adriana feel unable to identify publicly as part-Italian by ancestry, but her racial Blackness always superseded her racial Whiteness.

Therefore, despite how common it has become for Black-White people to identify with both races, the reporting of both races obscured important differences in how biracially identifying participants thought about, and experienced, their racial selves. How these participants related to their White and Black racial backgrounds was heavily influenced by variable exposure, their racial appearance, and the degree to which they felt accepted by both Black and White people around them. Although many of these biracially reporting participants "felt" more Black than White, a few participants identified more with their White ancestry and with White people. The racial consciousness associated with racist experiences, or awareness of Black stereotypes, was common across our sample, but not all our participants gravitated toward their Black background. As we have illustrated, themes of membership and exclusion, in relation to both White and Black groups and settings, were related to the dynamics around gender, colorism, and class.

## RACIAL IDENTIFICATION AMONG PEOPLE
## WITH ASIAN-WHITE MIXED HERITAGE

One immediate point of comparison between Asian-White people and both Native-White and Black-White people is that most Asian-White people in the United States are the descendants of people of color who came to this country voluntarily.[46] Nevertheless, there is huge diversity among Asian Americans in their historical incorporation into the United States. Many Japanese and Chinese Americans have ancestors who immigrated to the United States in the 1800s.[47] By contrast, most ancestors of Vietnamese Americans arrived as refugees in the 1970s, and most ancestors of the largely college-educated Korean Americans and Asian Indian Americans arrived in the post-1965 era.[48] Despite their significant heterogeneity, Asian Americans are often characterized as a "racial middle" group situated between White and Black Americans, alongside Latinos.[49] Describing the politically distinct position of Asian Americans in the United States, Gary Okihiro argues that "yellow is emphatically neither white nor black."[50]

Despite historical restrictions on immigration from Asia to the United States, as well as restrictions on intermarriage between Asian people and White people, sizable numbers of US military personnel married East Asian women in the mid-twentieth century, especially during the Korean and Vietnam Wars.[51] In fact, several of our Asian-White participants reported this scenario: Their mothers had immigrated from Japan and Korea after marrying their White fathers. But most Asian-White intermarriages, being relatively recent, have taken place in a period when "multiracial" is a relatively viable identity claim for their US-born children.

Among people who reported Asian and White mixed heritage in the census data, a White race (and Asian ancestry) response dominated in the 1980 and 1990 census data (figure 3.1). For decades, the Asian census race question has included six Asian countries of origin, as well as a fill-in-the-blank for other origins, unlike the Black and White categories, for which no opportunity for detail was provided before 2020. The distribution of responses by specific Asian group is shown in figure 3.6.[52]

**Figure 3.6** *Percentage of Asian-White Mixed-Heritage People in Each Detailed Asian Group Who Gave Each Race/Ancestry Response, 1980–2019*

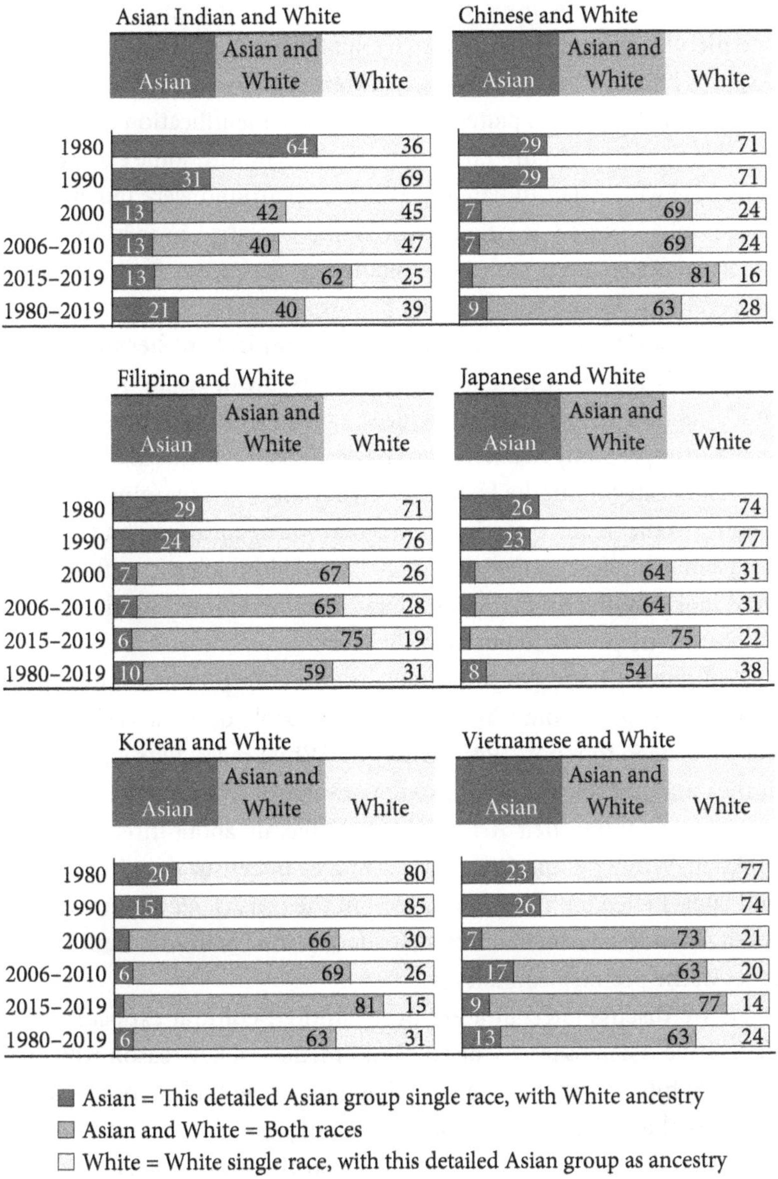

Asian Indian and White

| | Asian | Asian and White | White |
|---|---|---|---|
| 1980 | | 64 | 36 |
| 1990 | 31 | | 69 |
| 2000 | 13 | 42 | 45 |
| 2006–2010 | 13 | 40 | 47 |
| 2015–2019 | 13 | 62 | 25 |
| 1980–2019 | 21 | 40 | 39 |

Chinese and White

| | Asian | Asian and White | White |
|---|---|---|---|
| 1980 | 29 | | 71 |
| 1990 | 29 | | 71 |
| 2000 | 7 | 69 | 24 |
| 2006–2010 | 7 | 69 | 24 |
| 2015–2019 | | 81 | 16 |
| 1980–2019 | 9 | 63 | 28 |

Filipino and White

| | Asian | Asian and White | White |
|---|---|---|---|
| 1980 | 29 | | 71 |
| 1990 | 24 | | 76 |
| 2000 | 7 | 67 | 26 |
| 2006–2010 | 7 | 65 | 28 |
| 2015–2019 | 6 | 75 | 19 |
| 1980–2019 | 10 | 59 | 31 |

Japanese and White

| | Asian | Asian and White | White |
|---|---|---|---|
| 1980 | 26 | | 74 |
| 1990 | 23 | | 77 |
| 2000 | | 64 | 31 |
| 2006–2010 | | 64 | 31 |
| 2015–2019 | | 75 | 22 |
| 1980–2019 | 8 | 54 | 38 |

Korean and White

| | Asian | Asian and White | White |
|---|---|---|---|
| 1980 | 20 | | 80 |
| 1990 | 15 | | 85 |
| 2000 | | 66 | 30 |
| 2006–2010 | 6 | 69 | 26 |
| 2015–2019 | | 81 | 15 |
| 1980–2019 | 6 | 63 | 31 |

Vietnamese and White

| | Asian | Asian and White | White |
|---|---|---|---|
| 1980 | 23 | | 77 |
| 1990 | 26 | | 74 |
| 2000 | 7 | 73 | 21 |
| 2006–2010 | 17 | 63 | 20 |
| 2015–2019 | 9 | 77 | 14 |
| 1980–2019 | 13 | 63 | 24 |

■ Asian = This detailed Asian group single race, with White ancestry
▨ Asian and White = Both races
☐ White = White single race, with this detailed Asian group as ancestry

*Source:* Authors' calculations.

Distinctions between Asian groups—at least in terms of language, foods, and customs—are at least somewhat acknowledged in US culture, and such recognition may support the culture-specific learning and identity building experienced by mixed-heritage people from their Asian relatives. Despite the many differences between Asian origin groups, the large-scale pattern of chosen self-identification across the six Asian groups in figure 3.6 is relatively similar, with some exceptions.

People with Asian Indian and White background were much more commonly reported as Asian (with White ancestry) in 1980 than the other five Asian groups who were named on the census form. By 1990, however, the Asian Indian–White pattern was more similar to that of other Asian-White groups. After 2000, Asian Indians became much more likely to choose a single race (either White or Asian Indian) and much less likely to choose two races, compared to the other Asian-White groups. Many Asian Indians have a sense of distinctiveness from the Asian category in the US context. They are at the margins of membership in the "Asian American" category, whose meanings and images are primarily associated with East Asians.[53] Although caste affiliations may make many Asian Indians feel distinctive, our (South Asian–White) participants did not mention caste.

As figures 3.1 and 3.6 show, once multiple responses were invited in 2000, the most common response for people of Asian-White heritage has been to report both Asian and White races. Our closer look at the data (not shown) reveals that many Asian-White people include information about their Asian ancestry. Overall, about three-quarters of Asian-White people reported both races in census data from 2000 and later. Reflecting this pattern seen in the census, *all* of our twenty-seven Asian-White interview participants reported both Asian and White races in the preinterview survey.

As we discuss later, in addition to limited cultural exposure to a distinctive Asian ethnicity or cultural practices, a key reason why our Asian-White mixed-heritage participants do not identify as solely Asian is that some Asian monoracial people exclude Asian-White people from their definition of "Asian" on the grounds that they are not authentically, "fully" Asian. Such social rejection of group membership, which was reported by both male and female participants, can be based on racial appearance or a perceived lack of knowledge and understanding of Asian languages and cultural practices, as well as other factors.[54] Such exclusion is the converse of the historical tendency to regard all people with Black ancestry as Black.[55] Forty-three-year-old Andrew's description of himself as racially marginal was representative of a theme among many Asian-White interviewees. Although he grew up in a RESCI 2 suburb that had some Asian families, he did not find it easy to forge ties with them. Andrew reported a lifetime of being seen as not belonging to any one race, especially on the basis of his racially ambiguous appearance: "I was the Asian guy with my White friends, and I was the White guy with my Asian friends," he said. As such, Andrew felt neither White nor Asian.

All of our Asian-White participants specified a particular Asian ethnicity in the ancestry question rather than just writing "Asian." For instance, Sumi, who was forty-four, lived in a RESCI 1 area, and reported White and Japanese for her race, also described her ancestry as "Japanese Italian." Forty-two-year-old Makana, from a RESCI 3 locale, reported her race as "White, Japanese, and Chinese" and her ancestry as "Japanese, Chinese, French Canadian, Slovakian." David, who was thirty-five and also from a RESCI 3 area, reported his race as White and Chinese and described his ancestry as "Chinese, English, Norwegian, German, Scottish, Welsh." Despite these detailed ancestry responses, one Asian ancestry was usually deemed most salient when discussed in the interview.

The tendency among Asian-White participants to provide detailed ancestry responses could stem from several sources, including the genealogical recency of Asian ancestors, the provision of distinct Asian ethnic categories in the census and other official forms, and the emphasis on ancestral knowledge in both Asian and White cultures. Claiming a specific Asian ethnicity is also an assertion of an ethnic option that makes a person more distinctive rather than simply a member of an undifferentiated Asian racial grouping.[56] Being considered generically "Asian" could be a liability in terms of racist responses (for example, when COVID-19 was denounced as "the China virus," instigating undifferentiated anti-Asian violence).

In comparison with the other mixed-heritage groups, Asian-White people are much less likely to report a single race in census data (figure 3.1). Figure 3.7 shows that single-race Asian identification declined in all the types of places identified by the RESCI measure. However, there is context-related variation in the extent to which mixed-heritage

**Figure 3.7** *Percentage of Asian-White Mixed-Heritage People Who Gave Each Race/Ancestry Response, by Racial/Ethnic Spatial Context, 1980–2019*

| | Asian Race, with White Ancestry | Both Races Reported | White Race, with Asian Ancestry |
|---|---|---|---|

**RESCI 1: E.g., Atlanta, Georgia, Detroit, Michigan, and Tallahassee, FL**

| Year | Asian Race, with White Ancestry | Both Races Reported | White Race, with Asian Ancestry |
|---|---|---|---|
| 1980 | 25 | | 75 |
| 1990 | 17 | | 83 |
| 2000 | 6 | 54 | 40 |
| 2006–2010 | 7 | 55 | 38 |
| 2015–2019 | | 71 | 24 |
| 1980–2019 | 9 | 47 | 44 |

**RESCI 2: E.g., Fort Collins, Colorado, Clemson, South Carolina, and Duluth, Minnesota**

| Year | Asian Race, with White Ancestry | Both Races Reported | White Race, with Asian Ancestry |
|---|---|---|---|
| 1980 | 31 | | 69 |
| 1990 | 23 | | 77 |
| 2000 | 7 | 57 | 36 |
| 2006–2010 | 7 | 59 | 34 |
| 2015–2019 | | 73 | 23 |
| 1980–2019 | 10 | 53 | 38 |

**RESCI 3: E.g., Minneapolis, New York City, Los Angeles, Houston, and Seattle**

| Year | Asian Race, with White Ancestry | Both Races Reported | White Race, with Asian Ancestry |
|---|---|---|---|
| 1980 | 34 | | 66 |
| 1990 | 29 | | 71 |
| 2000 | 8 | 65 | 27 |
| 2006–2010 | 8 | 63 | 30 |
| 2015–2019 | | 76 | 18 |
| 1980–2019 | 9 | 62 | 29 |

**RESCI 4: E.g., Hopi reservation, Arizona, and Rosebud reservation, South Dakota**

| Year | Asian Race, with White Ancestry | Both Races Reported | White Race, with Asian Ancestry |
|---|---|---|---|
| 1980 | | | |
| 1990 | | | |
| 2000 | | | |
| 2006–2010 | | | |
| 2015–2019 | | | |
| 1980–2019 | | | |

**RESCI 5: Hawaii and San Francisco**

| Year | Asian Race, with White Ancestry | Both Races Reported | White Race, with Asian Ancestry |
|---|---|---|---|
| 1980 | 46 | | 54 |
| 1990 | 42 | | 58 |
| 2000 | | 85 | 9 |
| 2006–2010 | 6 | 85 | 9 |
| 2015–2019 | | 89 | 6 |
| 1980–2019 | 14 | 68 | 19 |

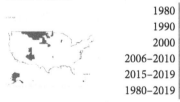

*Source:* Authors' calculations.

*Note:* Maps show the RESCI for PUMAs as of 2010; decade-specific RESCI geography was used to calculate results. The graph for RESCI 4 is not shown because the underlying sample is very small.

Asian-White people identify as single-race White, with Asian ancestry, as opposed to biracial. In places with a particularly notable Black-related history (RESCI 1) or White-related history (RESCI 2), a substantial proportion of mixed-heritage Asian-White people (36 to 40 percent) identify as single-race White, even after 2000. In contrast, in Hawaii and San Francisco (RESCI 5), where the population of Asian and Pacific Islanders is particularly high, 85 to 89 percent of Asian-White people identify biracially, with only 6 percent identifying as White from 2015 to 2019. These areas have a recognized "Hapa" identity for mixed-race Asians.[57]

Our Asian-White interviews reflect the census patterns, as none of our participants reported themselves as solely Asian or solely White. As with the biracially identified participants in the other mixed-heritage groups, there was considerable variability in how these participants thought about and felt a sense of (non-)belonging in relation to these groups. We found that biracial reporting does not have a fixed meaning. Although some Asian-White participants were strongly attached to their Asian heritage and embedded in Asian social networks, others had little real connection with their Asian background. The societal treatment of Asian-White people also differed according to the historical norms and conventions in each RESCI. For example, RESCI 5 (Hawaii and San Francisco), which had a relatively large population of not only Asian Americans but also mixed people, was a context where Asian-White people were more likely to be recognized and treated as mixed Asian-White people rather than just Asian or just White. As with the other mixed-heritage groups, racial appearance and cultural exposure, along with understandings about racial and ethnic authenticity, were prominent themes in our interviews with Asian-White mixed-heritage people.

Some Asian-White participants felt a strong and primary attachment to their Asian background. These participants had been exposed to Asian cultural practices and Asian relatives and people more generally.[58] For example, Jacqui, who was thirty-nine, lived in RESCI 3, and identified as White and Korean, grew up in a highly Asian metropolitan area in RESCI 5, speaking Korean and with a strong sense of Korean American identity.

Well, my dad's White and my mom's Korean, and we were really, I mean, we're really culturally a Korean family in a lot of ways. My dad was in the army, and so instead of sending him to Vietnam, they sent him to Korea. So he had to learn Korean, . . . We still speak Korean at home . . . we eat Korean food, do all the Korean celebrations.

In fact, Jacqui's Korean grandmother had lived with them for some time. Jacqui reported a stronger affinity for her Korean side of the family: "I've always felt much closer to my mom's side of the family and more accepted and loved than on my dad's [White] side."

Like Jacqui, Nani, a forty-one-year-old Asian-White woman who lived in RESCI 3 and had a mixed-heritage Asian-White mother and a Chinese husband, felt most comfortable with Asian culture and people; in fact, her social network was primarily Asian American. She grew up in a family that was infused with a hybridized Asian culture and sensibility, and she also grew up in a West Coast area with many Asian and Asian-White people. Nani reported that she felt the most affinity with other Asian people rather than being specifically attached to her Filipino grandfather's ancestry. Yet she believed that most people usually saw her as White (albeit not as northern European), a racial attribution that did not fit her own sense of self. After our interview, Nani wanted to elaborate on her sense of self and sent this message via email:

> The more that I think about it, most people have viewed me as being Caucasian (or on occasion Jewish or Middle Eastern) since that's the way that I appear, but on the inside I feel more Asian, in general, because of my upbringing, foods, the influence of my mom's side of the family and frequent visits to [X] to see family which celebrates all Asian backgrounds and blended families. I was and still am drawn to Asian friends and of course my [Chinese] husband. It's in these relationships where I feel most comfortable and at home.

By contrast, some other Asian-White participants had had very limited exposure to Asian people, culture, and practices growing up, including some who had little contact with their Asian parent. Such limited exposure was sometimes compounded by being raised in mostly White regions. These participants reported biracially but did not necessarily feel a strong and validated attachment to their Asian background. For instance, Jane, age thirty-eight, grew up in a predominantly White town in RESCI 2 and identified herself as White and Korean, but in this spatial context she did not assert a sense of being mixed heritage;

being part Asian was not commonly recognized there. In fact, Jane's Korean mother died when she was young, and her father did not foster contact with her mother's Korean relatives.

> That's always been a weird thing with me [not knowing about the Korean side of the family]. My mom died when I was ten, so I lost that connection, so it's . . . like my dad met her in Korea when he was in the army and brought her back over, so we don't . . . I've been there once when I was seven. So, I don't really know any of the family there. I have one cousin that I'm in touch with on Facebook, and he speaks passible English, kind of. So that's really all I've got there. I didn't even know when my grandparents died. I don't know how many cousins I have.

Having grown up in a part of the Midwest with few Asian people, Jane had very little contact with other Asian Americans or other mixed-heritage Asians. As such, while Jane identified herself as a racially mixed person, she was self-conscious about the fact that her ties to her Asian heritage were very tenuous.

Another common reason why many Asian-White participants did not identify as solely Asian was their experience of social rejection by monoracial Asians, including some relatives. Forty-three-year-old Andrew, whose mother was Korean, spoke of feeling upset by not being accepted as a "real" Korean person by other Koreans, including a Korean relative:

> I can never feel Korean, like I can never go to Korea and feel like these are my people. Partly because they wouldn't see me as "my people." . . . Even talking to my cousin, male cousin from Korea, who stayed with us for about a year. We're talking about, having a conversation about, our common ancestor who was this . . . some luminary in the tenth century, and he would . . . I would refer to him as our ancestor and he would say, "Not your ancestor, my ancestor."

Like some of the Black-White participants' experiences related to skin color, the Asian-White participants spoke a great deal about their often ambiguous racial appearance and its impact on their social treatment, especially by single-race Asian people. In keeping with prior qualitative research, which found that Asian-White people are seen in many different ways, our Asian-White participants reported quite variable racial appearance, ranging from White to mixed to Asian.[59]

Recognition of this phenotypical variability is important, because some recent comparative studies of multiracial people have characterized Asian-White people as having a physically White appearance without recognizing that there is a real range of racial appearance among Asian-White people.[60]

Our participants (both men and women) often discussed this diversity as manifested in their own racial appearance (and their siblings' appearance) and the differential social treatment associated with it.[61] Like Jane, Annie, who was twenty-nine and lived in RESCI 2, grew up in a predominantly White town in the central United States that did not readily recognize racially mixed people. Aside from her Chinese mother, Annie had little exposure to Asian people. She identified as White and Chinese and reported that she was usually seen as White and that she and her siblings were seen very differently: "I always got the comment that I looked the least Asian out of my siblings. . . . My brother looks the most Asian, and my sister looks mixed."

Alison, age thirty-seven and living in a RESCI 2 area, identified as Japanese and White. She had this to say of herself and her sisters: "My older sister, absolutely, [she] definitely looks more Asian, the most Asian of the three of us. I look the most Latino or Latina. My little sister looks the most White." Forty-three-year-old Andrew (discussed above) also reported being seen in a number of different ways. He often found this jarring and felt little sense of control over how he was seen. Andrew described an upsetting incident at work, when a colleague referred to him as a White man:

> The way I see myself is neither. . . . I hate the term "White," but I don't know another term for it. I don't see myself as White. I don't identify as White. I also don't identify as Asian. And I never have. I think I . . . early in my childhood I felt very conscious of this ambiguity, partly because it was kind of imposed on me. I think that people . . . I don't think I'd be as aware of it if people didn't keep asking what my background is.

Andrew was clearly frustrated and hurt by what he saw as others' misrecognition of him and their constant need to racially categorize him.[62]

Some participants' racially mixed appearance combined with their Anglo surnames (since most had White fathers and Asian mothers) to make them easy to single out as not being "fully" Asian. A strong theme of "othering" by single-race Asians emerged from interviews with this group of participants. Ray, who was forty-six, lived in RESCI 3, and reported his race as White and Japanese, was proud of being "Hapa" and "Hafu" (his words). His pride was possible in his West Coast setting, where there were many Asian-White mixed people and a "Hapa" identity was recognized: "I'm proud of it. When people see me, they see my mixture. I'm not White, I'm not Asian. Sometimes they see me as Mexican in some places." One reason why Ray felt Hapa, as opposed to Asian, was his feeling of not being accepted by many Asian people as another Asian person.[63] His mixed friends, he said, were also often stigmatized. "Never fitting in . . . like my Korean/half friends say they don't go to Korea Town. [They] feel resented by Koreans."

For some participants, however, moving to a location with a large Asian American population was life-changing. Forty-eight-year-old Jonathan lived in a RESCI 5 area and saw himself as biracial. He grew up in a predominantly White area in the Midwest (RESCI 2), where he lived with his White mother, his exposure to Korean people and culture having been further limited by her divorce from his Korean father. He reported feeling buffeted by the disparate ways in which he was racially assigned by others: "I've actually had people see me as a full Korean person and people say to me [that] they can barely even see any White in me, whereas I've had other people say they can't see any Korean in me. So, it's a little bit like how do two people . . . see me [so] completely differently?"

In his late twenties, Jonathan decided to take a job in a RESCI 5 metropolitan area with many Asian Americans, and in that context he was seen, and accepted, as a racially mixed Asian person for the first time:

Well, it just took time. And maybe it helped being in a place like [this city], where for the first time I was like . . . I ended up working at a predominantly Chinese high school, so it was, you know, predominantly Asian, and so I was being really seen in that high school as an Asian person. . . . It was sort of the first time that people really, where I was exposed to a lot of people recognizing me as an Asian person.

For Jonathan, moving to a place where it was not uncommon to have mixed Asian heritage validated his sense of being an Asian person who was part of a wider Asian American community. Although he had almost never been seen as Asian or part-Asian while growing up in a White area (RESCI 2), he was usually seen as part-Asian where he now lived (RESCI 5). Negotiating membership within Asian American communities was also influenced by the generational remove of some Asian migrants to the United States. While there are many foreign-born Asian Americans in the United States, there are also Asian Americans who are the descendants of second, third, or later-generation Asian Americans who may have little connection with a distant Asian "homeland" and its languages and practices.[64] Some Asian-White participants who had Asian American parents (and grandparents) but were culturally distanced from an ancestral Asian "homeland" reported their lack of knowledge of an Asian language and cultural exposure, especially those who had grown up in mostly White places. For instance, forty-eight-year-old Donna, who lived in RESCI 2, said that her Japanese American mother was born on the West Coast and interned with her family at the beginning of the Second World War. In fact, both sets of Donna's grandparents were Japanese Americans who were also born in the United States. When asked about her upbringing, Donna explained that her mother did not speak Japanese and therefore could not teach her the language. "My mother was six when the war ended. And certainly, at that time, to assimilate and just slide under the radar, not draw attention to yourself, you absolutely did not learn Japanese. . . . She doesn't have a lot of those traditions and cultural things that are not (*pauses*) . . . really Japanese, they're really Japanese American."

Angela, age forty-eight and living in RESCI 3, had a White Jewish mother and a Japanese-White father. As in Donna's family, Angela's father endured the stigma of being (part) Japanese in the postwar period and distanced himself from his Asian background. This theme of historical stigma was reminiscent of what some Native-White participants described in relation to their Native parents and grandparents.

> So . . . I would say neither of my parents were that interested in their own heritage or religion. So, my dad was half Japanese. . . . When he moved to his [mostly White] town in Florida, which is the town my grandpa grew up in, he was the only, he and his mom were the only Asian people, and it was after World War II, it was like the late forties or early fifties, so it was really hard on him. And I wouldn't say that

he necessarily had an interest. By the time I came along, he did not have an interest in Japan or Japanese culture, and I don't know if he ever did.

The further generational remove from Japan was significant in limiting Angela's meaningful exposure to Japanese culture within her family.[65]

Interestingly, despite (or because of) their parents' detachment from their Asian ancestries, both Donna and Angela, as young adults, studied subjects related to their Japanese heritage in college, and Angela even spent a year in Japan. When Donna went to college, she said that she was excited to have the opportunity to join an Asian American student organization. (There was no Asian mixed-heritage group at the time.) Unfortunately, she felt rejected in this organization:

> I really felt unwelcome at that group. . . . I mean, it was a bummer because . . . surrounded by White people my whole life so . . . it's a bummer. . . . felt like, listen, I've been denied this affinity group my whole life, and I'm excited to connect with people on that level, and they were like, "No, you're not Asian enough, not really."

While Donna continued to identify as mixed and reported both White and Asian races, she remained reluctant to assert her Asian ancestry in groups and organizations primarily for monoracial Asians. Donna believed that if she looked more Japanese (by prevailing norms), she probably would have gained more acceptance into Japanese and Asian American social networks.[66] She noted, however, that with generational and social change, she saw other possibilities for her son (who had a White father) to claim his Japanese ancestry and hoped that he would be less subject to essentialist ideas about racial authenticity.[67]

## Conclusion

In this chapter, we have looked at how three mixed-heritage populations—Native-White, Black-White, and Asian-White—racially identified from 1980 to 2019 in national census data and within varied racial/ethnic contexts. The distinctive histories of each of these mixed-heritage populations and the distinctive contexts shaped by these histories were clearly important in shaping how they reported their races and experienced their identities. As shown in the interviews with all three mixed-heritage groups, the geographical context in which people grow up is critical in shaping how they are seen by others and how they see themselves. Some locations have a history of settlement and cultures that recognize mixed-heritage people, while others do not.

Most of our mixed-heritage participants had knowledge of their parents' ancestry, including tribal affiliations. All the Asian-White participants knew their specific Asian ethnic background, and the inclusion of disparate Asian "races" in the census reinforced their awareness of these disparate ethnic backgrounds. Black-White participants, unsurprisingly, tended to know less about their Black ancestry, but many, like the other mixed-heritage participants, reported their European ancestry in some detail. While the mixed-heritage participants in this study expressed varying degrees of interest in and attachment to their non-White race and ancestry, hardly any reported an attachment to or strong interest in their White ancestry, which was seen as the mainstream default.

Across all three mixed-heritage groups, we found that to assert multiracial identity was to claim ties and connections with multiple ethnic and racial groups, even if these connections were asymmetrical, contested, or unrecognized by others. Given how common it was for interview participants to report that their asserted identities were refuted, challenged, or somehow "spoiled," the growing tendency of Black-White and Asian-White people to report more than one race (on the census) suggests that many mixed-heritage people filling in the census report multiple races *despite* their lack of validation by others.[68] This assertion of their desired identity by mixed-heritage young adults in spite of, or because of, others' lack of validation has been found in other research.[69]

Once the federal statistical system allowed multiple responses to the race question in Census Bureau data, a high proportion of both Asian-White and Black-White people reported both races. This convergence is notable given the distinct histories of these groups. Black-White mixed-heritage people were subject to legal and social constraints imposed by the one-drop rule, which defined them as solely Black. Asian-White people, in contrast, reported feeling rejected by both Asian and White single-race groups, but especially by other Asians. People in both mixed-heritage groups often acknowledged the mixed heritage in their ancestry responses in the census data and discussed their multiracial family trees in the interviews.

Based on our findings, we believe that the change in identification patterns in 2000 and later reflects both that more people are feeling biracial and that the Census Bureau has improved the alignment between how people feel and how the census form asks the question. As other scholars have argued, the one-drop rule that has defined how Black-White people may identify themselves, or their children, is loosening its hold. For many, not only is this a shift in convention, but it may also reflect a felt difference in how Black-White individuals believe they are seen and treated.

People who reported only one race (rare in our sample and mostly confined to Native-White individuals) can be seen as making a statement about where they "stand." Our interviews reveal that one of the intentions of those Native-White participants who claimed only an American Indian/Alaska Native race was to take a politicized stance about the importance of "counting" American Indian people.

Yet it would be a mistake to assume that participants across all three groups who reported *both* races were somehow less committed or attached to their BIPOC ancestry. It's not that simple. Our research reveals that we cannot easily interpret biracial identification in relation to how people live their lives. Our biracially identified participants varied substantially in how they related to and engaged with their White and non-White backgrounds and in their racial consciousness. It is important that scholars recognize the significant differences in upbringing, social experiences, racial appearance, and identities of biracial-reporting people across all mixed-heritage groups, including the three at the heart of this study.

Mixed-heritage people grow up and live in highly varied racial/ethnic spatial contexts, and they experience variable levels of exposure to disparate parts of their family trees. There is also great variability in their exposure to racially minoritized people and communities, who may or may not accept them. Some biracially reporting Native-White, Black-White, and Asian-White people were more invested in and attached to their BIPOC heritage than others. In other words, while there were differences in the racial reporting and experiences across the three mixed-heritage groups, we cannot overlook the significant differences *within* each mixed-heritage group. No clear gender patterns emerged among our interview participants in this respect.

Despite the fact that Black-White and Asian-White people are now most likely to identify biracially, the census data show that more

Black-White people than Asian-White people continue to identify monoracially (as Black). Although nineteen of our twenty Black-White participants reported themselves biracially on the preinterview survey, many of these participants lived their lives as Black people (and were seen by others as Black), confirming prior studies about the social treatment of Black-White mixed people as Black. Overall, this was the case for both Black-White men and women. At the same time, a number of Black-White participants reported feeling more White than Black in their affiliations with others and their cultural upbringing and attributes; typically, such individuals had had little exposure to Black people or networks. Clearly, even among Black-White participants who reported biracially, there was significant variation in their racial experiences, identities, and affiliations.

Reflecting the current census data showing a tendency to report biracially, especially in areas with large Asian populations, all of our twenty-seven Asian-White participants reported both Asian and White races. This response meshes with the thematic emphasis on being racially and culturally hybrid—or "Hapa," as several participants put it. In comparison with Native-White and Black-White mixed-heritage groups, many Asian-White participants reported feeling in between— neither White nor Asian. They often felt socially rejected by monoracial Asians. Thus, although Asian-White people commonly reported both races, what that meant in terms of their lived experiences clearly differed considerably across racial/ethnic spatial contexts and their disparate histories of settlement and racial treatment. Reporting both Asian and White races in the census from a small, White-dominated town in Montana or Alabama most likely referred to a very different experience from that of someone who made the same report from a large and diverse city such as Chicago or Los Angeles. Asian-White participants also reported that they were racially seen in quite diverse ways: Some were seen as White and others as "fully" Asian, and often they were seen as racially ambiguous. As with the other mixed-heritage groups, our Asian-White participants reported quite varied attachments to their Asian and White family backgrounds, depending on their familial and cultural exposure and the racial and ethnic context of the locations where they grew up.

Native-White people show a different pattern in the census: Most reported either only White race or only American Indian/Alaska Native race. Our five Native-White participants reporting only Native race cited a political tribal identity, with some expressing resistance to the trope of the "disappearing Indian." These participants tended to have had significant cultural and social exposure to other Native people. Dwanna McKay describes a political legal identity based on tribal citizenship that is not available to all people of Native heritage.[70] The "boundaries" of identification as American Indian/Alaska Native race are generally open to people who are tribal members, no matter what they look like and no matter how mixed their family tree is, and such acceptance is encouraged in many places. The distinct identity patterns in RESCI 4 illustrate the unique milieu on and near some reservations. Many Native-White people do not live in or near a reservation or a dense Native population. Yet our interviews with Native-White people, including the fifteen who reported both Native and White races, also suggest that some with Native heritage feel a strong and politicized motivation to assert their Native heritage and identity outside that space, with a sense of urgency about dispelling the myth that American Indians have vanished. They might, as a consequence, drive long distances to attend Native events and celebrations.

For Native-White people who are not tribal members, phenotype and cultural knowledge are significant factors in their willingness to report American Indian/Alaska Native as a race. The pain of being labeled "inauthentic" is consequential enough that people will avoid making claims to being Native.[71] Our Black-White participants reported being subject to essentialist understandings of how they should "be," look, and behave in order to lay claim to a Black identity.[72] It is striking that so many Asian-White participants reported that they were often not regarded as authentically Asian by single-race Asian people, based on their appearance and/or lack of knowledge of their Asian relatives' culture and language. This is the converse of the historical tendency to regard all people with Black ancestry as Black. It is also distinct from the terms of exclusion of mixed-heritage Native people, who do not need to be "fully" Native but do need to be enrolled tribal citizens or deeply connected culturally. Such experiences of social rejection—sometimes even hostility—could be upsetting for our participants.

Participants across and within the three mixed-heritage groups differed in their cultural and social exposure to their White and non-White backgrounds and, relatedly, their attachments to these backgrounds. Many factors influenced the nature and degree of such exposure for our participants, from being raised by only one parent to a lack of contact with one part of the family tree (owing, for example, to family discord) or the racial composition of their surroundings when they were growing up. Their contact with and attachment to their parents' families were often asymmetrical, even among participants who reported multiple races and ancestries. Across all three mixed-heritage groups, many participants expressed an interest in and attachment to their BIPOC race and ancestry.[73]

Another prominent theme discussed across our sample was phenotype and how participants were seen racially by others. As found in many prior studies, our participants commonly reported that their identity options were circumscribed by how other people saw them racially.[74] Not properly recognized in extant research, Asian-White participants can be seen racially in quite disparate ways. Black-White participants in our study, especially female participants, were especially attuned to how their light skin and more ambiguous racial appearance could result in a lack of acceptance by other Black women. Many of the mixed-heritage participants highlighted the explicit and often unspoken constraints around their ability to identify or affiliate with their BIPOC or White racial background, or with both backgrounds, on the basis of their racial appearance.

Another theme that emerged from our interviews was the contentiousness of negotiating their membership within existing ethnic groups for some mixed-heritage individuals. Non-White people's ethnic and racial identities are not private and voluntary.[75] In this they differ from White ethnics (such as Italian Americans), whose ethnicity Alba describes as "private, voluntary, and undemanding," and as a "personal style."[76] In any race or ethnic group, membership entitles one to participate in the group's culture and politics and legitimates a claim to the group's distinctive ways of talking, dressing, interacting, and the like. Membership also involves obligations, and some coethnic members may expect a degree of conformity of expression of ethnic identity.[77] "There is no intrinsic personality related to race; yet individuals are expected to locate themselves 'accurately' within established racial structures."[78]

Our study reveals substantial variation in the identities developed by mixed-heritage Black-White, Native-White, and Asian-White individuals. The many differences within disparate mixed-heritage groups makes it difficult to make sweeping generalizations about any one group experience, for there is no one, or typical, experience that can fully capture the Native-White, Black-White, or Asian-White mixed-heritage experience.

# CHAPTER FOUR

# CHOOSING A SPOUSE: THE IMPLICATIONS OF RACIAL OVERLAP

In chapter 3, we explored the meanings of mixed-heritage people's race responses and how and why they came to identify themselves in particular ways. We learned that many mixed-heritage Asian-White and Black-White participants (but not Native-White participants) find it increasingly normative to report two races. Interviews revealed that their biracial identification reported on surveys did not necessarily tell us about the salience of a person's races in their day-to-day lives; in fact, across and within all three mixed-heritage groups, people who reported multiple races varied considerably in their attachment to their BIPOC and White backgrounds. In this chapter, we look at another way to more fully investigate how racial identification impacts the lives of mixed-heritage people by examining their marriage choices.

In a recent review of marriages of Black-White, Asian-White, and Native-White individuals, Michael Miyawaki points to the need for future research to look at the relationship of the racial identifications of mixed-heritage individuals to their choice of spouse.[1] Such a focus is an important part of this chapter. Rather than categorizing the unions of mixed-heritage people as in-marriage or out-marriage, Miri Song has argued that it is more meaningful and revealing to investigate ethnic and/or racial *overlap* between mixed-heritage people and their partners and the possible meanings of such an overlap within their relationships.[2]

In this chapter, we ask: How do mixed-heritage people who are married make sense of their identity with respect to their spouse's race? And how does the racial overlap (or lack of overlap) impact or reflect the relative salience of race in their relationship? Once again, we rely on

https://doi.org/10.7758/edyf5459.8617

**Figure 4.1** *Race of Spouses of Mixed-Heritage Native-White, Asian-White, and Black-White People, 1980–2019*

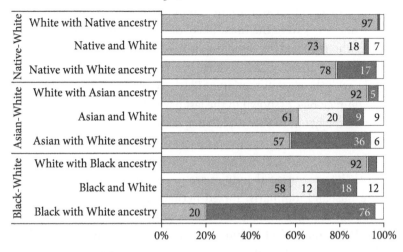

Spouse is White
Spouse is White and Native, White and Asian, or White and Black
Spouse is Native, Asian, or Black
Spouse is not White, Native, Asian or Black

*Source:* Authors' calculations.

census data for an overview and our interviews for further context and deeper understanding.

A look at census data about married people of mixed heritage (figure 4.1) reveals a strong relationship between a mixed-heritage person's racial identification choice and the race of their spouse. That is, the census shows that *a mixed-heritage person's reported race tends to be predictive of their spouse's race.* In the top bar of each panel of figure 4.1, the census data from 1980 to 2019 shows us that mixed-heritage people who identify as racially White (a rare choice for Asian-White and Black-White people) almost always marry other White people.[3] For example, of married Native-White people who reported White race only (with Native ancestry), 97 percent were married to someone who also reported White race only. For Asian-White and Black-White people who identified as racially White (with Asian or Black ancestry), this figure was 92 percent. The second bar of each panel—showing the marriage choices of people who reported two races—shows that a significant proportion married someone who gave the same two-race response in the census data. And the pattern continues in the third bar of each panel, showing that mixed-heritage people who identified as single-race American Indian/Alaska Native, Asian, or Black (with White ancestry) were the most likely of these groups to marry other people who reported the same single race. Notably, it was common for all of these groups of mixed-heritage people to marry single-race White people, with the clear exception of Black-White people who identified as single-race Black (shown in the last bar of figure 4.1).

Interestingly, our further exploration of the census data (not depicted) reveals that mixed-heritage people generally follow the gender-specific racial assortative marriage patterns seen among single-race people. Asian/White monoracial couples are most often an Asian wife and a White husband. Similarly, mixed-heritage Asian-White women are slightly more likely to have a White spouse than are mixed-heritage Asian-White men. Black/White monoracial couples more often include a Black husband and White wife, and we find that mixed-heritage Black-White men are more likely to have a White spouse than are mixed-heritage Black-White women. Neither monoracial nor mixed-heritage Native people show clear gendered patterns in marriage choice: Native men and Native women are about equally likely to have a White spouse, as are Native-White men and women. Our analysis also shows that mixed-heritage Asian-White, Black-White, and Native-White people who identify as racially White (with BIPOC ancestry) usually marry White people, as monoracial White people do. All of these census data patterns are reflected in our interview participants' spouse choices, but our interviews also illustrate other marital unions, such as ones with no racial overlap between the spouses.

Our interviews show that for many mixed-heritage people, race and ethnicity can be an important consideration in their choice of partner. Most of our participants across the three mixed-heritage groups shared some racial overlap with their spouse—most often a White racial background. We use interview data from the three mixed-heritage groups to illustrate what different types of unions may tell us about the importance of race in their relationships and what it can mean for how they live. For instance, how do mixed-heritage participants with a White spouse differ from those whose spouse shares a racialized minority heritage with them, or from those who have a non-White spouse with whom they share no racial overlap?

While we find some notable differences between those with a White spouse versus a non-White spouse (across all three groups), we also find considerable variation among mixed-heritage people with a White spouse in terms of the salience of the mixed-heritage person's BIPOC race and the racial and cultural practices adopted by their White partner. This is consistent with prior research findings. Jessica Vasquez-Tokos has found that the majority of intermarried couples take "a bicultural [approach], eschewing dichotomous notions of ethnicity," and that non-Latino White people actively engage with such biculturalism.[4] In her study of mixed people in Britain, Song also finds that mixed individuals with a White spouse varied in their racial attitudes and consciousness and in how they raised their children.[5] The authors of a qualitative study of interracial couples in Australia (White Australians and Indo-Asian Australians) find that, rather than minority spouses simply adapting to their spouse's White racial frame, interracial families are key sites where new forms of cultural, gender, and social class identities and practices are generated.[6]

Just as multiple factors influence the racial identities of mixed-heritage people, as discussed in the last chapter, many factors influence how and why people partner with someone of a particular racial and ethnic background.[7] We know that adolescents' contact with people of other races, such in school and in friendship groups, is strongly associated with interracial romantic relationships later when they become young adults.[8] But of course, the opportunity for such contact is highly dependent on geographical context. Thus, movement from, say, an ethnically homogeneous spatial context to a highly diverse context could lead to opportunities to date and meet a range of potential partners. Mixed-heritage people who grow up in primarily White locations (such as RESCI 2) not only are subject to dominant (and often implicit) narratives about White supremacy but also have relatively few opportunities to meet coethnics or other BIPOC people. In the remainder of the chapter, we examine marriage choices and their meanings for our interview participants, keeping the racial/ethnic spatial context in mind.

## The Marriage Choices of Native-White Individuals

As figure 4.1 illustrates, there is a clear and striking relationship between a mixed-heritage Native-White person's choice of a race response and their choice of a spouse. Figure 4.2 shows the variation in this pattern

**Figure 4.2** *The Race of Spouses of Mixed-Heritage Native-White People, by Racial/Ethnic Spatial Context, 1980–2019*

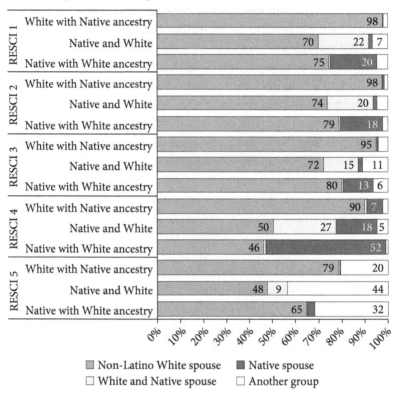

Source: Authors' calculations.

across racial/ethnic spatial contexts for people of Native-White mixed heritage.

Married mixed-heritage Native-White people living in places like Atlanta, Fort Collins, Colorado, and Minneapolis (RESCI 1, 2, and 3) show marriage patterns similar to the national pattern. Notably, even though the Native population is a small proportion of the US population, a substantial proportion of people who identify as single-race Native have been able to marry others who also identify as single-race Native.

Isolated areas near large reservations (RESCI 4) and San Francisco and Hawaii (RESCI 5) are dramatically different contexts for Native-White marriages. In rural areas near reservations, marriage to single-race-identified Native people is quite common. Also, a substantial percentage of biracially identified Native-White people (27 percent) are married to others of the same racial identification. As shown in chapter 3, RESCI 4 contains a relatively high proportion of people who identify racially as Native, either alone or in combination with White race. In contrast, RESCI 5 (San Francisco and Hawaii) is a context where Native-White people of all racial identities often marry people with whom they have no racial overlap. For example, 44 percent of Native-White-identified and 32 percent of Native-identified people in RESCI 5 are married to someone who does not report Native alone, White alone, or both Native and White.[9]

## WHITE-IDENTIFIED NATIVE-WHITE PEOPLE

Although White-identified Native-White people are numerous in the United States according to the census data, they did not respond to our call for mixed-heritage interview participants. The one Native-White interviewee who identified as solely White followed the primary pattern seen in national data. Dawn, the forty-year-old we met in chapter 3, was married to a non-Latino White man whom she described as "super blond. He's mega-White." Dawn did not feel she should identify herself biracially as Native-White because her experience and contact with Native people and culture were quite distant and tenuous. Dawn's paternal grandmother, who was Ojibwe, had been adopted by a White family as a young child, and she grew up apart from her many siblings who remained on the reservation.

> So, like, my dad said, "You should go up and visit your grandmother's siblings, they're still there. They're in their eighties, they're going to die soon." Like, "You should go up, and if you're curious, go up and find out more about this because they're all still enrolled." And [those with the family name] have all passed away, her adopted family, so, I don't know, it's interesting. . . . So yeah, I'm a quarter Ojibwe, but through that process of poverty and adoption and relationships and time, we don't, like . . . we're not at all connected culturally or anything but have this whole sweep of family who is.

Through generational disconnection, starting with her father's mother, Dawn felt distanced from her father's Native ancestry. While she lived in a (RESCI 3) city with significant numbers of Native people living there and in the surrounding area, Dawn never felt connected to her

Native background. She reported that she had not thought much about her Native ancestry when she dated people in high school:

> I guess I never really thought about it very much. I guess my high school boyfriend, he was from a very similar situation, like disconnected Native American, right, and he was a quarter as well, but neither one of us was like, "We're together because we're bonding over our disconnected White . . . ," you know, it was sort of like, yeah, my grandma's Dakota, yeah, my grandma's Ojibwe, yeah, that's cool, like whatever.

When asked if her husband was interested in her Ojibwe heritage, Dawn replied: "He's interested inasmuch as it's interesting to me. If it's interesting to me, he'll find it interesting . . . but like, if I'm not pursuing it, then I don't think—he's not that necessarily curious about it on a day-to-day basis." As a self-described "disconnected White," Dawn understood that her "mega-White" husband was unlikely to engage with American Indian practices and heritage if she did not.

## NATIVE-IDENTIFIED MIXED-HERITAGE NATIVE-WHITE PEOPLE

Figure 4.1 shows that about 75 percent of Native-White people who reported only American Indian/Alaska Native race (and White ancestry) had a White spouse, but that a significant proportion were married to other single-race Native people. This suggests that those who identify as solely Native and have a Native spouse would have made an effort to find such a spouse, especially in racial/ethnic contexts without sizable, segregated Native populations.

Only one of our five participants who identified solely as American Indian/Alaska Native was married to another single-race Native person. Susie, age forty-seven, had married a Native man she knew in high school, which was in a RESCI 2 area with many other American Indian people. She spoke of the importance of a shared understanding and shared cultural background with her husband, who also shared her tribal affiliation.

> I have this conversation with my daughter and . . . I told her, like for me personally, yes, that was something [to marry another Native

person], because I wanted to raise a daughter with both parents being Ho-Chunk because . . . so let me put it this way. I don't want to need to explain why I do the things I do. Why I talk a certain way when my husband understands me, because he grew up there.

Devon, whom we met in chapter 3, identified solely as Menominee Tribe and reported her spouse as White, Black, and Choctaw. Devon was very committed to her Native heritage. Although she and her spouse had different tribal affiliations, it was important to them to celebrate all of their heritages. Devon reported unequivocally that she knew she wanted an American Indian partner. She reflected on her White boyfriend in high school:

> I spoke to him about our future and having children, and he had once made a comment about boys with long hair and boys with earrings, and I said, "Well, if we ever have a boy and our boy wants to grow his hair long or wear earrings and dance and participate in our culture," I said, "it could very well happen," and he just kind of said, "No, no son of mine . . ." and that's the first time that I realized I have different goals for my children and for a possible spouse or life partner. So, going into college, I did . . . you know, I hung around a lot of the American Indian students, but I did say to myself I wanted somebody who could identify or at least accept fully my culture.

The census data show that those who identify their race as American Indian are much more likely to have a White partner than those who identify solely as Asian or Black. Structural factors, such as the relatively small Native population size and lack of geographic concentration outside of reservations, contribute to the high intermarriage rate. Like the majority of Native-identified people in the census data, three of the five participants who identified as solely Native had a White spouse. For example, Nick, a thirty-four-year-old who identified as Inuit, had a White spouse whom he met in a Northeastern town with very few Native people. When asked how his wife felt about his Inuit heritage, he laughed and said, "She didn't really care!" Nick reported that he felt a strong sense of being Inuit and had spent his early childhood in the Arctic with his Inuit father and his relatives; now he lived in a predominantly White town that could not be more different from his childhood setting.

For some, having a White spouse could be compatible with a life spent heavily involved with Native people and organizations. For example,

Ron, a resident of a RESCI 2 area who was forty-seven (introduced in the last chapter), identified as Native, and was a teacher in his tribal college, reported that his White wife was very appreciative of his Native background, although she was not directly involved with the American Indian community herself: "My being Native is a very positive thing for her. She . . . is very supportive of appreciating Native culture, supporting me in that. She's happy to be married to a tribal member."

Fifty-two-year-old Sam lived in a primarily White town in the Northeast (RESCI 2). Identifying as solely Native, he revealed that he had made a conscious decision not to partner with a Native woman in order to distance himself from what he described as "the historical trauma" and ensuing social problems that afflicted many American Indians and Alaska Natives.

> This is a very difficult thing to say, and it's not a very popular thing to say, but a lot of Native women are hard and not very nurturing . . . and bring so much of the past and all those issues I talk about, and they bring that with them into their families, and I just, you know. . . . It is sad. It's hard, you know, and I think I've made a lot of decisions in my life to move away; marry who I married; to work where I work, you know. To build a different future.

Sam's choice of a non-Native spouse accompanied his choice to live and work away from an area with a significant Native population. In a similar vein, Vasquez-Tokos finds that some Mexican American women wanted to marry a White man to avoid what they perceived to be the traditionally paternalistic men in the Mexican American community.[10] Therefore, while some participants, such as Devon, made a conscious decision to partner with a person with American Indian ancestry, others, like Sam, chose not to.

## BIRACIALLY IDENTIFIED NATIVE-WHITE PEOPLE

The national data show that just under three-quarters of biracially identified Native-White people are married to a White person (similar to single-race-identified Native people), though only about half have a White spouse and live in an area near a large reservation (RESCI 4) or Hawaii or San Francisco (RESCI 5) (both of which have large non-White populations). Seven of our fifteen biracially identified Native-White participants had a White spouse.

As with participants who identified solely as Native, it was relatively uncommon for a White spouse to be active in Native cultural practices and social networks. There was some variation among White spouses, however, and it was usually linked to their Native spouse's attachment to and interest in their Native heritage. Aaron, age forty-four and living in RESCI 3 (discussed in chapter 3), was raised away from his reservation, and having never felt very accepted by his father's many Native relatives, he did not feel "connected" to them. Aaron grew up in primarily White settings, around White people, and he dated mostly White women. At the time of the interview, Aaron was divorced from a White woman whom he had met at college. Although she knew of his Native background, it was clear that it was not a prominent part of their relationship, or even her perception of him:

> Once we were at a trivia game in a bar, she got the question: Have you ever been in an interracial relationship? And she answered no! And I thought, "What the heck?!" First, she thought of that question in terms of Black/White interracial, but reflecting back on it, it was clear that she didn't think of me as a minority.

For some, having a White spouse effectively led to a relationship in which Native ancestry was largely absent, as in Aaron's case, while others had a White spouse who could be very interested and even embedded in American Indian cultural practices. For example, when Tara, age thirty-four, went to college, she learned a lot about Native American history and her own father's Native heritage. She was passionate about her American Indian background and was tribally enrolled and very involved with her Native community. Given how strongly Tara felt about her Native heritage, it was very important to her that her spouse also have a real connection with, and appreciation of, her Native background. Tara's White husband wholeheartedly participated in her Native network and political activism: "My husband's family are very respectful of my Native background, and we are teaching our daughter some Lakota. My husband comes to powwows with us in the city. The reservation and [Tara's hometown near the reservation] are both 'home.'"

Biracial homogamy is reflected nationally in the approximately 20 percent of biracially identified Native people who are married to other biracially identified Native-White people like themselves. For instance, forty-one-year-old Cathy, who lived in a RESCI 4 area, met her husband (who was also biracially identified as Native-White) on a reservation when visiting a friend. Her husband was in the military and saw a lot of the world. When asked if it was important to her that she have a Native partner, Cathy responded that it was not important in principle. She did acknowledge, however, that having a spouse who was also Native-White kept her in her "comfort zone" and that she did not have many opportunities to meet and socialize with men who were *not* part of her reservation and the American Indian network around her.

Even though she grew up in the Midwest, Sarah, age thirty-seven and living in a RESCI 2 area, found her spouse in the Southwest, where she knew she would meet many Native people. Sarah chose her mixed-heritage Mexican Indigenous and White partner because she felt a connection with other Indigenous people: "My partner is Mexican American and much darker than me. We met in Arizona. Most Mexicans in the Arizona area are immigrants." Her husband was a 1.5-generation immigrant, having "grown up in the US since he was ten years old." She met him, she said, "at a hip-hop show." When asked if his being Mexican was meaningful to her, Sarah replied:

> Yes, definitely. When I went there, I had hoped to connect with someone who was Indigenous. Before Arizona, I lived in [city], and I had a lot of Latino friends, and many of them made an intentional claim to Indigenous identity . . . and I had a comfort level with them. . . . Before I even knew anyone who was Chicano/Chicana, I resonated with that identity, it made sense to me, because of my own mixed identity.

Thus, what mattered most to Sarah was a shared sense of being Indigenous and being racially mixed, as opposed to having a specific tribal background. Sarah made a purposeful point of looking for a partner who valued his Indigenous ancestry.

The census data show that few who identify as both Native and White are married to single-race Native spouses. One biracially identified participant, Alex, made it clear that he wanted to marry a Navajo woman as part of his desire to connect with his own Navajo heritage, as discussed in the last chapter. He proudly stated that his wife was Navajo. His union with her, and living with her on the reservation, had cemented his wish to be fully immersed in an American Indian community located in RESCI 4, where there were numerous surrounding Native communities.

Although unusual nationally, three of our biracially reporting Native-White participants were married to a person of a non-overlapping single race. Thirty-four-year-old Savannah, in RESCI 3, reported both Native and White races, strongly identified as a Navajo woman, and had not grown up with "anything Dutch" (her mother's ancestry). She had married a Black African man, whom she met at college. While their shared interest in the history of colonization and developing societies had brought them together, being in a relationship with someone from a very different cultural background, Savannah reported, often involved tensions and disagreements about their everyday lives and how they raised their children.

Even more than the specific ways in which Native-White participants reported their own race, we found, the spouse's race was especially revealing about the relative centrality of race in these participants' day-to-day lives and their relation to their White and Native communities. We found that participants with a White spouse were generally less immersed in Native networks and practices than those who had a spouse with a Native or partially Native background, although there were some exceptions. Regardless of whether they themselves identified as solely American Indian/Alaska Native or as both Native and White, we found that participants who had a spouse with some Native heritage were distinct from participants who shared no Native overlap with their spouse. A shared sense of being Native was central to such relationships (and further enhanced by a shared tribal membership), as well as to how they thought about raising their children.

### The Marriage Choices of Asian-White Individuals

Asian-White mixed-heritage people also often marry a non-Latino White (figure 4.1), especially if they themselves identify as racially White (with Asian ancestry). This strategy of identification has become less common than biracial identification since 2000.

Mirroring the national census data after 2000, none of our twenty-seven Asian-White participants identified as single-race White or Asian; they *all* identified as both Asian and White. The interviews enable us to explore the association between a mixed-heritage person's racial identification and their choice of spouse, including the range of experiences associated with having a spouse of a different racial background. As with our Native-White participants, we find differences in

the racial experiences of Asian-White participants with a White partner versus an Asian partner or a partner with some other racial background. However, there is also considerable variation in the nature of
unions with White spouses, some of whom are much more involved in
their spouse's Asian practices and networks than others.

Figure 4.3 shows the importance of racial/ethnic context for Asian-
White mixed-heritage people's spouse choices. RESCI 1 (for example,
Detroit) and RESCI 2 (for example, Clemson, South Carolina) have
relatively few Asian people, yet a substantial proportion of Asian-
identified mixed-heritage people in these areas (30 percent and 26 percent, respectively) were married to other Asian-identified people. Thus,
like Native or Native-White people in areas with few American Indians,
these Asian-White people would have made an extra effort to seek out
an Asian partner. In RESCI 3 (which includes diverse cities such as New
York and Houston) and RESCI 5 (Hawaii and San Francisco) in particular, people identifying as Asian or Asian-White were less likely to have a
White spouse. RESCI 3 includes major metropolises as well as much of
the West Coast, where many Asian Americans live. In RESCI 5, which
has a large Asian and Pacific Islander population, half of married Asian-
identified people were married to a single-race Asian, and another 18 percent were married to someone in the "other" category, usually Native
Hawaiian. RESCI 4 (for example, the Hopi reservation) has few Asian-
White mixed-heritage people and is not shown in figure 4.3.

## WHITE-IDENTIFIED ASIAN-WHITE PEOPLE

Figure 4.3 shows that those Asian-White people who identify as White
overwhelmingly marry other White people (which is also true of Native-
White and Black-White people)—except in RESCI 5. It is important to
keep in mind, however, that there are relatively few Asian-White people
who identify racially as White now that multiple-race responses are
allowed; for instance, only 20 percent of mixed-heritage Asian-White
people identified as White in the 2015–2019 ACS, as shown in figure 3.1.

## ASIAN-IDENTIFIED ASIAN-WHITE PEOPLE

Figure 4.3 also shows that a significant proportion of those who identify
as solely Asian (between 26 and 50 percent) are married to other Asians
(not necessarily coethnics), thus underlining the connection between

**Figure 4.3** *The Race of Spouses of Mixed-Heritage Asian-White People, by Racial/Ethnic Spatial Context, 1980–2019*

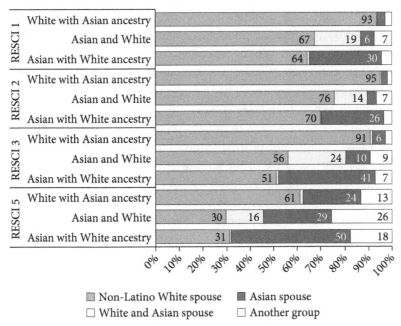

*Source:* Authors' calculations.

someone's reported race and the race of their spouse. As discussed, whether an Asian-identified mixed-heritage Asian-White person marries a White person depends a great deal on whether the racial/ethnic context includes other Asians.

Our call for interview participants did not yield any people of mixed Asian-White heritage who reported only Asian as their race, so we do not have interviews to draw on to interpret these census data results. As discussed in chapter 3, some mixed-heritage Asian-White people who feel strongly attached to their Asian heritage do not feel "allowed" to claim a solely Asian identity by other monoracial Asians, who may regard them as not authentically Asian.

### BIRACIALLY IDENTIFIED ASIAN-WHITE PEOPLE

Figure 4.3 shows considerable spousal racial diversity for biracially identified Asian-White respondents, including a substantial proportion who were married to other biracially identified Asian-White people.

They are relatively unlikely to have a non-Latino White spouse, especially in RESCI 3 and 5, where there are more Asians and Pacific Islanders. Notably, single-race-identified people with Asian-White heritage very rarely marry a multiracially identified Asian-White person. Our twenty-seven biracial Asian-White respondents mirrored the census results with a diverse range of spousal backgrounds: Eighteen of the twenty-seven had a White spouse, six had a single-race Asian spouse, and three had a non-White, non-Asian spouse.

As in the case of American Indian–White participants, we find that the racial background of their spouse (and the nature of the racial overlap) was indicative of the kind of relationship they had, including the salience of a shared Asian race. A shared Whiteness was rarely remarked upon or discussed as a point of interest or commonality.[11] Participants regarded Whiteness as a heritage devoid of distinctiveness, and they primarily associated it with the norm and with social and political dominance.

## BIRACIALLY IDENTIFIED ASIAN-WHITE PEOPLE WITH AN ASIAN SPOUSE

Interview participants with a single-race Asian spouse tended to report that they felt a strong affinity with other Asians or expressed a desire to choose a life partner who was also Asian, though they had not always dated other Asians. Some of our Asian-White participants reported that a shared ethnicity was important in their relationship with their spouse. For instance, recall Jonathan, who had a Korean father and European mother, from chapter 3. He had not dated Asian women before he married his Korean American wife, whom he met when he moved to a large metropolitan area with a large Asian American population. Previously, he had never lived in an area where he was regularly recognized as a part-Asian person or a place with many other Asian Americans. When asked how important his Korean ancestry was to him, Jonathan replied: "Well, it's very important to me. And [it's] probably, on a subconscious level, the reason why I ended up marrying a Korean American and why I send my children to a Korean language elementary school." Given his dating history, Jonathan would probably not have chosen an Asian spouse if he had not moved to an area with a large Asian American population. And as discussed in chapter 3, the fact that relocating to this area enabled Jonathan to be seen by other Asians Americans as Asian himself highlights the contingencies and opportunities of place.

Forty-seven-year-old Petra grew up in mostly White suburban areas in RESCI 2 with an Asian Indian father and German mother. Her childhood and teen years were characterized by a feeling that she was "weird" and not really American, as her peers saw her as somehow foreign. As such, Petra reported, she related well to foreigners and non-White immigrants. She met her Asian Indian husband at a party on the West Coast (where they now lived) and was drawn to his cosmopolitan background. When asked about her dating history, Petra replied: "I never dated a straight-up American guy. Mexican, Indians, Italian guy, one Cuban American, then I married [my husband]." She explained why she never dated any White Americans: "I think most of my friends ended up being foreigners. I felt more comfortable with that group, less different. Or we had more in common with our values—it was easier."

A number of our Asian-White participants with a single-race Asian spouse reported that shared Asian-ness was important in their relationship with their spouse. Asian-White people with an Asian spouse (of either the same or a different ethnicity) could become immersed in a wider Asian family and culture.[12] For example, Vincent, thirty-two years old and living in RESCI 3, had a Filipina mother and White father and was married to a Japanese immigrant. He reported that while they were interested in each other's distinctive ethnic backgrounds, their shared Asian-ness was especially important to them.[13] When he was younger, Vincent had mostly dated White women, but in college he became interested in learning more about his mother's Filipina background and started dating Asian women. This emphasis on Asian panethnicity was also linked with broader racial coalitions in Vincent's work as a community organizer in a racially mixed urban context: "We have a huge social (and political) network, built over thirty years of being here. We're close to different politicians. Massive network. The network is Latino, Asian, White, Black. I love being able to be connected to a lot of different cultures."

Another participant introduced in chapter 3, Nani, who had a Filipino maternal grandfather and White maternal grandmother, was married to a Chinese man who had immigrated to the United States for college. Like Vincent, she grew up (in RESCI 5) with many different Asian people around her and felt a strong attachment to and comfort level with her Asian heritage and other Asian people. Nani explained that her specific Asian ancestry was less important to her than her sense of being Asian.[14] She explained her sense of commonality with other Asian people, including Asian Americans and Asian immigrants: "Filipino is not a huge part of my identity. . . . I'm very comfortable with Asians and Asian friends, for example, Koreans. In college I gravitated toward my Chinese husband."

There is evidence of a growing number of unions between Asian Americans of disparate ethnic backgrounds—for example, between Korean and Chinese Americans.[15] Such unions constitute an important part of a pan-Asian sensibility and identity.[16]

## BIRACIALLY IDENTIFIED ASIAN-WHITE PEOPLE
### WITH ANOTHER BIPOC SPOUSE

The census data in figure 4.3 suggest that it is rare for a mixed-heritage Asian-White person outside of RESCI 5 to be married to someone with whom they share no racial overlap. Such couples do exist, however, as evidenced in our sample. Jacqui, introduced in chapter 3, reported her race as White and Korean and knew very little about her father's Scandinavian heritage; nor did she have any meaningful contact with his relatives: "Like I said before, my family raised me culturally Korean, so we've never really acknowledged or like celebrated in any kind of way the White side of my family. My dad only had one sister that passed away. She didn't have any children, so it's like everything in my family has just reinforced the Korean culture."

Jacqui was married to a (non-White) Latino man, and they lived in a diverse city in the Northeast. When she had started college, she found that she really gravitated toward dating "mostly non-Whites." Now, she reported, she and her spouse shared a commitment to racial justice and diversity and worked at valuing both of their minoritized backgrounds. When asked why she thought she had wanted to date non-White people, Jacqui replied that both she and her husband had a mother who was said to be either "colorist" or latently prejudiced toward non-White people. Jacqui was clear that she and her husband strongly objected to such colorist attitudes. Their racial consciousness, including a shared sense of being people of color, was an important part of their relationship.

Forty-one-year-old Hilary, who had Asian Indian heritage and lived in RESCI 3, was married to a racially mixed man who had Black, Chinese, Vietnamese, and White European heritage and had grown up in Asia and Europe. While Hilary and her spouse both had some White heritage, she characterized her relationship with him as the joining of two people with very disparate ethnic and racial backgrounds. In comparison with Jacqui, who delighted in the fact that her marriage with her Latino husband brought together people from two distinctive ethnic and racial backgrounds, Hilary was more ambivalent about marrying someone who was ethnically very different from her (though she also found her husband's mixed background fascinating). Like some other participants in this study, Hilary articulated a strong sense of cultural loss in marrying her husband, as he did not share her Indian heritage. She did not feel a sense of loss around her White European ancestry. However, Hilary valued and enjoyed living with her husband in a cosmopolitan setting on the West Coast where there were many South Asian and East Asian origin people.

> When I decided to marry my husband, I really mourned . . . the idea of losing parts of my Indian heritage. . . . Because he comes from a completely different set of ethnic backgrounds, I knew that it was going to be even more difficult to retain those Indian rituals and celebrations and practices. I mean, it was hard enough even before, but because my mother just lived that way, listening to Indian music, watched Bollywood, and cooked Indian food, I was surrounded by her Indianness growing up.

On the other hand, Hilary was well aware that she and her children "also gained a lot through my husband, with all of his backgrounds. So, it's not just loss, but adding on new things."

## BIRACIALLY IDENTIFIED ASIAN-WHITE PEOPLE WITH A WHITE SPOUSE

Like the Native-White participants with a White spouse, Asian-White participants with a White spouse reported a diverse range of spousal responses to and involvement in their own Asian background. Some individuals with a White spouse felt their Asian heritage receding into the background and their shared Whiteness becoming their default mode as a couple. For instance, Noelle, age thirty-eight and living in a RESCI 3 area, reported biracially in the online survey and had a White spouse. In the interview, Noelle said that her parents had "shoved race down my throat," and she did not consider either her Chinese or European ancestry to be especially meaningful. Although she loved different Asian foods and had a wide circle of friends, including many Asian Americans, Noelle did not feel strongly attached to her Asian heritage.

Growing up in an environment full of Asian and Asian-White people (RESCI 5), Noelle had dated Asian and part-Asian people, so when she started dating the White man who would become her husband, all of her friends were surprised. She reported that marrying a White man had entailed an "adjustment," which included changing her idea of what her children would look like:

> I hadn't really thought about what I expected for my life, but I do think that it was an adjustment for me marrying [my husband], just in the sense that I knew I was marrying a White guy. . . . The thing that was surprising for me, how I reacted, was the fact that I had little blond babies. I always have seen myself having brown babies, so . . .

Noelle understood that, with a White spouse and White-looking children, they were usually seen as a White family, and that her Chinese ancestry was much more in the background than would have been the case if she had married an Asian person. Although Noelle had reacted against her parents' expectation that she would "lean" toward her Chinese heritage, she revealed some ambivalence about giving birth to "little blond babies."

These mixed-heritage participants did not necessarily inhabit exclusively White social worlds or networks just because they had a White spouse. Participants with a White spouse who lived in highly cosmopolitan and ethnically diverse urban settings spoke of social worlds and networks that were not dominated by Whiteness. For them, the norm was a racially and culturally mixed space characterized by progressive politics; racial consciousness was simply a part of that wider culture.

For instance, Ray, whom we met in chapter 3, had a mother who was Japanese, and he described himself as an "army brat" who grew up partly in Japan, where he learned to speak Japanese fluently. He was very proud of his Japanese heritage. "I identify as Hafu [a Japanese term].

I'm proud of it. When people see me, they see my mixture. I'm not White, I'm not Asian."

After a varied dating history, Ray met his White wife in a large city on the West Coast, where they now resided. Asian and mixed Asian people were not uncommon there, and they participated in a large network that included different types of Asian Americans. Ray said that he had a great deal in common with his wife, who had an adopted Korean brother and a strong interest in Asian cultures. "My wife is proud of my heritage. I speak to my son in Japanese, and we have lots of Mexican American friends, other Hapa, and Asian American friends."

Alison, age thirty-seven and living in RESCI 2, reported her race as White and Japanese and was married to a White American man who, like Ray's wife, was very interested in his spouse's Japanese heritage. Alison's husband, for instance, had made a concerted effort to learn Japanese:

> We've been together for seventeen years, and when we first started dating, my [Japanese] mother's English, she was not nearly as good as she is now, so he wanted to be able to better understand her. . . . And then also my sisters and I were together with my mom, he'd want to understand, so he'd try to learn it on his own, and then now he's gotten a lot better.

For Alison, marrying someone who was genuinely invested in her Japanese American heritage—who was committed to taking regular trips to Japan and gaining a wider appreciation of Japanese American culture—had been a priority. This priority was also reflected in how they were raising their daughter.

## The Marriage Choices of Black-White Individuals

As with the other mixed-heritage groups, there is a strong association between Black-White people's reported race and the race of their spouse. Mary Campbell found that Black-White mixed-heritage people married to a non-Black spouse were 22 percent less likely to identify themselves as Black, in comparison with people who were either unmarried or had a Black spouse.[17]

The marriage patterns of mixed-heritage Black-White people vary by type of place and by their racial self-identification, as illustrated in

**Figure 4.4** *The Race of Spouses of Mixed-Heritage Black-White People, by Racial/Ethnic Spatial Context, 1980–2019*

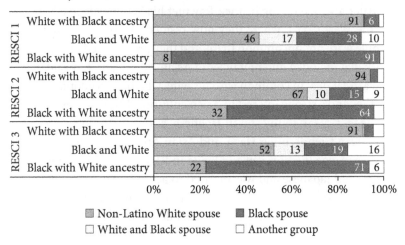

*Source:* Authors' calculations.

figure 4.4. RESCI 1 includes much of the South and appears to be a distinct racial context for people of mixed Black-White heritage, and one that impacts them even after they move away.[18] In RESCI 1, biracially identified Black-White people less often marry a single-race White person and more often marry someone who includes Black in their racial identification. Those who identify as single-race Black (with White ancestry) in RESCI 1 are almost always marrying another single-race Black person. In RESCI 2, which includes White-dominated and more rural spaces, a much higher proportion of Black-White people have a single-race non-Latino White spouse. Few Black-White mixed-heritage people marry someone who is neither Black nor White, though this is more common in RESCI 3, which includes areas with substantial Asian and Pacific Islander populations. Low numbers of married mixed-heritage Black-White people in RESCI 4 and RESCI 5 limit our analyses in these places.

## WHITE-IDENTIFIED BLACK-WHITE PEOPLE

In comparison with Native-White people, many of whom identify as White, it is relatively rare for mixed-heritage Black-White people to identify as White. Those who do are extremely likely to have a White spouse;

over 90 percent of such people have a White spouse across all the RESCI areas. None of our Black-White participants identified as single-race White. As with members of the other mixed groups, some Black-White people may not have been comfortable saying that they felt more White than Black. But as discussed in chapter 3 and later in this chapter, some biracially identified Black-White participants do "lean" toward their White heritage, and most of them have a White spouse.

### BLACK-IDENTIFIED BLACK-WHITE PEOPLE

Homogamy among people identified as racially Black is very strong. It is striking in figures 4.1 and 4.4 that virtually none of the mixed-heritage Black-White people who identify as single-race Black have a spouse who is reported as biracial. As is true for all groups, it is possible that some single-race-identified people have mixed-heritage spouses but report them as single-race when filling out the census form. Doing so may be especially important in the families of mixed-heritage Black people, given the importance in many Black families of communicating a collective, shared Blackness.[19] As discussed in the last chapter, only one of our Black-White participants, Yetta, identified as Black. She had a Black spouse but was now divorced. "So, I identify as Black because it's how I was raised, you know, the neighborhood, my environment. . . . I think, honestly, I do think I felt positive about it, especially because, like I said, during the '70s it was the Black Power movement and it was a time where you could be proud to be Black."

In recalling the Black Power movement and embracing her Black identity as a teenager, Yetta reported that, relatedly, her dating experiences were structured by race, as she had attended a (de facto) racially segregated school where it was uncommon for Black people to date anyone who was not Black.

### BIRACIALLY IDENTIFIED BLACK-WHITE PEOPLE

As in the other mixed-heritage groups, there is considerable diversity among people who identify as biracial in the racial backgrounds of their spouses. We found particular variation in their reported racial consciousness and attitudes toward diversity among the White spouses of Black-White biracially identified people. Those in diverse metropolitan areas were often part of politically progressive and racially diverse social networks.

In the national data shown in figure 4.1, we see that about half of Black-White people who identify with both races married White people, though this varies by racial/ethnic context (figure 4.4). A notable minority (10 to 17 percent, depending on the type of location) were married to another multiracial Black-White person, and a larger share (15 to 28 percent) had a Black spouse. Nineteen of our twenty Black-White participants identified biracially as both White and Black, with a range of attachment to their Black and White backgrounds. Among these nineteen biracially identified Black-White participants, eight were married to a Black person, nine to a White person, and two to a biracial Black-White person like themselves.

## BIRACIALLY IDENTIFIED BLACK-WHITE PEOPLE
### WITH A WHITE SPOUSE

Our participants with a White spouse usually had a relationship that included more White people and settings, though these White spouses were not necessarily lacking in racial consciousness. Our biracially identified Black-White participants with a White spouse tended to be individuals who had grown up in predominantly White neighborhoods, schools, and other such contexts, and many had only limited contact with other Black people. For example, Max (from chapter 3) was raised by his White mother and had very little contact with his Black father growing up in a mostly White town in the Northeast (RESCI 2). He had dated mostly White women, as he lived primarily in White-dominated areas. As such, he did not feel that his wife's Whiteness posed a social or cultural barrier. In fact, according to Max, they shared similar cultural references, and he was often most comfortable, he implied, in White settings.

Some participants with a White spouse lived in predominantly White spaces and had mainly White social networks. For example, Blair, as mentioned in the last chapter, reported that he felt most comfortable with "the White dominant society." Given his ease around White people and White settings, he had mostly dated White women prior to marrying his White spouse. Because he had been raised in a mostly White, middle-class setting, he saw his choice of spouse as largely shaped by his racially homogeneous surroundings. Blair also implied that his own choice of a White spouse was influenced by the marital history of his Black father, both of whose spouses had been White. "So . . . yeah, and his projection or how he wants to be seen in terms of upper-middle-class and all this stuff. So . . . I mean, I don't know if it's kind of the cliché kind of thing where you move up and then your White wife kind of thing, I don't know, but that's always been his . . . also the [White] social circles he moves in, so . . . there you go."

Another biracially identified Black-White participant introduced in chapter 3, Saskia, had a White spouse and reported that she had mostly been attracted to White men:

> I was looking for someone who was serious about their faith. Not just someone who was a nominal Christian at the holidays only. In terms of attraction, I noticed I was attracted to Whites (*laughs*) and oh, okay, and not all were religious. I just watched and observed. My family had a no-dating policy for a while, so I wasn't involved in [much] dating.

Their shared Christianity was central to the relationship between Saskia and her husband, while her Black heritage receded into the background and was not central to how she saw herself.

Having a White spouse, however, did not necessarily mean that our Black-White participants inhabited mostly White spaces; that depended very much on the racial/ethnic context of their geographical location and the nature of their social networks. Living in a large city (RESCI 3, for example) could provide couples with a range of ethnic and racial neighborhoods to live and work in and venues to visit.

Recall from chapter 3 that a participant named Mallory identified as a White and Black woman and lived in a large and diverse city in the Northeast (RESCI 3). She took for granted that her White husband was racially conscious and appreciative of her mixed-heritage background. Mallory also reported that their social network was highly diverse: "We have a really nice community of people who are also in mixed marriages or who are themselves mixed, so like, of my very dearest friends, like two of them are mixed like I am." Moreover, she added, her son's "close friends, a lot of them are mixed."

Mallory and her White husband felt that, as a visibly mixed couple, they were unremarkable in their city and did not stand out in their daily lives. In fact, while Mallory and others who considered themselves politically and socially progressive were highly aware of the workings of White supremacy, they did not speak of White people as one homogeneous mass, as many of them (like Mallory) had a White spouse and White friends. Rather, these participants spoke of White people as highly varied in their sensibilities and racial politics.

Evan, a forty-three-year-old who identified as Black-White, grew up in a highly diverse city in the Northeast (RESCI 3) and was married to a White woman with eastern European immigrant parents. When asked about his dating history, he replied: "Sure. I dated everybody. Everybody." He then elaborated: "I didn't give a shit where she was from. I am and have always been a very easy person to . . . where meeting people is concerned. I don't have hang-ups about where you're from and who you are. Are you a nice person? Do you have your own opinions? Do you have opinions? Do you enjoy life?"

It was a given that Evan would not have partnered with a White person who was somehow prejudiced toward non-White people, but he did not assume that all White people were suspect in this way. Evan's open stance toward dating and potential partners was a product of his upbringing in a highly diverse setting, where he encountered a large range of people.

## BIRACIALLY IDENTIFIED BLACK-WHITE PEOPLE WITH A BLACK SPOUSE

For some participants, marrying a Black person opened up a social world that they had not previously experienced. A biracially identified participant whom we met in chapter 3, Wendy, was raised by her White mother, grew up in the Midwest (RESCI 2), and had very little contact with her Black father growing up. Marrying her Black husband enabled her to participate in a Black social network and world for the first time. She spoke of being raised to see herself as biracial; over time, however, and in a different setting, her multiracial background receded in importance, especially after she moved to a "more Black space" (in RESCI 1) and entered a relationship with her Black husband:

> I went to college in the early 2000s, so there was a lot of talk about being biracial. I'm not exactly sure when the shift [to feeling Black] happened. It might have occurred toward grad school for me. Maybe it was partly

moving into the South and having less exposure to the momentum of biracial identity movements and being in a more Black space.

When asked if having a Black partner was important to her, Wendy replied:

> Like the White boyfriend I had at the end of high school, I liked him, but I did feel like there was always this cultural barrier. Where he didn't understand things and it was annoying to have to explain them. In college, a White guy would be cute, but I never found the depth to those relationships, so there was more ease dating Black men.

In marrying a Black man who came from the South (she described him as being "as Southern Black as you can get"), Wendy became enveloped in a world that she had not known before:

> So, when we moved . . . we were surrounded by his family. That was the first time I'd gone to Black family reunions. But Black Americans don't really know an ethnic category other than Black. Or Southern Black, which may be its own ethnic category. I love the South. I thought I was gonna hate it. Coming from the Midwest, the South was gonna be racist, but I love the South . . . the richness of the Black Southern culture. Levels of hospitality. And everyone seems to be kin of kin. And there's also that richness of past civil rights movements. And the music as well, jazz or gospel, is huge.

Having a partner who was racially conscious and committed to racial justice was imperative for a number of Black-White participants. Thirty-eight-year-old Vanessa was married to a Black man of Puerto Rican heritage, and they lived in a diverse Northern city (RESCI 1). When asked if she had consciously wanted a partner who was not White, she replied:

> Not . . . I wouldn't say . . . that it [having a Black partner] was important to me. It was important to me to be partnered with somebody who . . . understood racial inequality; who understood my background and that . . . and I think there could be White people that fit that description, you know. . . . So, it wasn't important to me, but I would say probably there's a number of White men that I just wouldn't have ended up with because if I had been darker [she was very light-skinned], they wouldn't have dated me and that would be a deal-breaker.

## BIRACIALLY IDENTIFIED BLACK-WHITE PEOPLE WITH
## A BIRACIALLY IDENTIFIED BLACK-WHITE SPOUSE

Whether our Black-White participants had a single-race Black spouse or a mixed-heritage Black-White spouse, their Black racial overlap was central to how these couples related to one another. This was especially important in terms of their social treatment and perceptions of both partners as Black people, regardless of whether one partner was racially mixed or not. However, the experiences of participants with a mixed-heritage Black-White spouse were distinctive in one important respect from the experiences of those who had a monoracial Black spouse: Those with a Black-White spouse also shared a White racial overlap, in addition to their shared Blackness.

One biracially identified Black-White participant was married to a biracial Black-White person like herself. Corey, introduced in the last chapter, reported that sharing the same experience of being biracial with her spouse (both had a White mother and a Black father) was an important bond in their relationship. Although she had not purposely sought out someone who was racially mixed, as opposed to Black, she believed that they both had insight into the experience of growing up in a racially mixed family, which many (single-race) African Americans had not experienced.

Corey met her husband on an online dating site in a White-dominated city in the Midwest (RESCI 2) that had few Black people. "Dating in [city] was really hard. So I went on some dates with White people (on this dating site), which wasn't my thing, but I tried it out, and it was awkward. We [she and her husband] just kind of hit it off." In high school, she had dated a White boy: "Looking back, I was like, why was I with him? Then I had a string of biracial boyfriends, but nothing that lasted that long." After she started dating the man who would become her spouse, she discovered that

> the main thing we had in common was that our moms are both White, and they were both single parents. And we were both raised poor/working-class. I think he was a little better off than I was. And at that point in my life, I thought, "The person I date has to understand racism and believe that it's real, no matter what their race is." And he had that perspective, and that was really useful. He grew up in

[a Midwestern city] and went to a high school that was like 97 percent Black. He was like the one mixed kid in his friend group. But
we had like opposite upbringings, in terms of his being around all
Black people (other than his mother) and me growing up mostly
around White people.

A shared experience of having a White mother and a Black father and
navigating an often racially segregated world contributed to their sense
of closeness and understanding of each other.

There were many commonalities among participants who had a Black
or part-Black partner. The Black racial overlap between the participants
and their partners usually translated into a shared sensibility that allowed
an ease and racial consciousness about being Black and their treatment
in the wider society. Their shared Blackness was a meaningful bond that
tended to eclipse the fact that one or both of them also had White heritage. They especially valued their shared Blackness if they lived in a location with few Black people.

## Differential Exposure to White and Black Worlds

Across all mixed-heritage groups, we found that experiences of Whiteness influenced our participants' spouse choices. As people with a White
heritage, most of our participants had some exposure to experiences
of Whiteness, such as contact with White relatives and access to some
predominantly White spaces. For many participants who married
a White person, this spouse choice did not put them on an entirely new pathway; instead, they continued along a familiar pathway where Whiteness
was a feature of their comfort zone. For people with a White spouse, their
shared Whiteness was largely unremarked upon; there was no acknowledgment between them of White racial overlap as a basis of commonality
or shared experience.

By comparison, participants with a non-White spouse could encounter different dynamics, opportunities, or concerns about their shared
social worlds. As discussed, having a spouse with whom there was a
(BIPOC) racial overlap—whether it be Asian, Native, or Black—could
provide mixed-heritage participants with another basis for racial group
membership, such as Jonathan marrying a Korean American woman,
or Alex marrying a "full" Navajo woman, or Wendy gaining entry into

a Black social world she had not previously experienced. A shared non-White race (with minority racial overlap) was regarded as a meaningful basis for fostering a close relationship, based on a common understanding of that racial overlap. In this way, marrying a non-White person could open doors to networks and social worlds that had not been accessible before—usually BIPOC social worlds. Prior research on intermarriage with White people has tended to focus on how marriage to White people provides entry into White social worlds; by comparison, our research may be one of the first to investigate mixed-heritage people gaining entry into BIPOC settings and networks.

However, our mixed-heritage participants who had a Black spouse spoke of their spouse (who was not part-White) having varying degrees of access to White spaces and people in their upbringing. Our Black-White participants, even those with no strong ties to White relatives and networks, had experienced Whiteness to some degree, whether via identification with the White parent and wider family or in exposure to predominantly White spaces and practices. This theme among our mixed-heritage participants of experiencing Whiteness and having a heightened awareness of White spaces against the historical prominence of the Black-White racial boundary was especially notable in some of the interviews with our Black-White participants.[20]

For example, Wendy, who had grown up "working-class," always felt at ease with both White and Black people, even though she had had little contact with her Black father and his family. She spoke of her adaptations to White people and settings enabling her to move in and out of both White and non-White spaces with relative ease: "We had so many different settings. Like summer camp [with no Black people], but in another space, like a family reunion with my mom's side or going camping—so being in mostly White spaces was my life. I did a lot of adjusting and . . . blending. . . . I guess I learned how to translate myself into these spaces." An important "glue" for the relationship of a Black-White participant and their Black spouse was the shared experience of knowing how to navigate life with White people and White social worlds.[21] According to Wendy, her Black husband was comfortable, like her, in both Black and White social worlds:

[My husband] was put into a private Christian White school growing up, went to a Black church, but also around a lot of White people and forced to fit in. For him, it was also that comfortable feeling with us. We found that in common. By the nature of our jobs, we still do that, so we make situations work—code-switching. Like, if we have to go to a work dinner (predominantly White), we can go and have a good time. We had this ease in understanding each other.

The relative ease in navigating both White and Black social worlds that Wendy described was familiar to Kendra, who, as noted in chapter 3, had grown up with her Black father and White mother in an affluent and highly educated family. Her schools and social worlds had been mostly populated with many White people. But Kendra married a Black man from a working-class background and a family that was very different from hers. In comparison with her, Kendra's husband had had very limited exposure to White people and spaces growing up. Until they met, she said, "He had never been in a White person's house before." She noted that her family and her husband's family "came from very different class backgrounds. He came from a much more working-class and less educated family; he went to a high school that was 99 percent Black and a Historically Black University."

Kendra reported that she and her husband inhabited quite separate social worlds that seemed to reflect their different class backgrounds and exposures to White people in particular: While her friends were highly ethnically diverse, all of her husband's friends were Black. Kendra also took their son to an affluent, predominantly White church (the same church her parents attended), but her husband did not accompany them.

## Conclusion

In this chapter, we have explored the racial backgrounds of the spouses of mixed-heritage people. The census data show that, across all three mixed-heritage groups, a person's racial identification is highly predictive of their spouse's race. We see that the way a mixed-heritage individual reports their race—as White, as two races, or as a single-race BIPOC person—is strongly related to how their spouse is reported. Our analysis of national data also shows that gendered patterns in marital choices among people of mixed heritage tend to mirror the gendered patterns of their single-race counterparts.

As shown in figures 4.1 through 4.4, people in all three mixed-heritage groups—Native-White, Asian-White, and Black-White—who self-identify as single-race White very often have a single-race White spouse, though this tendency varies somewhat by racial/ethnic context. One participant who racially identified as White and was married to a White man provides some insight into the pattern shown in the national data. As detailed in the last chapter, Dawn had Native ancestry, but she looked White to others and she and her family embodied Whiteness and enjoyed the privileges of Whiteness. That is why she did not feel she should even identify biracially as Native-White. She did not participate in any Native activities or networks, and she felt that her Native heritage was entirely invisible to others.

The national data in figures 4.1 through 4.4 show that people of mixed heritage who self-identify as a single-race Native, Asian, or Black person (with White ancestry) are likely to marry someone with the same single-race identification. Such marriages are particularly common among mixed-heritage Black people, but Native and Asian people in the data show the same pattern. However, there are also pronounced cross-group differences among mixed-heritage people who identify as Native, Asian, or Black. Those identifying as solely Native still exhibit high rates of marriage to White people (78 percent nationally), while those identifying as solely Black are far less likely to be married to White people (20 percent nationally). Mixed-heritage people identifying as Asian fall in between the other two groups, with 57 percent married to White spouses. Again, figures 4.2 through 4.4 illustrate variation across racial/ethnic context.

Importantly, in all three mixed-heritage groups, those reporting biracially choose spouses from a variety of race groups, usually with some racial overlap. A White spouse is quite a common choice for biracially identified people with White heritage in all three mixed-heritage groups; nationally, 73 percent of married Native-White people, 61 percent of married Asian-White people, and 58 percent of married Black-White people from 2000 to 2019 had a White spouse. It is striking, given that many scholars of race often contrast the experiences of Black and Asian people, that there is almost no difference among biracial people with an Asian or Black heritage in their propensity to marry White people. This propensity for *biracial* Black-White and Asian-White people to marry White people suggests that there may be relatively little social distance between biracially identifying Black-White and Asian-White people and White people. This is in contrast to research suggesting that there is a significant gulf between Black-White people and single-race White people, and that this contrasts with the experiences of Asian-White people, whose social distance from White people is seen as smaller.[22]

People who self-report two races are relatively likely to be married to someone else who self-reports two or more races (ranging from 12 to 20 percent of marriages), while mixed-heritage people who report a single race are highly unlikely to have a multiple-race spouse (less than 5 percent of marriages).[23] Several factors may explain this remarkable pattern. Going into marriage, people may have preexisting identities that draw them to others who identify similarly. Or spouses who report the same race may be doing so because of shared discussions or decisions that mixed heritage should be reported as two (or more) races. Or one spouse may have filled out the form for both of them and applied their own schema to describe both themselves and their spouse.

Importantly, we find that the race of their spouse was often (though not always) an important indicator of how mixed-heritage participants thought and felt about their own White and BIPOC races and family backgrounds. As discussed in chapter 3, how participants related to their various racial and ethnic backgrounds was influenced by many factors, such as the settings where they grew up and how much interaction and cultural exposure they had with various branches of their White and non-White families. In this chapter, we see that these experiences also shaped their dating histories and choice of spouse.

Furthermore, racial/ethnic context factors such as the availability of non-White coethnics in their areas were also important in shaping their dating opportunities and choices. Demographic and cultural differences associated with disparate racial and ethnic spatial contexts structured the dating and marriage opportunities and norms that mixed-heritage people encountered. While some mixed participants intentionally moved to more diverse places (or moved away from them, like Sam, who moved away from an area with Native homelands), others were geographically much more confined owing to limited resources and educational capital or to family ties and connections.

Perhaps not surprisingly, our interviews reveal that, across participants in all three mixed-heritage groups, having a White spouse rather than a non-White spouse suggests a different orientation toward the centrality of race. On the whole, having a White partner rather than a partner with whom the mixed-heritage participant shared a non-White racial overlap was associated with a differential investment and immersion in a specific BIPOC racial and/or ethnic background.

Participants with a non-White partner (especially those who shared an Asian, Black, or Native racial overlap) tended to report that their race and/or ethnicity and that of their partner constituted a defining part of their relationship, albeit in variable ways. Some participants from all three mixed-heritage groups with a spouse who shared a BIPOC race with them indicated that having a spouse who shared their minoritized heritage was of personal importance to them and afforded them entry into BIPOC communities and networks. Participants, especially Black-White participants who shared Blackness with their spouse, often referred to the importance of a shared racial understanding, whether it be a shared cultural sensibility or a shared racial consciousness about being visibly non-White. Some Native-White participants with a Native spouse and Asian-White participants with an Asian spouse also expressed a wish, for example, to prevent the demise of Native languages and cultural practices, and or to keep Asian cultural practices and ancestries alive.

By virtue of being both part White and part BIPOC, our mixed-heritage participants had variable degrees of exposure to White and non-White people and settings, and their exposure was heavily dependent on their racial/ethnic context. Differences by RESCI area, shown in figures 4.2 through 4.4, may be due to these factors. Having a White spouse was associated with a greater likelihood of being part of a predominantly White social network and being comfortable with White people and settings. Nevertheless, having a White spouse did not necessarily mean that the union was devoid of racial consciousness or an ethnically diverse network. Nor did it inevitably dilute the mixed-heritage participant's ethnic or racial consciousness.[24] Some participants (of all three mixed-heritage groups), especially those who lived in a highly diverse metropolitan area, had a White spouse whom they described as a cosmopolitan individual who valued their partner's Asian, Native, or Black ancestry and who was committed to racial justice. Other unions with White people signaled that the participants' non-White heritage was receding into the background. Some with a White spouse regarded their spouse's Whiteness as unremarkable; as the "default mode" (in many areas), their Whiteness required no explicit discussion or appreciation.

In sum, the interviews were important in showing the disparate kinds of unions that mixed-heritage participants (across all three groups) had with White partners. While some participants with a White partner reported that they spent their day-to-day lives mostly among White people and White-dominated settings, others, especially those in a large metropolitan area, had a White spouse who was both racially conscious and invested in their mixed-heritage partner's ethnic and racial background. One important implication of our interview findings is that it is difficult to talk of White people and interracial unions with White people in a monolithic sense, because, even acknowledging the persistence of White supremacy and White privilege, *there is no one type of White spouse.*

A wider question arising from this chapter is how we should conceptualize the relationships of mixed-heritage people, since existing frameworks using terms such as "intermarriage" and "endogamy" are premised on the marital choices of people who are seen as monoracial.[25] Given the growing prevalence of interethnic and interracial dating and other intimate unions in the United States and elsewhere, this question of how to characterize such unions will only become more pressing. Rather than trying to fit these relationships into a limiting binary, we find that it is pertinent to look at what racial/ethnic overlap is present in the unions of mixed-heritage people, if any. Figures 4.1 through 4.4 in this chapter provide nationally representative statistics that fit this bill.

# CHAPTER FIVE

# HOW DO MIXED-HERITAGE PEOPLE IDENTIFY AND RAISE THEIR CHILDREN?

To understand racial identification and its impacts on people of mixed White and BIPOC heritage in the United States, we have discussed patterns and nuances in racial identification (chapter 3) and how these have influenced spouse choice (chapter 4). We now turn to the ways in which mixed-heritage people racially identify and raise their children. We find that there is a high degree of congruence between the sets of results in chapters 3, 4, and 5 across all types of people of mixed racial heritage in our study. We find that *the way a person of mixed heritage chooses to racially identify is strongly related to who they choose to marry and how they and their spouse racially identify and raise their children.* In the child-focused analyses in this chapter, this congruence can be seen in census data and in interviews, both of which highlight similarities between how the child's race is reported and how the child's parents report their own race and that of their spouse. Our work extends existing studies of how interracial couples identify their multiracial children in the United States, as extant studies are based on the unions of (usually) monoracially distinct partners, not unions involving one or more mixed-heritage individuals.

Various studies employing census data in the United States have examined the ways in which people in interracial unions racially identify their multiracial children.[1] Studies have shown that how multiracial people identify themselves may not match how their parents identify them.[2] Many of these studies have concluded that parents' connections to racial/ethnic groups, as well as the racial/ethnic context of the area, are very important to children's identifications. These studies of how

https://doi.org/10.7758/edyf5459.9032

interracial couples identify their children are premised on the unions of first-generation interracial unions—that is, couples with disparate racial backgrounds.

As discussed previously, unions with White Americans have been said to lead to some BIPOC partners "tilting White," and some scholars have implied that the children of such unions are also then likely to identify as White.[3] However, such suggestions about the likely outcomes for the children of such unions are not yet empirically substantiated. As found in Song's study of mixed-heritage people's experiences as parents, we also find significant heterogeneity in how mixed-heritage people, even those with a White spouse, think about their race and how they raise their children.[4]

Jenifer Bratter studied the racial identification of children of multiracially identified parents in the 2000 census.[5] A shared Black classification between parents did not guarantee that a child would be labeled as Black; Bratter found that "approximately a third of the families where either the mother or the father is partially Black and their spouse is Black (alone) classify their children as 'multiracial.'"[6] Bratter also found that over 85 percent of families with two partially Black multiracial parents identified their children with multiple races. These results suggest that a multiracial identification is seen as a "viable racial identity," even among Black people, who have been historically subject to the one-drop rule.[7] Besides these intriguing results, little research has been done about how mixed-heritage parents report their children's race.[8]

In addition to examining the many ways in which mixed-heritage parents identify their children in the census data, we also delve more deeply in this chapter into *why* mixed-heritage parents identify their children in particular ways, and what their identifications of their children may reveal about their upbringing. Through our interviews, we also describe some of our participants' wider concerns about their children's upbringing from the perspective of mixed-heritage parents.

Based on Census Bureau data and discussions with our interview participants, we find that *patterns in how children are racially identified are primarily driven by who marries whom*. In other words, the racial identities of the parents (and the racial overlap between the mixed-heritage parent and their spouse) are tightly related to how they identify and raise their children. We also find that patterns differ in important ways between the mixed-heritage groups—for example, some of the patterns of Asian-White families are different from those of Black-White families—and they differ across type of place (especially where American Indian and Asian populations are larger and more established). Both of these results are impacted by the (modest) gendered patterns in marriage choice, but we did not find other evidence of gendered patterns in child identification. Because our results indicate that children's racial identification (and upbringing) is dominated by parent identity and spouse race choices, we organize the chapter by race combinations of parents.

Our analyses of Census Bureau data are summarized in figures 5.1, 5.2, and 5.3, each of which has twelve panels that show the distribution of race/ancestry responses given for children with parents of a certain race/ethnicity combination. Within each panel, families are shown in different columns depending on the RESCI area where they lived. Most of the variation in figures 5.1, 5.2, and 5.3 is between panels, revealing that the parents' race/ancestry responses are key drivers of the race/ancestry response given for the child. There is spatial variation, however, in how commonly a child is reported one way versus another, especially in areas dominated by the focal BIPOC group.

Figure 5.1 shows the race/ancestry response given for the children of heterosexually married Native-White mixed-heritage people in Census Bureau data from 1980 to 2019. If the mixed-heritage Native-White parent reported Native race and White ancestry, the family is represented in the third column of panels (the row depends on the race of the spouse). If this parent was married to a single-race White person, for example, the children's race/ancestry is shown in panel C (and disaggregated by RESCI within panel C). In panel C of figure 5.1, we can see that children in RESCI 4 (where there are relatively many Native people and Native homelands) are more likely to be identified as Native race with White ancestry or as Native race with no mention of White ancestry; this finding points to the importance of geographical location in shaping these dynamics. See chapter 2 and the appendixes for details on the coding of family members' race/ancestry data.

Figures 5.1, 5.2, and 5.3 are dense with information, and they are discussed throughout the chapter, with individual panels reprinted where needed. Some marriage pairings are so rare that we do not show their results; for example, panel F in all figures is omitted because it is rare for two people of the same mixed racial heritage to marry and also

**Figure 5.1** *Distribution of Child's Race Response If at Least One Parent Was Native-White, by Parents' Race Responses and RESCI Area, 1980–2019*

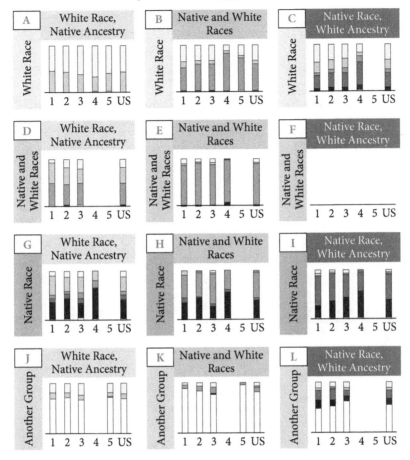

**Child Response Legend**

☐ White race and no mention of Native ancestry
▨ White race and Native ancestry
▨ White and Native races
▨ Native race and White ancestry
■ Native race and no mention of White ancestry
☐ Another group

**Racial/Ethnic Spatial Context Indicator**

1: E.g., Atlanta, Georgia, or Detroit, Michigan
2: E.g., Fort Collins, Colorado, or Duluth, Minnesota
3: E.g., Minneapolis, New York City, or Houston
4: E.g., Hopi reservation, Arizona
5: Hawaii or San Francisco
US = Entire United States

*Source:* Authors' calculations.
*Note:* "Children" are the children of the householder and are ages zero through nineteen. If both parents are mixed-heritage Native-White, the mother is shown as parent 1. The percentage is not shown if the total unweighted number of children in the data with this set of parents is less than 60 (see, for example, panel F). Data are pooled 1980, 1990, and 2000 census 5 percent PUMS and 2006–2010 and 2015–2019 ACS, all accessed at IPUMS.org.

**Figure 5.2** *Distribution of Child's Race Response If at Least One Parent Was Asian-White, by Parents' Race Responses and RESCI Area, 1980–2019*

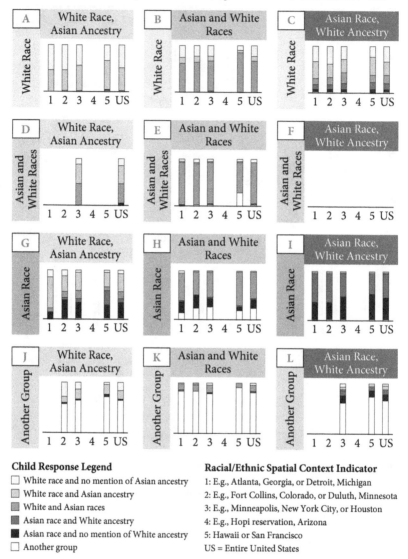

**Child Response Legend**
☐ White race and no mention of Asian ancestry
▦ White race and Asian ancestry
▩ White and Asian races
▨ Asian race and White ancestry
■ Asian race and no mention of White ancestry
☐ Another group

**Racial/Ethnic Spatial Context Indicator**
1: E.g., Atlanta, Georgia, or Detroit, Michigan
2: E.g., Fort Collins, Colorado, or Duluth, Minnesota
3: E.g., Minneapolis, New York City, or Houston
4: E.g., Hopi reservation, Arizona
5: Hawaii or San Francisco
US = Entire United States

*Source:* Authors' calculations.

*Note:* "Children" are the children of the householder and are ages zero through nineteen. If both parents are mixed-heritage Asian-White, the mother is shown as parent 1. The percentage is not shown if the total unweighted number of children in the data with this set of parents is less than 60 (see, for example, panel F). Data are pooled 1980, 1990, and 2000 Census 5 percent PUMS and 2006–2010 and 2015–2019 ACS, all accessed at IPUMS.org.

**Figure 5.3** *Distribution of Child's Race Response If at Least One Parent Was Black-White, by Parents' Race Responses and RESCI Area, 1980–2019*

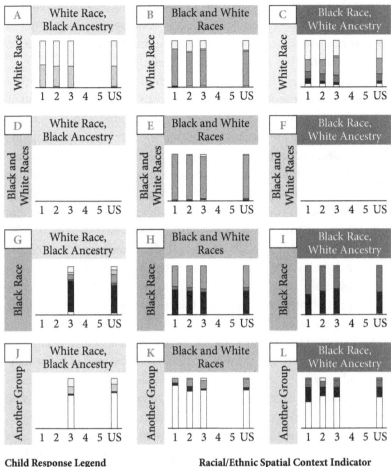

**Child Response Legend**

☐ White race and no mention of Black ancestry
▢ White race and Black ancestry
▨ White and Black races
▩ Black race and White ancestry
■ Black race and no mention of White ancestry
☐ Another group

**Racial/Ethnic Spatial Context Indicator**

1: E.g., Atlanta, Georgia, or Detroit, Michigan
2: E.g., Fort Collins, Colorado, or Duluth, Minnesota
3: E.g., Minneapolis, New York City, or Houston
4: E.g., Hopi reservation, Arizona
5: Hawaii or San Francisco
US = Entire United States

*Source:* Authors' calculations.

*Note:* "Children" are the children of the householder and are ages zero through nineteen. If both parents are mixed-heritage Black-White, the mother is shown as parent 1. The percentage is not shown if the total unweighted number of children in the data with this set of parents is less than 60 (see, for example, panel F). Data are pooled 1980, 1990, and 2000 Census 5 percent PUMS and 2006–2010 and 2015–2019 ACS, all accessed at IPUMS.org.

self-identify divergently (one as multiple races and one as the non-White race with White ancestry). Similarly, individual RESCI locations are not shown if there are very few families of that race/ethnic configuration in that racial/ethnic context. It is sociologically interesting to see how rare are some family configurations in some types of contexts, even when data from 1980–2019 are pooled.

Many participants hoped that their children would identify in particular ways or that they would become attached to a particular ancestry. In that sense, parents had racial and ethnic aspirations for their children.[9] Just as the chapter on racial identities reported that most participants were uninterested in their White background, our participants rarely discussed their children's White race and ancestry. Hardly any of our mixed-heritage participants pointed to a White European ancestry they wished to cultivate or reclaim. Parents who wished to transmit ethnic and racial distinctiveness or consciousness in relation to their BIPOC races/ancestries made a concerted effort to do so and mentioned Whiteness as a default mode in the wider society. The few parents who identified their children as solely White on the preinterview survey clearly signaled in the interview that their children had no connection to their non-White ancestry.

As discussed later in this chapter, mixed-heritage participants and their partners, especially those with more economic and cultural capital, could engage in "identity projects" for their children that were not about inculcating specific identities or heritages.[10] For example, some Asian-White participants (especially those with a South Asian heritage) who led affluent lives stressed cosmopolitanism in their children's upbringing. Exposure to a multitude of people, cultural practices, languages, and foods was desirable because such connections were understood to be associated with pluralist values and an openness to different people and backgrounds.[11]

### Children of Monoracially Identified Parents of Mixed Heritage Married to Someone of the Same Single Race

Some people of mixed heritage identify themselves as a single race and marry someone of the same single race. Panels A and I from figures 5.1, 5.2, and 5.3 (reprinted in figure 5.4; see figures 5.1 to 5.3 for the legends) show that whether the parents shared the same single racial

**Figure 5.4** *Child's Race Response If They Had Two Single-Race-Identified Parents (at Least One of Whom Had Mixed Racial Heritage) with the Same Race Response, 1980–2019*

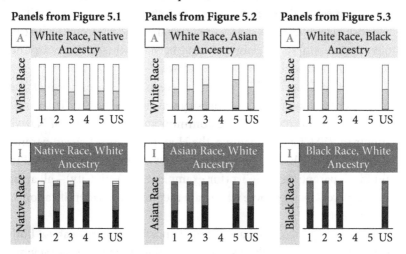

*Source:* Authors' calculations.
*Note:* See figures 5.1 through 5.3 for legends.

identification of Native, Asian, Black, or White, the children of same-single-race marriages were essentially never reported as multiple races, even though at least one parent acknowledged a mixed racial heritage. This result is perhaps not surprising if both parents reported the same single race, though if both parents reported the same additional ancestry, they might have been more likely to report their child as having more than one race.

The predominance of colors representing single-race responses in figure 5.4 highlights the great extent to which parents in these same-race marriages passed this race response to their children. The absence of multiple-race responses for children in panels A and I indicates that these marriages were not the source of the next generation of people who identified (or were identified by parents) as multiracial. Our interviews reveal instead that such couples emphasized racial commonality.

In each panel A (reprinted in figure 5.4), there are some cases where the mixed-heritage White-identified parent's non-White ancestry was not mentioned as the child's ancestry. In most RESCI areas, at least half of children were reported as White with no mention of their parents' mixed racial heritage. Panel A for Native-White people shows a notable pattern in RESCI 4: A Native-White mixed-heritage person who lived in RESCI 4, identified as single-race White, and married a single-race White person was especially likely to make *no mention* of Native ancestry. This response may reflect a relatively tight social boundary around who can make a successful social claim to Native heritage when so many around them are American Indian/Alaska Native.

Each panel I reprinted in figure 5.4 reveals some cases in which the mixed-heritage parent's White ancestry was not mentioned. This omission of White heritage is more common among children of Native parents in RESCI 4 (for example, the Hopi reservation), Asian parents in RESCI 3 and RESCI 5 (for example, New York City and Honolulu), and Black parents in RESCI 3 (for example, New York City)—all areas with relatively many people who share the same racial identification as both parents.

Our participants often gave detailed ancestry responses about both their White and non-White ancestries in the preinterview survey; we have written elsewhere about how participants interpreted their ancestry responses.[12] Participants' ancestry responses for their children were often even more detailed than their own because they also tended to include the known ancestries of their children's other parent.[13]

Only three people in our study—Yetta, Susie, and Dawn—reported a single race and married someone with the same single race. Yetta, a sixty-year-old resident of RESCI 2 whom we met in chapter 3, identified as monoracially Black (with White ancestry). She had a child with a Black man and identified her as Black, with "Caribbean and African American" ancestry. Yetta, the oldest Black-White participant in our study, became a parent before the introduction of multiple race options in the 2000 US census, and she raised her daughter as "Black."

Also from chapter 3, Dawn, a forty-year-old resident of RESCI 3 who identified as White (with Native ancestry), was the only person in our interview study who identified as White. She had a White spouse and identified her children as White. Her choice to not add any ancestry data for her children was highly unusual in our study. As discussed in chapter 3, Dawn had not been raised with a connection to her Native ancestry:

I don't really consider . . . I guess if I considered myself American Indian and White, then I'd consider them [my children] on some level, but like, I'm not raising them culturally . . . they know we've discussed where's your family from or where's your background from, yeah, this is where we're from, you know, yeah, part of you is from here, right, but like, they're not being raised culturally within that.

Dawn regarded her ties to her American Indian ancestry, and her children's, to be very tenuous and thought it would be inappropriate to identify herself or her children as having Native ancestry.

Susie, as we learned in chapter 3, identified herself, her husband, and her child as Native, and all three with the same tribal affiliation. The fact that she lived in a rural RESCI 2 area with Native communities and reservations nearby enhanced her sense of belonging to a wider Indigenous population. In the preinterview survey, Susie wrote that her child's ancestry was "Native American and Norwegian"—the same ancestry report she gave for herself. In their interviews, Yetta, Susie, and Dawn shared a clear emphasis on the racial cohesion of the family in their children's upbringing—as illustrated by Susie, who reported that their daughter's sense of her Native heritage was reinforced by the fact that her parents shared this heritage (and the same tribal affiliation) and both could teach her about this heritage.

But these parents also wanted their children to benefit from the wider diversity around them and from a generalized cosmopolitanism. For instance, Susie wanted to foster her daughter's pride in her Native heritage, but doing so off the reservation in a primarily White area was not easy. Susie explained that she and her Native husband had decided to raise their teenage daughter off the reservation to widen her opportunities, emphasizing an everyday cosmopolitanism and "rounded experience": "We wanted to provide our daughter with the experience of being very well rounded to experience, different schools, different cultures, different languages."

But in moving off the reservation to broaden their daughter's experiences, Susie reported, her daughter faced other difficulties, such as White racism and less contact with their tribe. "There's an identity issue that she's struggling with right now with her being Ho-Chunk and living off the reservation. There's like an identity issue. I experienced that in my twenties to my thirties, but she's experienced it at an early age because she's growing up with non-Indians."

As Susie's husband was Native with the same tribal background, she reported, it was very important to them that their daughter learn about

**Figure 5.5** *Child's Race Response for Children with Two Single-Race-Identified Parents, at Least One of Whom Had Mixed Racial Heritage, with Different Race Responses, 1980–2019*

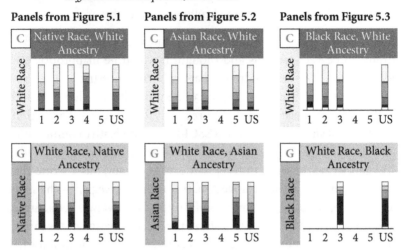

*Source:* Authors' calculations.
*Note:* See figures 5.1 through 5.3 for legends.

and value her Native and tribal background, but at the same time Susie did not want her daughter's opportunities to be constrained by remaining on the reservation. This type of scenario—having a strong personal attachment to a Native identity and community—could require some difficult decisions in navigating the relationship between family members' identities and the opportunities in different racial/ethnic spatial contexts. This tension was reported by other Native-White participants who lived on reservations but identified biracially (such as Cathy).

## Children of Monoracially Identified Parents of Mixed Heritage with a Spouse of a Different Single Race

Some marriages involve complex racial overlap. Panels C and G (reprinted in figure 5.5) depict the racial identifications of children of some of these marriages. Panel C from figure 5.1, for example, shows the wide diversity of race/ancestry responses given for children with a parent who reported Native race (with White ancestry) and a parent who reported White race. Note that most studies on intermarriage or on children's racial identification do not take ancestry responses into account; ignoring the information about racial overlap, these studies identify these as children of interracially married couples.

The wide variety of colors in the panels in figure 5.5 highlight three results. First, there are no clear social norms about how these children should be reported. Second, despite the option of choosing multiple races for the child (since 2000), and despite the fact that the child was living with married parents of two different races, most of the children were not reported as biracial. Third, the distribution of color in each bar is different depending on racial/ethnic context, indicating that this context is an important factor in determining how the child will be reported racially.

Three participants fell into the family types shown in figure 5.5. In fact, all were men who identified as single-race Native and had a White female spouse (panel A, figure 5.1).

Although it is difficult to tease out patterns on the basis of a few cases, we can see that geographical context, in combination with participants' own (sometimes conflicted) feelings about their Native ancestry and community and conventions about claims to Native membership, shaped how they racially identified their children. Middle-aged Sam and Ron, who lived in RESCI 2 (chapter 3), both identified as solely Native and had a White spouse and both identified their children as White. When asked why he identified his children as solely White, Ron replied: "Because they are not tribally enrolled." None of Sam's four children were tribal members either. When asked why he identified all his children as White, Sam said:

> If anyone that could possibly check off Native American out of the four boys, it could be my oldest, but then again, there were times when I tried to bring him up to the reservation to do things like walking in the . . . harvest wild rice with me. . . . Anyhow, long story short, he's never really connected in any way to any of our Native cultures. Goes to the occasional powwow with me . . .

Sam recognized that he could not engineer a meaningful connection between his children and their Native ancestry—especially since his children were not raised in an area with many other American Indian people. Furthermore, as discussed previously, Sam felt ambivalent about fully exposing his children to Native people and communities;

after witnessing the poverty and substance abuse among his Native relatives, he himself had moved to a very White town in the Northeast. Despite his ambivalence, Sam also talked about his sadness that his children were not "connected" with their Native ancestry and what that could bode for the future: "Oh yeah, that's . . . that's tough. . . . I hope they won't have . . . unfortunately, we're losing a certain piece of history that's just not . . . I don't know if it's sustainable or not." Although Sam very much wanted his children to have a meaningful affiliation with his American Indian ancestry, it was clear that he thought it would be wrong to say that they were American Indian if they had no active ties to or interest in that heritage.

By comparison, Nick identified as Inuit-Métis and identified his son as Inuit-Métis, even though his son's mother was a White American woman (and even though, as discussed in the last chapter, his wife was reportedly indifferent to Nick's Native heritage). Nick and his family also lived in an affluent suburb in the Northeast that was far from any Native communities. Nick's reporting of his son as solely Inuit-Métis appears to have arisen from an attachment to a group that he believed was largely invisible and forgotten. He reported that he hoped to introduce his young son to his Native heritage as he grew older. However, he realized that doing so would be difficult, as his own contact with his father and older brother, both of whom lived in Native communities, was tenuous. In this sense, Nick's identification of his son as American Indian/Alaska Native could be seen as aspirational.

### Children of Single-Race-Identified Mixed-Heritage People with a Spouse from "Another Group"

Panels J and L (reprinted in figure 5.6) refer to unions between mixed-heritage individuals who are married to people who identify in other ways. The families represented in these panels include a single-race-identified parent of mixed heritage with a spouse who had another race response besides White, same biracial, or same single race. In those panels, a high proportion of children are identified in relation to "another group." For all three parent race groups, panels J and L look similar, with most children reported differently from their mixed-heritage parent (possibly because they were reported as being all of their parents' races).

**Figure 5.6** *Child's Race Response for Children with One Single-Race Parent (with Mixed Racial Heritage) and One Parent from "Another Group," 1980–2019*

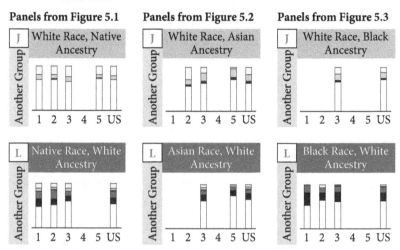

Source: Authors' calculations.
Note: See figures 5.1 through 5.3 for legends.

As included in panel J or panel L, mixed-heritage people who identify as a single race can have a spouse with multiple racial backgrounds. These unions can include some racial overlap. For example, Devon from chapter 3 identified as single-race Native with White ancestry and reported her spouse as "White, Black, Choctaw." She described her children in this way: "race: White, Black, Native (Menominee); ancestry: Menominee, French Canadian, African American, Choctaw, Scottish." The way that Devon reported her children's race would place them in "another group" in panel L in figure 5.1. Her race reporting of her children reflected both her and her spouse's racial backgrounds as well as their commitment to raising their children to be proud of their Native and Black ancestries. Their shared Native backgrounds seemed to be an important element of how they identified their children. Devon included Native tribal information for both herself (Menominee) and her husband (Choctaw) in describing her children. She spoke of her strong attachment to her Native ancestry being at the foundation of how she and her spouse raised their children, as well as the best tribal affiliation for their children given the different tribal affiliations of their parents:

[My children] are enrolled with my tribe because I have more blood quantum than [my spouse], and it was kind of a conversation we had early on when we thought about having children. We thought about enrollment, and because my tribe is patrilineal, which means that you can only go with the father's clan and the father's name and things like that. But his tribe is matrilineal, where you go with the woman, and so we just decided to go with me because I had more blood quantum. So that way it would hopefully last for longer generations.

Given the potential multiplicity of disparate racial backgrounds between two parents, the race response for some of these children can be quite complex and detailed. Most of the parents in our study, especially those who reported biracially, reported their children's race and ancestry to reflect both parents' background.

## Children of Biracially Identified Parents of Mixed Heritage

In figures 5.1 through 5.3, children of biracially identified mixed-heritage parents are shown in panels B, D, E, H, and K, which have been reprinted together in figure 5.7. Note that no one could identify biracially in the census data until 2000, so all data in figure 5.7 are from 2000 to 2019.

Figure 5.7 stands in contrast to previous figures because of the predominance of children reported as having two races. Looking back at figures 5.1 through 5.3 reveals that, compared to children of parents with two different single-race identities (highlighted in figure 5.4), when a parent reported two races, the child was much more likely to be reported as two races (as found by Bratter for part-Black multiracial parents).[14] Unsurprisingly, a very high proportion of children with two parents who reported the same two races (panel E) were also reported in this way. This is true across all three mixed-heritage groups. At the same time, not all parents who gave a biracial response in the census data reported their child as biracial. We explore group-specific patterns in the next sections. Panel E has many children in RESCI 5 who were reported as "another group." Given that RESCI 5 includes Hawaii, and given the marriage choices of Asian-White people (discussed in chapter 4), children's classification in "another group" in panel E almost certainly reflects Native Hawaiian and/or other Pacific Islander ancestry in one or both parents' background. This may also reflect the social

**Figure 5.7** *Child's Race Response for Children with a Biracially Identified Parent, 2000–2019*

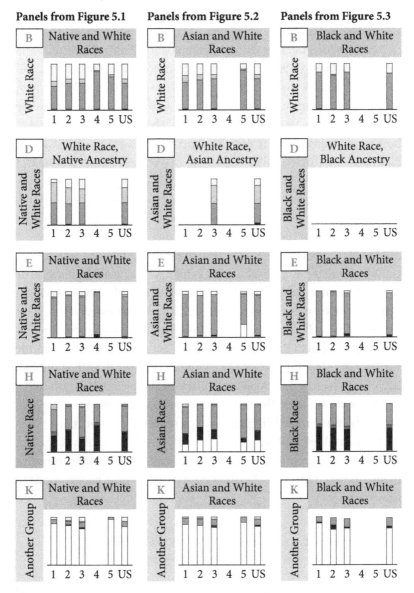

*Source:* Authors' calculations.

*Note:* See figures 5.1 through 5.3 for legends.

construction of Asian and Pacific Islander groups as closely related; in fact, the 1977 federal definition of these groups as the same group ("Asian/Pacific Islander") was in place until the 1997 revision of federal categories split them.

Panel B shows families with one parent who identified biracially and the other as White. Such families more commonly identified their child as biracial than as single-race White; children reported as White with an ancestry response indicating Native, Asian, or Black heritage are noticeably absent. Parents are especially likely to identify their child as biracial in areas with more people of their BIPOC group—RESCI 4 for Native-White children, RESCI 5 for Asian-White children, and RESCI 1 and RESCI 3 for Black-White children. This response pattern may reflect countervailing pressures to identify as White (acknowledging the racial overlap between the parents) and to identify with the BIPOC group prevalent in the area.

One might assume that panel H, which shows families with a biracially identified parent and a non-White parent, would give similar results, but it does not. Native-White families identify their children as Native relatively often, especially in RESCI 4. But it is extremely rare for a child in panel H from an Asian-White family to be reported as anything but biracial in RESCI 5 (Hawaii and San Francisco). There is little variation by place for Black-White families in panel H, with about half of children reported as single-race Black in all race/ethnic contexts.

In our study, all of the sixty-one biracially identified participants across the three mixed-heritage groups reported two (or more) races for their children, capturing both parents' racial backgrounds. In fact, seven biracially identified participants reported three or more races for their children, reflecting the diverse racial and ethnic backgrounds of these couples.

## CHILDREN OF BIRACIALLY IDENTIFIED NATIVE-WHITE PEOPLE

Given that they lived with a parent who identified American Indian/ Alaska Native as one of their two races, it might be assumed that most children with a Native-White biracial parent would be reported as both White and Native race. However, a sizable proportion of children with a White parent and a Native-White biracially identified parent (figure 5.7, panel B) were reported as having *no* Native race or ancestry (though, as mentioned, this was rare in RESCI 4). It should be noted that these children may have had a different socialization experience than children reported as both American Indian/Alaska Native and White race. Our Native-White interview results support this interpretation, but we also find that it is not simple to interpret the racial designations of children, especially those reported as having both White and Native races.

In the census data, we see a similar pattern in families with two mixed-heritage Native-White parents when one reported White race (with Native ancestry) and one reported both Native and White races (panel D): About half of the children were reported as biracial, with some reported as White (some with and some without Native ancestry).

The majority (fifteen of twenty-one) of Native-White participants reported both White and Native races for themselves on the preinterview survey, and most of them reported the same two races for their children, including those who had a White partner. Despite how common it was for Native-White participants to identify their children biracially, there was substantial variation in how these parents raised their children. We found that *the spouse's race, rather than the children's reported race, was a better indicator of how the children were being raised*, especially in terms of cultural exposure.

## CHILDREN OF BIRACIALLY IDENTIFIED NATIVE-WHITE PEOPLE WITH A WHITE SPOUSE

Our mixed-heritage participants' racial identity (and upbringing) and their spouse's race were important indicators of how they thought about raising their children. Seven of our biracially identified Native-White participants had a White spouse. Despite the fact that they all had a White spouse and all identified their children biracially, there was notable variation in how they related to their Native heritage and in how they raised their children.

For instance, Aaron from RESCI 3, whom we met in the last chapter, had a lot of contact with his extended American Indian family in his early years. However, his contact became quite limited later in life, as was evident in how he and his White (then-)wife raised their children, whom he reported as biracial: "We haven't talk[ed] about it [my Native heritage] much, and I have exposed them to almost no Native

American things. It mostly relates back to the fact that my father's side of the family is a gigantic mess. They're physically remote and they are . . . trouble. . . . It's difficult, and I've intentionally limited my contact with them."

By comparison, Gabriella grew up with a lot of exposure to her Native family, and her American Indian heritage was very important to her (see chapter 3). She spoke of the continuing need to counter negative stereotypes about Native peoples. When asked about her daughter's school, Gabriella said: "I made a point of meeting with the principal and teachers and said I didn't want her to hear about Pocahontas or Christopher Columbus or any of that nastiness. If you have any questions, I have a curriculum." As a highly educated person (she had a master's degree), Gabriella had the confidence and vocabulary to confront teachers and other professionals.[15] She also reported that she worked at cultivating a connection to her daughter's Native ancestry: "I take her to ceremonies since she was four months old. He [her White spouse] has no real interest to know the ceremonial Native side. So he's very hands-off; it's important to you, we'll let her choose."

Gabriella and her family lived in a mostly White rural RESCI 2 area with some Native people, so she had to make a concerted effort to drive to Native gatherings and events. Her husband's "hands-off" attitude did not deter Gabriella from raising their daughter with a strong connection to her Native culture: "If she wants to identify as Native, I really insist that she has cultural knowledge—that she knows language and that she goes to ceremony. But if she doesn't want to do that and identify biracially, like my mother does, I would support that too."

Although Gabriella's White spouse did not actively foster their daughter's attachment to her Native roots, Gabriella's determination to do so was clear. Sandy from chapter 3, one of our older participants, was divorced from the White father of her children. Although he had not been interested in her enthusiasm for her Native ancestry (which she learned about as an adult), she tried to convey this pride to her children. She also rebuffed other people's skepticism about her Native ancestry: "There are some that always have remarks about half-breeds, as they call them: 'So you're not really Indian, and you're not really White. What are you?'" Some Native people also did not validate her identification as someone with Native heritage, but Sandy reported that she "felt" American Indian and that she had raised her children to embrace their Native ancestry. In fact, she proudly reported that her son had two children with two different "full" American Indian women.

Thus, for our participants, having a White spouse—even one uninterested in cultivating their non-White heritage—did not automatically mean that the children would be raised as White. Native-White participants with a White spouse who were not actively interested in their Native heritage, however, had to be motivated to ensure that their children experienced that cultural and social exposure. Providing such exposure was quite challenging for participants who did not live in contexts with significant numbers of Native people.

## CHILDREN OF BIRACIALLY IDENTIFIED NATIVE-WHITE PEOPLE WITH A NATIVE OR OTHER BIPOC SPOUSE

Some biracially identified Native-White participants had an American Indian spouse or a spouse of a different racial background. Alex from chapter 3, whose Native father had distanced himself from his Native heritage, wanted to be "more Navajo," had married a Navajo woman, and was raising his children on a large reservation so that their Native ancestry was the bedrock of their upbringing and family life. Alex contrasted his own upbringing with how he and his wife were raising their children. His own childhood, he said, was "pretty typically American, our food, our culture, TV shows, basketball. . . . My parents did not expose us to any ceremonies because, as Christians, they didn't believe in them. But my dad took me to his parents [on the reservation] . . . and we went fishing on the reservation."

Not only did having a Native spouse (and living in RESCI 4, with many Native people around him) enable Alex to raise his children as Native, but having a spouse and children who identified as Native also opened many doors to other networks and relationships that deepened (and legitimated) his ties with American Indian people and community: "We have CDIBs [Certificates of Degree of Indian Blood from the US Bureau of Indian Affairs]. It's one of the reasons I married a Navajo, because I was always drawn to that. . . . For me, it also goes to wanting to be as self-sufficient as possible. How the Navajos used to live—they raised their crops, they had their sheep—I think it's neat. . . . I want to become more self-sufficient in my lifestyle."

There was significant diversity among our Native-White participants, but such diversity was not always apparent. One might think that participants who identified themselves, their spouse, and their children as both Native and White would be likely to have much in common. However, it is difficult to interpret these measures without more information about the participants. For example, both forty-one-year-old Cathy and sixty-four-year-old Brendan identified themselves, their spouses, and their children as both Native and White. While Cathy grew up on a Native reservation in RESCI 4 and still lived and worked on one, Brendan, who lived in RESCI 2, had more tenuous, and more conflicted, ties to his Native heritage. He reported that he did not feel at ease around other Natives. When asked why he didn't feel very comfortable around Natives in the tribal community where he was enrolled, he said:

> Well, one, I didn't grow up with them. That's the most obvious one. . . .
> I have different ways I act, and some things that really matter is, if you
> speak the language, if you follow a lot of the cultural practices that
> I would not have been taught as a child. . . . I did go through a naming
> ceremony and that initial sweat ceremony.

Brendan and his wife—who was also Native-White, but not enrolled— did not feel accepted by his tribal members and found it difficult to bring their (now-grown) son into Native networks and practices. By comparison, Cathy's spouse shared the same tribal affiliation, and her life revolved around her family (including their children's upbringing) and work ties to her reservation.

Like the participants discussed in relation to figure 5.6 (panels J and L), participants who identified as biracial and had a spouse of a different racial background (with no racial overlap) posed some challenges in terms of balancing the ethnic and cultural backgrounds of each parent. Such concerns were amplified in the case of participants with an immigrant spouse whose cultural background was very different from the participant's. Savannah (see chapter 4), who was married to a Black Ghanaian man, reported her children's race as "White, Black, American Indian (Diné)"; this family would be represented in panel K of figure 5.1. Savannah talked about the challenges that she and her husband faced in their effort to ensure that both her ancestry and her husband's were reflected in how they raised their children, given the vast differences in Native and Ghanaian cultures. In spite of these challenges, Savannah found that drawing on both their backgrounds was more doable in the relatively diverse city where they lived. "So right now, for us, none of us are really living in our parents' cultures. We're very far from any family. My husband's parents live in Ghana, my parents live in [a Southwestern state], and we're raising our daughter here [in a Northern city]."

Although she had reported her daughter's race as "White, Black, American Indian (Diné)," Savannah observed that her White heritage was not a priority, and that she felt no personal attachment to it. Describing her daughter as "truly . . . like quadro-ethnic," she explained:

> She has four kinds of tribes, and we try to teach her about all of them. Her name . . . comes from my father-in-law's [African] tribe. Her other name comes from my Navajo side, and then she has a third name we put on her birth certificate from my mother-in-law. And so she only doesn't have a Dutch name. And I think the Dutch probably gets overlooked like, and you're a quarter Dutch, which is like the Whiteness mixed in. . . . I didn't grow up with anything Dutch, even though I was with my mom and her way of being.

In prioritizing their daughter's BIPOC heritages, Savannah and her husband decided that she should attend a school that taught Native languages, though not the language associated with Savannah's tribe: "I participate in some of those traditions myself personally with my family, and my daughter goes to the American Indian Montessori School here in [a diverse Northern city] where they teach Ojibwe and Dakota."

Like many of our mixed-heritage participants, Savannah and her husband had to think carefully about where they lived and their proximity to a school that would teach their children languages other than English. Jonas, age thirty-three, also had a Black African spouse who had not grown up in the United States. He became very interested in his Native heritage in his teens, and his mother tried to support him in that interest, though she had been distanced from Native culture herself. Jonas was married to a Black Muslim woman, and he reported that he and his wife talked a lot about how to foster a sense of attachment to *both* of their racial backgrounds, as well as to Islam, to which he had converted upon their marriage. Living in a large and diverse city in RESCI 3 enabled them to cultivate links with a Muslim social network.

> How can I be a Muslim guy while also practicing my Native American heritage? I was originally raised Catholic because . . . my [Native] grandmother was raised Catholic, but my mom wanted to bring us

back more to a more Native, at least [in terms of] knowledge and understanding. . . . There are [lots] of people . . . like, they don't even know what they don't know [about their Native heritage].

By contrast, participants whose ties to their Native background were more tenuous did not face the same pressure to pass down competing and distinctive ethnic and cultural practices to their children. For example, forty-three-year-old Cassidy, who lived in a RESCI 3 area, identified as biracial Native-White, was married to an Asian Indian man, and reported her children's race as "White, American Indian, Asian Indian." But unlike Savannah, who felt a strong attachment to her Native background, Cassidy did not:

> I don't feel like my identity as a human being is racialized, and I deeply believe that race plays a part in every interaction because we're social creatures, so I would probably say, culturally, I'm White, or I have most identification quote unquote as White. I . . . because I was raised in White culture, because I was not raised on the rez, I was not raised even within a community of predominantly Native folks.

Rather than juggling distinctive cultural and ethnic backgrounds, both Cassidy and her Asian Indian spouse, having been born and raised in the United States, felt that they wanted their children to be able to deal with being "read racially in different ways" and to be comfortable and positive about being mixed heritage.

## Children of Biracially Identified Asian-White People

Reflecting the predominance of two-race responses among people with mixed Asian heritage after 2000, all twenty-seven of our Asian-White interview participants reported biracially, and about two-thirds were married to White people (see panel B of figure 5.2). In the census data, a biracial Asian-White parent married to a single-race White person (panel B) did not always report their children as biracial, though more than half the children across the disparate racial/ethnic spatial contexts (and especially RESCI 5) were reported biracially. As is true for Native-White children, mixed-heritage Asian-White children reported by their parents as White may have had a different socialization experience than those children reported as White and Asian.

All of our Asian-White interview participants reported both races, and whether their spouse was White, Asian, or another group, all reported that their children were of multiple races. Identical racial reporting of children across disparate households can obscure major differences in the practices and upbringing of children.[16] We found that variation in childrearing is related to the spouse's race: The race of the spouse (and thus the spouse choice) makes a big difference in how children are raised, the schooling they receive, and their cultural exposure in relation to their relatives and the wider ethnic community. We conclude from both the census data and the interviews that *the racial background of the other parent* is far more revealing about the racial upbringing of children than their specific racial identification on a form—especially given that multiple-race reporting appears to be a convention among mixed-heritage Asian-White people.

## CHILDREN OF BIRACIALLY IDENTIFIED ASIAN-WHITE PEOPLE WITH A WHITE SPOUSE

Asian-White biracial participants with a White spouse all reported their children as both Asian and White, but some participants did not regard their Asian ancestry as fundamental to their children's upbringing or their family lives. For example, Victor, who was forty-three and lived in a RESCI 3 area, reported that while he and his White wife felt very positive about his Chinese heritage (and interestingly, he said, others always saw him as Chinese), it was not a central part of their children's upbringing or their family life. Victor's connection to his Chinese ancestry was less a "thick" tie than a "symbolic" tie.[17] Another participant, Noelle, whom we met in chapter 4, identified her children biracially but made it clear that her Asian background was not particularly salient in her day-to-day life, and she was adamant about not prioritizing any one parental heritage over the other: "Why should my Chinese background be more important than [her husband's] Italian background?" Noelle refuted the idea that one's visible minority ancestry was automatically more important to her children than her husband's less visible European ancestry (though she was not particularly interested in her husband's Italian ancestry either).

Yet some biracially identified participants with a White spouse were highly committed to their Asian race and culture. Alison identified as

White and Japanese, and her White husband prioritized her Japanese heritage in their daughter's upbringing (see chapters 3 and 4). They had a Japanese au pair who lived with them so that their daughter could be raised bilingually. As mentioned in the previous chapter, Alison reported that, even before her daughter's birth, her husband had started learning Japanese so that he could better communicate with her Japanese mother, whose English was very limited. In this her husband was adopting a form of affiliative ethnicity.[18]

Ray, who identified as "Hapa" (see chapter 3), grew up partly in Japan. When he returned to the United States, he was shocked by the racial prejudice he encountered: "I was called a Chink, and I felt very foreign. I'm not Chinese so . . . they didn't know what ethnicity I was. I went from being seen as different but in a positive way [in Tokyo], but then in [a town in the Northeast] I was different but in a negative way." One reason why Ray was drawn to his White wife, he said, was that she loved the fact that he was Hapa and "different": "I'm so proud of my Japanese heritage because it's such a big part of me, so I definitely want to pass it down. I want to take him [his son] back to Japan." Ray's wife, he reported, "would love for him to speak Japanese." Ray and his wife decided to settle in a metropolitan area on the West Coast because it had many Asian and mixed people. While his wife worked full-time, Ray took care of their infant son, spoke to him in Japanese, and adapted his work to his son's care. Although his wife had little knowledge of Japanese culture, she was completely committed to cultivating a strong attachment to it.

As reported in chapter 3, Makana identified as "White, Japanese, Chinese," and she racially identified her young son in the same way. She spoke about her racial consciousness and the importance of her son attending a racially diverse school. Makana and her family lived in an affluent and relatively diverse college town in the Midwest (RESCI 2): "My son's elementary school, which was very important to me, is predominantly minority [with a large Black student population]. It has actually one of the largest populations of self-identifying multiracial kids of any elementary schools that I have seen in this area." However, Makana reported, her White husband had not always been that racially aware:

> And interestingly, going to sort of a coparenting aspect, it [their son's attendance at a racially diverse school] wasn't a high priority for my husband, and I remember him saying at one point, 'Kids don't even notice race at that age'! . . . You know, remembering back to my own

childhood that kids would call me and my brother names on the playground without even understanding what they meant. So, I think he [my husband] is Caucasian, he grew up in a very predominantly White community in Northern California. His group of friends is predominantly White, and it just . . . it's not a frame that he automatically sees the world in.

Although Makana believed that her husband was a socially and politically progressive person, she felt that she was the one who was motivated to ensure that their son interacted with Black children, as well as with Asian and White children. In comparison with her White husband, Makana saw herself and her son as mixed people who felt some affinity with other people of color in the United States.

And you know, I think I was thinking about, why is it important for me and for my child to have some connection to this heritage and it's not . . . it's not so critical for me necessarily for him to think of himself as Asian American in some way. But simply to understand that he, you know, *that he's not monolithically White* [emphasis added] and there's something important in this country about that and about the history of coming here and about being part of this kind of whole melting pot of whatever. . . . My hope is that it gives him a personal reason to be more respectful of people of other races.

Participants with a White spouse could find it challenging to cultivate an Asian identity or upbringing for their children, especially if they did not live in a diverse area with other Asian people, such as RESCI 3 or 5; however, as we have shown, biracially identified Asian-White participants could be committed to fostering an appreciation not only of Asian-ness but of other BIPOC people and of diversity more generally. Some White spouses were also enthusiastically involved in fostering these attachments in their children. Living in an ethnically diverse RESCI with diverse schools and neighborhoods facilitated the appreciation of minority cultures and a BIPOC sensibility.

## CHILDREN OF BIRACIALLY IDENTIFIED ASIAN-WHITE PEOPLE WITH AN ASIAN OR BIPOC SPOUSE

Most biracially identified Asian-White people whose spouse is single-race Asian (panel H in figure 5.2) reported their children as both White and Asian, with variation depending on the racial/ethnic spatial context. Our interview sample is consistent with this pattern: All of the biracially identified Asian-White people with a single-race Asian spouse identified their children as both White and Asian. An example from chapter 4 is Vincent, who identified as White and Filipino, had two young children with his Japanese wife, and identified their children as White and Asian. Vincent reported that they were teaching their children to speak Japanese, and that their family life was very oriented to Asian (both Japanese and Filipino) food, Asian language, and the wider Asian social network. They lived in a heavily Latino metropolitan area that also had pockets of Asian communities.

Nani, who identified as Asian (Filipino) and White, as we learned in chapter 3, was married to a Chinese man. She described her children's race as "White, Chinese, Filipino," and like Vincent, she and her husband, who had disparate Asian ancestries, heavily stressed the family's shared Asian-ness. Although she reported that people did not usually see her as Asian, Nani *felt* strongly Asian, having lived much of her life, as she still did, in the Northwest, where there were many different Asian people. Nani wanted to pass down her Chinese husband's ancestry and language, but she also wanted her children to be part of a wider Asian community and culture. In order for their daughters to attend a Chinese immersion school, Nani and her husband had sold their house and moved across town to be in the right catchment area: "I wanted them to learn their Chinese heritage and language, and I didn't want that to be lost. . . . It was a big sacrifice for us; we loved our old neighborhood."

Like Nani, Jonathan from chapter 3, who identified as White and Korean, sent his children to a Korean immersion school, as both he and his spouse had Korean heritage. Interestingly, neither Jonathan nor his wife possessed more than a rudimentary grasp of the Korean language, and they knew relatively little about Korean history and culture. After his parents' divorce, Jonathan had had regular, but infrequent, contact with his Korean father. Now he and his Korean American wife wanted their children to have this cultural exposure, especially since they were now living in an urban area with a large Asian population. "I've often said that I can't teach my children Korean because our Korean is not good enough, so [we] might as well send them to school to teach them Korean. . . . I think my son identifies more . . . well, he would be three-quarters Korean from a blood perspective, and I think he sees himself as a Korean American already."

A shared Asian race between spouses was therefore an important foundation for how such couples raised their children. In addition to their efforts to teach their children specific Asian languages and practices (for example, Filipino, Japanese, or Korean), participants with an Asian spouse whose ethnicity was different from their own also stressed a pan-Asian upbringing and family culture.[19] Couples with a similar racial appearance that they also shared with their children were socially treated quite consistently as an Asian family. This "family race" contrasted with the social treatment and conspicuousness of a visibly racially mixed family.[20]

While a number of our Asian-White participants had a spouse with Asian heritage, one was married to someone with a different non-White background. Jacqui reported her children's race as "White and Korean," the same as her own race response (chapter 3). But she also described her children's ancestry as "Korean, Colombian, Puerto Rican" to reflect her spouse's Latino background. In fact, Jacqui revealed, she and her spouse were trying to emphasize both Korean and Latino identities, languages, and practices. The only race and ancestry that they did *not* emphasize was the White European part of Jacqui's heritage (which she reported as "Korean, Scottish-Irish, German, Welsh, Finnish"). As discussed in chapter 3, Jacqui did not feel as close to her father's White family, as she felt no affinity with Whiteness.

Strongly identifying as Korean American, as Asian American, *and* as a person of color, Jacqui wanted her children to also see themselves in these ways. She reported that she and her Latino husband discussed their children's upbringing regularly, and that she was very attentive to issues around racial justice and racial stereotyping:

> We've also had problems with like babysitters who'll say ridiculous things to my kids, and then [the kids] say them to me, and I'm like, "Where did you learn that? Because I know that you didn't learn that from me or your dad." . . . We have wanted to make sure that they have the vocabulary, but also not go around practicing and developing habits to say things in like an ignorant way . . . like the "Chinese eyes" comment.

Jacqui, who said that other people saw her as part-Asian and racially ambiguous, reported that people always asked her where she was from, and that she resisted that question by telling them that she was from [a large US city]. She noted that she and her husband agreed on most aspects of childrearing, but not always: "He's like, 'Just tell them what they want to know, it's not . . . not everything has to be a teachable moment,' and I'm like, 'No, they need to know what's the question that they really need to ask.' So . . . we don't agree on everything."

Among some of the Asian-White biracial participants—especially among those with an Asian *Indian* background (and particularly across RESCIs 3 and 5)—one notable theme was cosmopolitanism and the importance of a highly varied ethnic and cultural milieu. This emphasis on cosmopolitanism was especially prominent among the most privileged and elite participants, who had lucrative jobs that required living abroad and sometimes frequent travel to distant places. As we described her in chapter 4, Petra reported her race and her children's race as White and Asian Indian and worked in the tech industry on the West Coast. She had grown up with her Asian Indian father and German mother in predominantly White towns in the Midwest, and by comparison, she now "loved" her life with her Asian Indian husband and children in a highly diverse metropolitan setting. When asked about her children's upbringing, Petra emphasized the importance of speaking as many languages as possible:

> I speak only German [Petra's mother was German] to them, [their father] speaks only Hindi to them, the au pair speaks only Portuguese to them, and English is everywhere else. They don't even think about it [their ethnicity]. That's the wonderful thing about [the area where they lived]. They've never even been asked where they're from or anything. I've asked them. And they both look brown. . . . They look Indian. It's so amazing. That's what I love about being here. As an example, when he [her son] first went to preschool . . . after a few months, he's like, "My friend Joshua, my friend Joshua, I love this guy. My best friend." And I finally met him after a few months, and he's Chinese.

Hilary reported White and Asian Indian races for herself (see chapter 4) and reported her children's multiple races as "White, Black, Asian Indian, Chinese, Vietnamese" to reflect both her races and her spouse's races. Hilary and her mixed-heritage spouse were both highly paid professionals who lived in an Asian-dominated Western city. They lived a very privileged life that included a great deal of international travel and the enjoyment of ethnic diversity. Hilary knew that prioritizing any one ancestry, such as the Asian Indian heritage of her (recently deceased) mother, would be challenging. She and her spouse wanted their children to appreciate all of their parents' ethnic and racial backgrounds, which "were important to me, but not important for them," she noted, adding, "that is one of the downsides of living in America. With every generation something gets lost." According to Hilary, her children were unfazed by the great diversity of ethnicities around them; it was simply "how it is" in their RESCI 3 area, where being mixed or non-White was unremarkable.

Although Hilary felt sad about the loss of her mother's Asian Indian cultural connection, she reported that she now put more emphasis on a cosmopolitanism that included not just her own background but also her husband's very ethnically and racially diverse family background. She hoped that their respective ancestries, including her Asian Indian ancestry, could be effectively translated into a cultural concoction that would be central to their family life. As such, her children were also learning French and Spanish, and they traveled a great deal as a family to many different parts of the globe, so that her children felt like "global citizens." Making a well-traveled cosmopolitanism a priority, however, is dependent on the very high income of those who usually have an upper-middle-class family background. While many of our participants were in professional occupations, most were not as affluent as Petra and Hilary.

It is interesting that more couples do not label their children as solely Asian when there is racial and/or ethnic overlap between the Asian-White parent and the solely Asian parent (as Bratter found in relation to Black-White people and couples).[21] One reason may be that Asian-White people have not been subject to anything like the one-drop rule of hypodescent by which Black-White people are regarded as Black. In a pattern reminiscent of the hyperdescent framework imposed on Native-White people, Asian-White people are sometimes marginalized and/or socially excluded by monoracial Asian people as not "really" Asian (as discussed in chapters 1 and 3). The historical emphasis in various East Asian societies on national "purity" and ethnic homogeneity runs deep and is also manifested in aspects of Asian American society.[22] According to our interviews, the tendency of parents who experience an Asian overlap between them to report their children biracially stems from a widely held belief that "multiple race" is the best way to describe their children.

But parents' decisions about how to identify their children may not align with how children see themselves.[23] Sixty-four-year-old Albert, who lived in RESCI 3 and identified as Asian-White with a biracial parent, identified his son as White and Chinese. Albert felt a very strong attachment to being Chinese; having married a Chinese woman who immigrated to the United States, he had spent much of his personal and professional life cultivating this ethnicity. Albert was rueful about his son's virtual lack of interest in his Chinese ancestry, even though gene-alogically his son, who was now in his late thirties, was "seven-eighths Chinese":

> When he was little, we spoke to him in Mandarin. We were afraid when he went to nursery school that he didn't know English, but he did. He was willing to speak with us in Mandarin. We tried to send him to Chinese school. He hated it, like all the other kids. . . . We were trying to create an environment, a bilingual environment, a bicultural environment.

Despite his hopes that his son would develop an attachment to his Chinese ancestry, Albert reported, his son was "very American." It was also interesting to Albert that his son was genealogically "more" Chinese than he himself was, yet so resolutely "American." In a similar vein, as discussed in chapter 4, Noelle had resisted her parents' expectation that she would identify more with her Chinese ancestry.

These participants' experiences support our conclusion that mixed-heritage parents' racial designations of their children are not easy to interpret without more detail and context. Parents' racial designations of their children are largely aspirational, and they reflect how parents wish to see their children. Such identifications may not correspond, however, with how their children see themselves racially.

## Children of Biracially Identified Black-White People

Bratter found that about one-third of biracial Black-White people married to a Black person identified their children as both White and Black in the 2000 census, but that a single race response was more common.[24] In our census analysis, we note that these children were often identified as monoracially Black (panel H in figure 5.3), though bira-cial responses were just as common. In suggesting that this tendency to report children biracially, even with Black racial overlap, seems to have grown since 2000, analyses by year (not shown) point to a diminishing imposition of the one-drop rule.[25] All but one of our twenty Black-White participants identified biracially, and most of them identified their chil-dren biracially as well. However, three participants with a Black partner and one with a Black-White partner reported their children as solely Black—reflecting the importance of their Black racial overlap.

## CHILDREN OF BIRACIALLY IDENTIFIED BLACK-WHITE PEOPLE WITH A WHITE SPOUSE

The census data reflect a tendency to report a Black-White child as bira-cial if one of their parents is White (panel B in figure 5.3). This pattern is borne out in our interview data. All nine biracial Black-White partici-pants with a White spouse identified their children as both White and Black. However, participants with a White spouse varied considerably in their family lives and in how they were bringing up their children. In contrast, biracially identified Black-White participants with a Black or Black-White spouse showed little variation in their concerns and practices around their children's upbringing.

One Black-White participant from chapter 3, Saskia, who had a White spouse, reported that her main concern about her son was that he not be racially stereotyped in ways that would limit his individuality and aspirations: "I am honestly more concerned about society trying to label him and put him in a racial category that discourages him from taking up interests or trying new things because he doesn't look the part. I also don't want him to feel like he has to love African drumming if he prefers country music and baseball." Saskia reported that she and her White husband did not emphasize racial consciousness; indeed, they did not talk about it very much, putting more emphasis on their Christianity in their son's upbringing. As discussed in chapter 3, Saskia did not see race as central to how she saw herself, and she and her spouse did not want their son's Black heritage to define him.

By comparison, Carl, age forty-five, and his White wife made a point of regularly discussing race and other bases of identity with their children. They lived in a relatively diverse university town in RESCI 2 where it was not unusual to discuss and debate issues around race and sexuality. "There is nothing off the table. We talk about sex, race, gender, with the children, politics, religion. She [my wife] doesn't want them to feel any sexual identity pressure. . . . We have a ton of conversations about skin color: C is brown, L is brown, Daddy is brown, Mamma, you white!"

Interestingly, while Carl encouraged his family to openly discuss race, he himself did not feel that his Blackness was very central to who he was (though he did report both Black and White races in the pre-interview survey). Carl was raised by his White mother and White step-father and had not connected with his Black father until he was a young adult. He reported that his White spouse was keenly motivated to talk about race, including their different racial appearances.

Some Black-White participants explicitly reflected on having parents who had not helped them to confront racial reality as they grew up. Evan from chapter 4, in thinking about his son being seen as a racially mixed man when he grew up, talked about how inadequately his own White mother had prepared him to deal with the negative racial experiences he had as a racially ambiguous-looking man:

And one of those things was the way she approached race with me. It was garbage, it was bullshit, it really did me a disservice, because you shouldn't be twenty and starting to go, "Fuck, am I a Black guy?," I think so. That shouldn't be a twenty-year-old thought. I know kids who are seven who are way more militant than that, you know.

Evan reported that he and his White wife were thinking about how to prepare their young son, who was said to be phenotypically ambiguous, for the possibility of being negatively racialized. Yet not all Black-White parents had had that "conversation" or were worried about their children facing racism, especially if the other parent was White. Mallory, who was Black-White, was racially conscious, but she lived in a large and ethnically diverse city in the Northeast (RESCI 4) where she and her White husband felt very unremarkable as a mixed family:

Yeah, so I realized this summer that my [twelve-year-old] son was getting to the age where I was going to have to have the talk with him about how to deal with the police . . . and I realized, "Wait a minute, actually he . . . he's much lighter than I am," so he might actually experience the world as a White man. And so I realized that I hadn't had a conversation with him in a really long time about how he identifies, how he self-identifies, so I realized that I did need to have that conversation with him. But I keep forgetting.

That Mallory kept "forgetting" to have "that conversation" with her son suggests that it was not a pressing worry for her; she also wondered if her son, with his very light skin color, was even seen as Black. As found in other studies, parents had to judge the importance of preparing their children for the possibility of racial prejudice and discrimination even as they wanted their children to not have to worry about such possibilities.[26]

## CHILDREN OF BIRACIALLY IDENTIFIED BLACK-WHITE PEOPLE WITH A BLACK OR BLACK-WHITE SPOUSE

Of the eight biracially identified Black-White interviewees with a Black spouse (and two interviewees with a mixed-heritage Black-White spouse), four identified their children as solely Black, while the remaining six reported both White and Black races for their children—as anticipated by Bratter. However, all these couples were notably similar in their childrearing. The shared Black overlap between the mixed-heritage participant and their spouse was key in explaining their approach to childrearing and the role of race.

An emphasis on *racial consciousness* and pride in a BIPOC ancestry was most pronounced among Black-White participants.[27] It was even more pronounced if they had a Black (or mixed-heritage Black) spouse. Many of the Black-White interview participants explicitly expressed concerns about racism and the need to build racial pride. For example, twenty-eight-year-old Andreas, who grew up with his White mother and her extended family and now lived in a RESCI 3 area, recalled "being the butt of racist jokes" in school. He and his Black wife made a conscious effort to talk to their daughters (identified biracially) about racism: "Kids don't listen to their parents half the time anyways, so . . . we can say whatever we want to say about internalized racism but how . . . whether they're going to even believe us. So . . . yeah, I'm not worried about racial stigma for myself, or dealing with it, but I'm worried about how it will impact my daughters."

Concerns about children's racial treatment were manifest in a variety of ways. For instance, Helen identified biracially and had a Black spouse (see chapter 3). She talked about having thought carefully about the names she had chosen for her three children. She purposefully chose what she called "traditional" names, where their Blackness could not be inferred. When asked if she was concerned about her children experiencing racism in their RESCI 2 area, Helen said: "Yes, that's one of the reasons why their names are . . . traditional formal-sounding names. I've done plenty of interviewing, and you can only go on someone's name. And if I see 'Laquisha,' 'Dashawn,' 'Jamal,' I already know: You're Black."

Ariel, age thirty and living in a RESCI 3 area, identified as a racially mixed Black-White person. She spoke of sharing Blackness with her Black husband and of their awareness of the need to build pride in their three young children:

> As a family, we're a Black family. If we were a White family we wouldn't have to build this confidence and pride in who we are. But as a Black family, you do. But as a Black family, we have to intentionally buy books about little Black girls' hair and "I'm a happy little Black girl." If we were White, we wouldn't have to do those things.

Vanessa, introduced in chapter 4, had researched her Black father's genealogy and knew about the slave master of her father's ancestors. Although she had grown up with a White Scandinavian mother (who had recently died), Vanessa and her Black husband prioritized the need to develop a positive sense of Black culture and history with their young son: "I think that we're very, [my husband] and I, we expose him to a lot of Black culture and positive Black culture and Black pride, and we talk a lot about what White people have done to Blacks throughout history." Although she valued her Scandinavian heritage, Vanessa did not emphasize it with her son. Many Black-White participants engaged with the idea of a distinctive history of Blackness by fostering racial consciousness in their children. The presence of many Black people in the city where Vanessa and her family lived allowed her and her husband to cultivate a sense of belonging and pride in their city.

Kendra, also introduced in chapter 4, reported Black and White races for herself, had a Black spouse, and identified her son as solely

Black. She was adamant that it was best for her son to be raised to see himself as Black:

> I don't see a real reason to try to encourage a mixed identity in him. I think that would be detrimental to his well-being. Because I think it was detrimental to my well-being [to identify as biracial growing up]. And to have no one else really validate that. Obviously my family and close friends did, but . . . so, it would be better for him to identify the way that people are going to identify him. And to feel good about that. So I would never tell him that he's mixed or biracial. If he grew up and wanted to identify that way, seeing how diverse our family is, I wouldn't have a problem with that. But I would not want to encourage that sort of identity in him.

As part of a family that included her Black spouse, presenting a unified message about being a Black family—rather than pointing to differences in their racial makeup that would not be validated by others anyway—was important to Kendra.

Parents' racial consciousness could also extend to their views on whom their children dated and eventually chose as a partner. When asked if she would mind her son dating someone White, Kendra replied that she would not. However, she said,

> I don't want [my son] to be one of those men who idolizes White women. If he ends up with a White woman, fine, but . . . like that happens to a lot of Black men. "Oh, I have a White woman on my arm," and it's a status thing. And I do not want him to be like that. But if he ends up marrying a White woman, I wouldn't be like, "OMG it's a problem!" Like, if I noticed that he was only dating White women, I would probably have a conversation with him, like, "This is interesting!"

Our participants' experiences showed that having a Black spouse, more than identifying their child as Black-White versus Black, was a reliable indicator of an especially strong emphasis on Black racial consciousness and the value placed on a shared Blackness as the family's race. Black-White participants who lived in an area without many other Black people expressed their concerns about the difficulty of fostering a positive Black identity in their children in a place where they were unable to be around other Black people. For instance, Corey from chapter 3, who lived in a mostly White suburb, reported herself and her son as both Black and White. Corey and her husband, who was also Black-White, wanted to ensure that their son had more exposure to Black people, as their jobs had taken them to a part of the country with very few Black people. Encouraging their son to identify as a Black person was a concern because their son, to their surprise, was very light-skinned and blond.

> I want to live in as Black a neighborhood as we can find. But the one historical Black neighborhood is just not convenient for my job. So, I've told [her husband], "We've got to find a diverse school with some Black kids," in the hope that he'll have some Black friends. . . . Like, if we become [their son's] only connection to Black culture, I think [her husband] would be really unhappy.

Wendy (chapter 3) was married to an African American man, and she identified her son as solely Black. Although she had grown up with only her White mother's family, her family life now revolved around a shared Blackness. Emphasizing their Blackness required some parental effort because they lived in a heavily Latino town. Nevertheless, there were Black people and communities around them. Wendy reported that her son loved her mother (his White grandmother) and knew he had White heritage, but that she was raising him as Black:

> I feel like I'm raising him to be race-conscious. Sometimes I worry I'm overdoing it. We live in a rural area. . . . The schools are more Latino, so it's not White but more Latino. But I want to instill a positive under-standing of being Black. All of our art is Black art in our house. We have a Black Santa Claus. We are really deliberate (*laughs*). And he has two Black, educated parents and exposure to what that means. He does ask about his race. . . . I've taken him to African student night on campus . . . Black history month.

## Conclusion

We find that the way a mixed-heritage person identifies and raises their children is strongly related to how they racially identify themselves and the person they choose to marry. By looking at parent's race, spouse's race, and children's race together, our work shows how they interact with one another and provides a more complete understanding of how and why parents identify and raise their children in the ways they do.

We conclude from both the census data and the interviews that *the racial background and racial identification of the other parent* is far more revealing about the racial upbringing of children than the child's specific racial identification on a Census Bureau or preinterview survey form. In families with racial overlap between the spouses, we see evidence that some couples are leaning into a shared identity, a "family race," that guides their parenting choices and family life. Depending on the racial overlap between the parents, the family race espoused by the parents could vary; while a shared family race (for instance emphasizing a shared Black, Native, or Asian heritage) could be emphasized, a different narrative about family race, such as one based on racial and cultural multiplicity, could operate in these families.

Our analysis extends existing studies of how (usually monoracial) people in interracially married couples identify their multiracial children in the United States by exploring the experiences of mixed-heritage people as parents.[28] Because at least one of these partners has mixed heritage, their unions defy the simple binaries of "in-marriage" and "out-marriage." Most of the few studies of children's upbringing in mixed-heritage families do not examine the relationship between how children are racially identified and how their parents raise them.[29]

In this chapter, we first focused on cases with a *monoracially* identified parent of mixed racial heritage married to someone of the *same* single race. In these cases, the Census Bureau data show that *virtually all children are reported as the same race as their parents*. In our study, three couples fit this pattern, and all identified their children as well as themselves as the same single race. Our interviews show that some mixed-heritage people who reported the same race for themselves, their spouse, and their children were asserting a unified family race.

Next, we focused on cases with a *monoracially* identified parent of mixed racial heritage who had married someone of a *different* single race. Census Bureau data show *remarkable variety* in the types of race responses given for children from these marriages. Patterns vary across the race groups and across racial/ethnic spatial context, seeming to reflect no clear norms. Illustrating this variability in our study were three Native-White men who all identified as racially Native and had a White spouse. Two of these mixed-heritage Native-White men reported their children's race as White, while the third identified his child as Native. Counterintuitively, the participant who identified his son as solely Native reported that his White wife was uninterested in his Native background and they did not emphasize his Native ancestry in raising their son. By comparison, one of the other Native-White participants who identified his children as White reported that his White wife was interested in and supportive of their children's exposure to Native culture and practices. Thus, while White spouses could vary in their commitment to their mixed-heritage spouse's minority ancestry, their children's racial identification, even as White, was not necessarily a reliable reflection of how they were being raised.

Finally, the bulk of our discussion in this chapter focused on children's racial identification patterns when they had a *biracially* identified parent. We found in the Census Bureau data that if at least one parent is biracially identified, *the child is almost always biracially identified* (as Bratter found among Black-White parents).[30] Multiple-race reporting appears to be a convention among mixed-heritage Asian-White people, and increasingly among mixed-heritage Black-White people, but this convention hides significant variety.

Biracially identified participants with a White spouse showed more variation in how they were raising their children. Some biracially identified participants reported that their White spouse did not show much interest in cultivating minority cultural practices or identity in their children. Yet others were committed to and invested in learning their partner's language or participating in a Native ceremony. White spouses followed the lead of their mixed-heritage spouses—if minority heritage was important to their spouse, we found that the White spouse was often galvanized to raise their children with a minority emphasis.

A common concern for many mixed-heritage parents we interviewed was the importance of fostering racial pride and combating negative depictions of Blackness and of other people of color from minoritized groups that had been historically disadvantaged and denigrated. This concern led some to foster a sense of solidarity and affinity with other people of color. In comparison with Native-White and Asian-White parents, Black-White parents, especially those with a Black or part-Black spouse, stressed racial consciousness and racial pride in being Black. Furthermore, Black-White participants, both men and women, were especially attuned to the gendered treatment of Black boys and men and their vulnerability to negative racial treatment. Many Black-White parents articulated the importance of preparing their children

for the likelihood that they would encounter forms of racial prejudice and discrimination. Concerns about racial denigration or marginalization were not absent among Asian-White parents, though this
topic was less commonly raised than among Black-White and Native-
White participants. (Moreover, the interviews were conducted before
the anti-Asian sentiments engendered by the COVID-19 pandemic.)
For Native-White participants, a shared Native ancestry with different tribal affiliations could constitute an important part of a panethnic
family identity, and the same was true for Asian-White participants of
disparate Asian ethnicities.

We also found that a mixed-heritage parent could find it meaningful
to report *only a single race* for their child (though such an identification
was uncommon and did not reliably predict upbringing). In identifying their children as solely Black, four of our Black-White participants
with a Black spouse were not only emphasizing their shared Blackness
as a family but also arguing that it could be "detrimental" to their child
to be told that they were mixed, since they were likely to be treated
as Black in the wider society. The few Native-White participants who
identified their children as White argued that these children had little
knowledge of or attachment to their Native heritage; these children
were also perceived as being White.

Our findings about how mixed-heritage parents think about and
raise their children complicate arguments made by prominent scholars.
Richard Alba and his colleagues, for instance, suggest that while part-
Black people lean toward their Black heritage, Asian-White and Latino-
White people "tilt White." According to these scholars:

> The children of mixed minority-majority unions offer convincing
> evidence of mainstream expansion. They are generally being raised
> in families with incomes and residential locations that resemble
> those of white-only families. . . . For adults who are part white and
> part American Indian, Asian, or Latino, these identities "tilt white,"
> reflecting a sense of affinity with whites. They do not generally per-
> ceive racial barriers to their participation in mainstream settings.
> They tend to have white friends, [to] live in neighborhoods with
> many white neighbors and to marry whites.[31]

Such characterizations of part-Asian and part-Native people are
bound to hold for some mixed-heritage people with Asian or Native

ancestry, but given the heterogeneity of mixed-heritage populations and experiences, our qualitative investigation across disparate mixed-heritage groups brings needed nuance to these generalizations. Our interviews show a great deal of variation among all three mixed-heritage groups. Just as being Black was not always highly salient to our Black-White participants, Asian-White participants with a White partner did not necessarily "tilt White." Similarly, there was considerable variation in how Native-White interview participants related to their Native background and the upbringing of their children. Our results show that Asian-White and Native-White participants who identified their children biracially varied considerably in their attachment to their BIPOC ancestry, in how they raised their children, and in their aspirations for how their children would identify. Future studies of mixed-heritage people and their families must not lose sight of these variations within and across disparate mixed-heritage populations living in different racial/ethnic spatial contexts.

# CHAPTER SIX

# CONCLUSIONS

In this research, we have investigated the links between mixed-heritage people's racial identities, their spouse choices, and the ways they racially identify and raise their children. Prior research on these topics has treated these aspects of life separately, while devoting the vast bulk of research to a focus on the racial identities of mixed-heritage people. Very few studies have investigated the spousal choices of mixed-heritage people or their experiences as parents. A primary finding of this study is that these elements are all closely intertwined.

Our study is also novel in that we compare three mixed-heritage groups that are not usually examined in relation to one another. In particular, Native-White mixed-heritage people are rarely included in studies, while comparisons of Asian-White and Black-White people are somewhat more common. Using both interviews and Census Bureau data, we find substantial parallels between the three groups, as well as important distinctions.

Combining our analysis of census data with in-depth interviews is another important dimension of our research. Qualitative data used in combination with quantitative data are often described as "complementing" the quantitative data. One strength of our research, however, is that the qualitative data do not necessarily complement the census data.[1] For example, one respondent with American Indian heritage might have identified as monoracially White in the census, but our interviews tell us that this identification did not necessarily indicate that their Native racial identity was less important, but rather that the respondent recognized unspoken "rules" about authenticity and

https://doi.org/10.7758/edyf5459.8850

identity for Native-White people. A Black-White individual's decision to identify monoracially as Black may have been less about personal racial identity and more about making a political statement; such a decision can be made by Native-White people as well. Asian-White people who identified with multiple races in the census may have had a strong interest in maintaining their Asian heritage (and much less interest in their White heritage) but felt excluded from monoracial Asian communities because of their White racial background. In this research, the interview data prompt the reader to question the meaning of racial identification on census forms and to look at the variety of possible meanings across different mixed-heritage groups.

Because of the powerful impact of racial context on racial identity, spouse choice, and childrearing, we attend to participants' lived experiences across locations throughout the study. To include racial context in Census Bureau data, we developed a parsimonious measure—the Racial/Ethnic Spatial Context Indicator, or RESCI—that divides the United States into five types of geographic space. Different contexts are characterized by disparate demographics, settlement histories, and cultures. The combination of a place's attributes and history contributes to social messages about which identities are "valid" for which individuals and constrains opportunities for meeting potential spouses. Our quantitative and interview results show that our Racial/Ethnic Spatial Context Indicator captures aspects of the impact of place on identity and spouse choice, with subsequent impacts on children's identification.

Our interviews provide numerous examples of how a mixed-heritage person's experience varies according to their racial context. People who moved from one type of context to another were seen and treated differently by their local society, with impacts on their opportunities to make friends or date certain people. Mixed-heritage people in our study also reported that the racial and ethnic composition of their neighborhoods and their children's schools was of great importance to them; most often they favored racially diverse and cosmopolitan settings, but such settings were not always available.

## Identity and Self-Identification of People with Mixed Racial Heritage

As borne out in both the census data and much of the interview data, we find that substantial proportions of mixed-heritage people identify with more than one race, especially Asian-White and Black-White people. The interview data reveal that there are notable differences across disparate mixed-heritage populations in the meaning of reporting multiple races. For example, Asian-White people reported a strong sense of being racially hybrid—neither White nor Asian (as sometimes evinced in the use of the term "Hapa"). And while many Black-White people who reported both races still felt primarily Black, others were clear that they did not feel monoracially Black and instead felt mixed; a few even felt more attuned to their White heritage.[2] Our study points to the continued weakening of the one-drop rule for part-Black people.

Native-White people less often reported multiple races, as shown in both the census data and our interview data. Native-White mixed-heritage participants who identified as single-race Native discussed the importance of being seen and counted, given societal forces imposing invisibility on Native populations and challenging tribal sovereignty. At the same time, our Native-White participants were highly aware that their identification as Native could be challenged by others.

Although there is evidence of a Black/non-Black divide along some indicators (especially concerns about racism), we find convergence as well as diversity within mixed-heritage groups. Notably, the census analysis showed that both Asian-White and Black-White mixed-heritage people were more likely to identify biracially than as a single race. We also find that intragroup diversity is common among all three mixed-heritage groups. Participants within each of the three mixed-heritage groups varied markedly in their exposure to White and minority relatives, their exposure to distinctive cultural practices and languages, and their comfort level with White and minority people and settings.

As other researchers have observed, we find that many White Americans exploring their genealogies seem to regard their European ancestry as bland and uninteresting.[3] Reflecting this finding, our mixed-heritage participants were primarily interested in their Native, Asian, and Black ancestries and races, not their White European backgrounds; regarded as a residual category, their White heritage did not engender much interest. We find that some mixed-heritage people (with White ancestry) made significant efforts to cultivate minority practices—for example, enrolling their children in Dakota, Mandarin, or Korean language immersion schools. Native-White and Asian-White participants were especially attuned to discourses about ethnic and cultural retention, authenticity, and knowledge associated with their ancestry. Many Native-White participants articulated a sense of urgency about the demise of Native American languages and cultural practices. Nevertheless, some mixed-heritage people were removed from their minority ancestry, often because of limited cultural exposure to that ancestry or experiences of social rejection by monoracial minority people. Forms of social rejection were reported across all three groups, such as Black-White women being rejected by Black women. A number of our participants spoke of their interest in a hybrid, cosmopolitan family life that emphasized a sense of connection and solidarity with other non-White people and people of mixed heritage.

## Relationship Between Identity and Spouse Choice for People with Mixed Racial Heritage

Our analysis of patterns in Census Bureau data shows that the racial identification choice of a person of mixed racial heritage has a clear and powerful relationship with the race of their spouse. In all three of the groups we studied, almost the only people whose spouse reported two races were also reporting two races for themselves (and for their children). A number of participants, from all three groups, were married to BIPOC people not by accident—they had actively sought out a BIPOC partner. A participant's opportunity to find a partner of color, especially someone with a non-White racial overlap, was largely dependent on the RESCI where they lived. For example, someone moving from one location to another could come into contact with many more Native people (RESCI 4) or Asian Americans (RESCI 5).

The census data show that a married mixed-heritage person who identified as racially White (with BIPOC ancestry) almost always had a White spouse, regardless of the BIPOC group in their ancestry. However, our interviews revealed that, across all three mixed-heritage groups, the White spouses of our participants showed notable variability in how invested they were in their mixed-heritage spouse's non-White race and related cultural practices and social networks.

## Mixed-Heritage Children's Identification

Our census results highlight that, in many family configurations, the child's (reported) racial identification was essentially determined on the parents' wedding day. Parents in some racial pairings almost always reported their children in a particular way. For example, parents who reported themselves with multiple races were the primary group reporting their child as multiple races. Similarly, two parents who racially identified as the same single race almost always reported the same race for their child.

The fact that a parent's mixed racial heritage is not always reflected in how their child's race/ancestry is identified reveals the power of identity decisions. A parent's identity choice—for example, reporting a single race and relegating some of their heritage to "ancestry"—can strongly impact how mixed heritage shows up in national data; in this situation, children with mixed racial heritage are often reported as entirely monoracial. Thus, a potentially large pool of people who are listed as monoracial in national data do in fact have known mixed racial heritage, and they (or their descendants) could identify as mixed in the future based on their recognized family background.[4] This finding lends important explanatory background to previous findings of widespread race response change.[5]

Most people in our interview sample identified themselves and their children with multiple races. Despite this consistency, we find that parents' concerns and practices varied across and within the three mixed-heritage groups. Variation in the commitment of our participants and their spouses to fostering their children's ethnic distinctiveness was largely influenced by the racial background of the other parent and spousal negotiations. The spouse's race often explained this variation.

Biracially identified participants who had a spouse with a shared minority race were relatively easily able to emphasize the value of the specific minority heritage in their family culture and in their children's upbringing. Although many participants of all three mixed-heritage backgrounds valued their ethnic and racial ancestries, some Asian-White and Native-White participants—especially those with a partner who shared their non-White race or ancestry—made a particularly concerted effort to pass down an appreciation of specific ancestral cultures to their children, for instance, by enrolling them in schools with language immersion programs. Participants who shared a minority racial overlap with their spouse were best able to cultivate a shared family culture and identity based on that racial overlap. For example, Black-White participants with a Black or part-Black partner emphasized the centrality of a shared Blackness in their children's upbringing and in their family lives. Children in such families were more likely to be raised in relation to that shared background than were the children of participants who did not share a non-White racial overlap with their spouse. Our mixed-heritage participants and their spouses articulated different narratives about their "family race," which tended to vary according to the nature of racial overlap between the parents.

## Contributions to Scholarly Conversations

### DO PART-WHITE PEOPLE OF MIXED RACIAL HERITAGE FEEL WHITE?

Will people with part-White (non-Black) heritage be subsumed over time into the "mainstream" monoracial White population, which will thus be allowed to retain its historical majority status, as predicted by Richard Alba and Eric Kaufmann?[6] Alba says that some mixed people (especially Asian-White people) experience "decategorization," that is, "individuals coming originally from different sides of an ethno-racial boundary—one majority, one minority—no longer commonly think about each other, or treat each other, based on their category memberships but as individuals."[7] Similarly, Strmc-Pawl describes Asian-White people in a near-White position that is "White Enough."[8]

Research from the United Kingdom, however, presents a different understanding of presumed "whitening." Arguing against the idea of "aspirational whitening" among mixed people in Britain, Tze Ming Mok has found that those who chose White in surveys were more likely to do so as a defensive reaction that shielded them from racisms; Mok also found that those who were middle-class were less likely to identify as White than working-class people, who were more socially vulnerable and had less status and confidence.[9] Song has found that many part-White mixed people in Britain wanted to pass down minority cultures and heritages to their children.[10] Davenport's comparative study of mixed people in US colleges found that people of mixed heritage rarely identify as racially White.[11]

Our census results show that relatively few Asian-White mixed-heritage people identified as racially White, and none of our Asian-White interview participants identified as White. Identifying as White race and Native ancestry is more common in the census data, but may reflect the common trope of a "Cherokee grandmother" that makes some otherwise White family trees seem more interesting. Our interview results directly challenge the idea that Asian-White and Native-White people are effectively White. Our research suggests that this presumption is simplistic because it ignores in-group variation in lived experiences, racial consciousness, discrimination, and phenotype, all of which are interpreted and experienced differently depending on racial context.[12] In other words, we find that many Asian-White and Native-White interview participants did *not* have experiences similar to those of White people. And certainly, many of our mixed-heritage participants who did not appear White phenotypically were not experiencing "decategorization."

Only one of our sixty-eight mixed-heritage interview participants— a person with Native-White heritage—identified as White. Native-White people can feel socially unable to claim monoracial Native racial identity if they are usually seen as White, or if their ties to Native communities are tenuous, while not necessarily feeling, or seeing themselves as, White. We find that some Native-White people felt a strong attachment to their Native ancestry, even if their appearance made it invisible to others. Some participants, especially those who felt phenotypically ambiguous, countered any "decategorization" from society by signaling their racial identity through jewelry, job choices, or other markers.

Although some of our Asian-White participants had only a symbolic attachment to their Asian background, none of our Asian-White participants identified as White. In fact, many of our Asian-White participants, including some with a White spouse, were deeply attached to being Asian.[13] Our interviews and other research have found that many people of mixed racial heritage do not feel that one single race sufficiently captures who they are or their experiences.

Like Tomàs Jiménez and Jessica Vasquez-Tokos, we find that some White spouses adapt to and become engaged with their mixed-heritage spouse's ethnic and racial background, social networks, and repertoire.[14] Although not all mixed-heritage participants were interested in or committed to their minority heritage, some had a White spouse who cultivated distinctive cultural practices or networks for their children. Our research shows that White spouses are not an undifferentiated and homogeneous group.

## IS "MULTIRACIAL" A MEANINGFUL CATEGORY?

Historically, mixed-heritage people were pathologized as "marginal" in relation to both mainstream society and their monoracial communities of color.[15] Increasingly in the contemporary United States, however, mixed-heritage people are not marginal in mainstream society but are becoming part of the mainstream. In this respect, we agree with Alba.[16] As soon as it was allowed in federal data collection, as of 1997, multiple race responses became common, and it is now unremarkable for respondents to identify with two or more races. Over 10 percent of people in the United States—33.8 million—were coded as multiple races in the 2020 census.[17]

Since the option to choose more than one race was added in the 2000 US census, analysts have debated whether "multiracial" primarily constitutes an administrative category or reflects the identity of a community of people.[18] The 2015 Pew survey found some degree of support for the latter argument: 81 percent of respondents with the same racial mix said that they had "some" or "a lot" in common with each other, and 72 percent said that they had "some" or "a lot" in common with people of a different racial mix.[19]

Like the Pew results, our study suggests that there may be a mixed-heritage population that identifies as "multiracial"—as neither single-race White nor a single non-White race. Many of our interview participants saw themselves as distinctive from White people (and in some cases, from monoracial BIPOC people as well). Our research with three mixed-heritage groups found that people who were first-generation mixed (both of their parents were single race), including most of our Asian-White participants and many Black-White participants, often identified as multiple-race. This finding concurs with prior findings that the generational locus of mixing matters to identities.[20]

However, this large population of multiracially identified people is heterogeneous. We find that this feeling of being "multiracial" varies across people and racial contexts, especially given the distinctive demographics and histories of different areas. Participants associated various meanings and experiences with "multiracial" identity and status. In other words, we find no *one* multiracial identity.[21] One way this variety was evident among our participants was in who they chose to marry and how they raised their children.

## HOW DO MIXED-HERITAGE PEOPLE AND THEIR FAMILIES FIT INTO THE US RACIAL HIERARCHY?

The proportionate increase in interracial couples and mixed-race families does suggest the erosion of certain social taboos and norms around intimate interracial unions. This is especially notable in relation to Black-White unions in the United States. However, we concur with researchers who warn that the growth in the number of mixed families and multiracial people does *not* signal that racism and negative racial narratives and beliefs have been vanquished. Kimberly DaCosta, Chandra Waring, and Erica Chito Childs argue (separately) that mixedness has various meanings and consequences and should not be regarded as a litmus test of progressive racial change.[22]

Policymakers and social scientists need to be alert to the differential impact and transmission of race over the generations and to be mindful of the significant heterogeneity in racialized experiences (and racial treatment) within specific mixed-heritage groups. Given the attention to generational depth and diversity (especially among our interview participants), more research is needed on how to define and enumerate this highly heterogeneous population.

A key policy question emerges as the mixed-heritage population grows and diversifies: How should mixed-heritage and multiracially identified people be considered in policymaking, particularly with regard to the monitoring and enforcement of civil rights law?[23] Given that part-White biracial people are on average socioeconomically better off than their monoracial BIPOC peers, are they a sector of the population that is considered to be vulnerable to racial discrimination?[24] These questions are highly pertinent, for instance, for mixed-heritage people who can choose to racially identify strategically in relation to only their non-White race in college admissions.[25] There are currently no US policies that determine whether multiracial people should be treated as a racially disadvantaged group in terms of affirmative action or access to scholarships.[26] About half of monoracial BIPOC people and the majority of White people oppose the inclusion of multiracial people in the population protected by antidiscrimination policies in the United States.[27]

Some argue that multiracial people face a unique kind of discrimination that the current legal system is inadequate to address because it does not recognize the specificity of mixed-race claims.[28] Our participants reported that social rejection by monoracial people of color, while not something that can be legally adjudicated, could be very hurtful and not inconsequential for identity development and maintenance. This topic was raised most often by participants with Asian-White mixed heritage who felt socially rejected by "full" Asians. At the same time, these individuals did not see themselves as White. We cannot dismiss the idea that those of mixed heritage may be subject to particular types of discrimination or marginalization on the basis of their being hybrid, mixed people.[29]

On the other hand, Tanya Hernández argues, it is not being multiracial per se that is the basis of discrimination against mixed people with Black ancestry, but anti-Blackness.[30] The fact that the vast majority of discrimination cases filed by multiple-race people are filed by those with Black heritage underscores the enduring salience of anti-Blackness, despite self-identification as mixed.[31] These legal debates reinforce the difficulty of talking about a unitary experience of being mixed heritage, even with the growing tendency to identify as "multiracial" across disparate mixed-heritage groups.

In exploring whether and how specific racial ancestries over several generations either become largely symbolic or continue to mark or disadvantage some mixed-heritage people in different contexts, we have found that the salience of race is not diminishing in a predictable or straightforward way for Native-White, Black-White, and Asian-White people.[32] The increase in the mixed-heritage population does not clearly foretell the future of race in America.

## Future Research

Our research results have a number of implications for future research. Here we discuss four of them.

First, we find that people of mixed racial heritage racially self-identify in a variety of ways. Given how common it has become to report multiple races, we must remember that respondents associate these reported identifications with disparate attachments and experiences stemming from their racial and ethnic backgrounds. In other words, simple racial self-identification responses (such as marking a check box on a questionnaire) do not provide enough information about a person's racial heritage and the meanings and lived experiences they associate with a chosen race—as we learned when our interview participants discussed identity, spouse choice, and the racial socialization practices they brought to childrearing. This finding has important implications for understanding what data about race can and cannot be reasonably assumed to represent. If data are being collected for the purposes of making reparations for past harms (such as for ancestors' enslavement), a simple survey question asking about race will be inadequate to identify the intergenerational impacts of past policies and events. For these purposes, more detailed information about family ancestry will need to be collected. It would not be safe to assume that generational distance simply and straightforwardly "dilutes" ethnic and racial attachment.[33] Much more research is needed on later-generation mixed-heritage people (for example, people with mixed-heritage parents), as mixed people can still be strongly invested in their minority and/or mixed backgrounds regardless of their generation.[34]

Second, others' perceptions of an individual's race (observed race) should be recorded in data collection efforts.[35] There needs to be more research into the variability in perceived racial appearance among disparate mixed-heritage people—including Asian-White and Native-White people as well as Black-White people. For example, Asian-White people can appear Asian, racially mixed, or even White by prevailing norms (dependent on racial/ethnic spatial context). Too much extant research has assumed that racial appearance is homogeneous or has failed to discuss the impact of appearance. Furthermore, as Kimberly DaCosta and Ann Morning have also pointed out (separately), disjunctures between racial appearance and identity are likely to become more common as the United States becomes more racially diverse. What were previously deemed self-evident boundaries of difference (such as skin color or hair texture) will become less likely to represent incontrovertible "proof" of group membership.[36]

Third, although we know that the identity choices made by people of mixed racial heritage may change over time and across circumstances, racial identification choice is still meaningful.[37] This is evident in the powerful link between identification and spouse choice. For example, mixed-heritage people in our study who identified as BIPOC in Census Bureau data were much more likely to be married to a BIPOC spouse than those who identified as two races or as single-race White. Our interviews and census data analyses show that identity choice impacts how children are racially identified and socialized, particularly in negotiation with spouses. Identities are complex and powerful, and future research about multiracial and mixed-heritage people should look for further impacts of identity choices on other aspects of life.

Finally, we note that most research on mixed-heritage people is based on the experiences of a limited set of people—highly educated, professional individuals with some White ancestry. As such, we know very little about what it means to have mixed heritage and be working-class.[38] Our knowledge of the experiences of those without any known White ancestry is scanty as well. Preliminary research has found that these are promising areas for further study. Aaron Gullickson has found class differences in the ways in which young people choose to take on the racial identities proposed for them by their parents.[39] And Liebler used census data to study the racial identification of the children of two BIPOC parents from different racialized groups.[40] Such inquiries are a promising beginning, but much work remains to be done.

Through this research, we have expanded the evidence about and appreciation for the relationships between identity choices and other important aspects of adults' personal lives. We have addressed a substantial gap in knowledge not only by comparing three mixed-heritage groups but by including Native-White participants. And we have highlighted contextual variation with a newly developed Racial/Ethnic Spatial Context Indicator. We remain grateful to our participants for entrusting us with personal accounts that have immeasurably improved our collective understanding.

# CENSUS BUREAU QUESTIONS ON RACE AND ANCESTRY

The US Census Bureau has collected information about individuals' race since its inception in 1790, though categories and/or instructions have changed with each census.[1] The US federal government first defined which race and (Latino) ethnic groups should be included in federal data collection efforts in 1977.[2] The 1980 census included these newly defined race categories, with the requirement that individuals choose only one group: White, Black, Asian and/or Pacific Islander, or American Indian/Alaska Native. In 1997 (and in time for the 2000 census), the federal government revised its required minimum to separate Pacific Islander from Asian and to allow individuals to mark multiple races. It also expanded the definition of "American Indian/Alaska Native" to include people indigenous to Central and South America as well as North America.[3] Another round of revisions to the minimum federal categories was finalized in March 2024.[4]

The number and nature of race categories in the US census probably influence how mixed-heritage people report their race and ancestry.[5] The 2019 race question (shown in figure A.1) had fifteen race categories, six of which represented Asian countries. American Indian or Alaska Native people were asked to write in their enrolled or principal tribe.

The ancestry question was first introduced in the 1980 census, replacing questions that had been asked from 1880 to 1970 about the birthplace of the respondent's mother and father. In acknowledgment of the lower immigration flows, the Census Bureau dropped the parent birthplace questions and began asking an "ancestry" question instead.

https://doi.org/10.7758/edyf5459.6695

**Figure A.1** *Race Question in the 2019 American Community Survey*

⑥ **What is Person 1's race?** *Mark (X) one or more boxes.*

☐ White

☐ Black or African Am.

☐ American Indian or Alaska Native — *Print name of enrolled or principal tribe.* ↗

☐ Asian Indian          ☐ Japanese          ☐ Native Hawaiian

☐ Chinese               ☐ Korean            ☐ Guamanian or Chamorro

☐ Filipino              ☐ Vietnamese        ☐ Samoan

☐ Other Asian – *Print race,* *for example, Hmong,* *Laotian, Thai, Pakistani,* *Cambodian, and so on.* ↗          ☐ Other Pacific Islander – *Print race, for example, Fijian, Tongan, and so on.* ↗

☐ Some other race – *Print race.* ↗

*Source:* 2019 ACS (US Census Bureau n.d.).

Ancestry was asked in the 1980, 1990, and 2000 censuses, then moved to the American Community Survey (ACS), which is also a Census Bureau product; see figure A.2 for an example of the ancestry question.

Ancestry examples and responses are usually country names, which are listed in the federal definitions of race groups.[6] Thus, we were able to code many ancestry responses into race groups to identify mixed-heritage people who reported a single race. Unfortunately, the translation

**Figure A.2** *Ancestry Question in the 2019 American Community Survey*

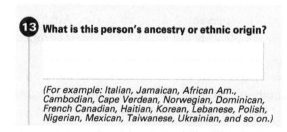

⑬ **What is this person's ancestry or ethnic origin?**

*(For example: Italian, Jamaican, African Am.,* *Cambodian, Cape Verdean, Norwegian, Dominican,* *French Canadian, Haitian, Korean, Lebanese, Polish,* *Nigerian, Mexican, Taiwanese, Ukrainian, and so on.)*

*Source:* 2019 ACS (US Census Bureau n.d.).

of ancestry responses into race groups is fraught with generalizations and assumptions—for example, the coding of Irish ancestry as a White group omits the many non-White Irish people. We code ancestry responses in the same way as prior researchers.[7] Because many ancestry responses are uncodable in terms of racialized ancestry, and because many people did not answer the ancestry question, not all single-race-identified people of mixed heritage are included in our study.

# PREINTERVIEW SURVEY

## Welcome

Welcome to the study called:

**Racial Identities and Life Choices Among Mixed-Heritage People in the USA**

## Consent

Thank you for your interest in our study called:

**Racial Identities and Life Choices Among Mixed-Heritage People in the USA**

We are two sociology professors doing a research project about the identities and life experiences of mixed-heritage Asian/White, American Indian/White, and Black/White people in different parts of the country.

While there is now considerable research on mixed-heritage children and young adults, we still know very little about mixed-heritage people when they partner and become parents. We are focusing on people from three different mixed-heritage backgrounds: Asian/White, American Indian/White, and Black/White mixed heritage.

We would like to hear from you if you:

· Are mixed-heritage Asian and White OR mixed-heritage American Indian and White OR mixed-heritage Black and White
· Do *not* have an additional heritage such as Hispanic, Latino, or three race groups

· Are the biological parent of a child you are raising or have raised (including shared custody)
· Are married (or used to be) to the other parent of at least one of your biological children

The study involves this brief online survey and then an interview. We will ask you for your contact information so we can get in touch to arrange the interview. The interview will be carried out at a time and in a location which is convenient for you.

In the interview, you will be asked about your views and experiences about your mixed heritage, your life experiences, and your family life. There are no "right" answers to these questions. You do not have to answer specific questions, and you can stop the interview at any time. You may find the interview experience to be enjoyable!

*Strict confidentiality* concerning your name and other details will be maintained throughout the study and after it has concluded. A summary of findings will also be available if you are interested.

We would be happy to answer *any questions* you may have about the research, either by email or by phone.

Many thanks,

Carolyn Liebler, Associate Professor of Sociology, University of Minnesota, [email], [phone number]

Miri Song, Professor of Sociology, University of Kent, England, [email], [phone number]

Please click "yes" if you agree to continue with this preinterview survey.

☐ Yes
☐ No

## Child Filter

Do you have any biological/natural-born children?

☐ Yes → Survey continues
☐ No → Thank you for your interest in our study, but we are focusing on people who are biological parents so that we can

understand how mixed-heritage identities get passed from one generation to the next. Please share information about the study with anyone else you know who may be interested in participating. If you selected this category accidentally, please click the Back button.

## Child Information

How many biological/natural-born children do you have? _____

Please enter the ages of *your* oldest ten children.

## Marriage Filter

Have you ever been married to the other biological parent of *any* of these children?

- ☐ Yes → If yes, which child(ren)? Select all that apply.
- ☐ No → Thank you for your interest in our study, but we are focusing on people who have ever been married to the other biological parent of their child. Please share information about the study with anyone else you know who may be interested in participating. If you selected this category accidentally, please click the Back button.

## Participant: Demographic Information

What is your current marital status?

- ☐ Never married/single
- ☐ Cohabiting with a partner
- ☐ Married
- ☐ Separated or divorced

What is your current occupation? For example, high school teacher, accountant, student, or homemaker. _____

How old are you? _____

If age is less than or equal to 17 → Thank you for your interest in our study. We are focusing on people ages 18 and older. Please pass the information about our study to others who may qualify and be interested in participating. If you reported an incorrect age accidentally, please click the Back button.

What is your gender:

☐ Woman
☐ Man
☐ Other _____

### Participant: Latino, Race, and Ancestry Filters and Information

Please answer all of these questions to the best of your ability, even if they seem repetitive or confusing. Thank you.

Are you of Hispanic, Latino, or Spanish origin? (*Note:* For this survey, Latino origins are not races.)

☐ No, not of Hispanic, Latino, or Spanish origin
☐ Yes, Mexican, Puerto Rican, Cuban, or another Spanish, Hispanic, or Latino origin

If yes → Thank you for your interest in this study. Because experiences are so varied, we are focusing only on people who have *only* White and Asian heritage or *only* White and American Indian heritage or *only* White and Black heritage. Please share information about the study with anyone else you know who may be interested in participating. If you selected this category accidentally, please click the Back button.

What is your race? Select all that apply.

☐ White
☐ Black or African American
☐ American Indian or Alaska Native. Type name of enrolled or principal tribe. _____
☐ Asian Indian
☐ Japanese

- ☐ Chinese
- ☐ Korean
- ☐ Filipino
- ☐ Vietnamese
- ☐ Other Asian. Type race—for example, Hmong, Laotian, Thai, Pakistani, Cambodian, and so on. _____
- ☐ Native Hawaiian
- ☐ Guamanian or Chamorro
- ☐ Samoan
- ☐ Other Pacific Islander. Type race—for example, Fijian, Tongan, and so on. _____
- ☐ Some other race. Type race. _____

If race includes two non-White races → Thank you for your interest in this study. Because experiences are so varied, we are focusing only on people who have *only* White and Asian heritage or *only* White and American Indian heritage or *only* White and Black heritage. Please share information about the study with anyone else you know who may be interested in participating. If you selected this category accidentally, please click the Back button.

What is your ancestry or ethnic origin (for example: Italian, Jamaican, African American, Cambodian, Cape Verdean, Norwegian, Dominican, French Canadian, Haitian, Korean, Lebanese, Polish, Nigerian, Mexican, Taiwanese, Ukrainian, and so on)?

_____

### Selected Child: Latino, Race, and Ancestry Information

Now we would like to know about *one* of your biological/natural-born children. Please choose any one of your children listed below.

Which child would you like to tell us about? *(Children are automatically listed by age. Respondent chooses one.)*

Now we would like to know about your biological/natural-born child. What is this child's gender?

- ☐ Boy/man
- ☐ Girl/woman
- ☐ Other: _____

Please answer all of these questions to the best of your ability, even if they seem repetitive or confusing. Thank you.

Is your child of Hispanic, Latino, or Spanish origin? (*Note:* For this survey, Latino origins are not races.)

☐ No, not of Hispanic, Latino, or Spanish origin
☐ Yes, Mexican, Puerto Rican, Cuban, or another Spanish, Hispanic, or Latino origin

What is your child's race? Select all that apply.

☐ White
☐ Black or African American
☐ American Indian or Alaska Native. Type name of enrolled or principal tribe. _____
☐ Asian Indian
☐ Japanese
☐ Chinese
☐ Korean
☐ Filipino
☐ Vietnamese
☐ Other Asian. Type race—for example, Hmong, Laotian, Thai, Pakistani, Cambodian, and so on. _____

_____
☐ Native Hawaiian
☐ Guamanian or Chamorro
☐ Samoan
☐ Other Pacific Islander. Type race—for example, Fijian, Tongan, and so on. _____

_____
☐ Some other race. Type race. _____

What is your child's ancestry or ethnic origin (for example: Italian, Jamaican, African American, Cambodian, Cape Verdean, Norwegian, Dominican, French Canadian, Haitian, Korean, Lebanese, Polish, Nigerian, Mexican, Taiwanese, Ukrainian, and so on)?

_____

## Other Parent of Selected Child: Latino, Race, and Ancestry Information

Please tell us about the other biological parent of this child. We recognize that not everyone has full information. Please answer to the best of your ability and then tell us how confident you are about these answers. Please answer all of these questions to the best of your ability, even if they seem repetitive or confusing. Thank you.

Is the other parent of Hispanic, Latino, or Spanish origin? (*Note:* For this survey, Latino origins are not races.)

☐ No, not of Hispanic, Latino, or Spanish origin
☐ Yes, Mexican, Puerto Rican, Cuban, or another Spanish, Hispanic, or Latino origin

What is the other parent's race? Select all that apply.

☐ White
☐ Black or African American
☐ American Indian or Alaska Native. Type name of enrolled or principal tribe. _____
☐ Asian Indian
☐ Japanese
☐ Chinese
☐ Korean
☐ Filipino
☐ Vietnamese
☐ Other Asian. Type race—for example, Hmong, Laotian, Thai, Pakistani, Cambodian, and so on. _____
_____
☐ Native Hawaiian
☐ Guamanian or Chamorro
☐ Samoan
☐ Other Pacific Islander. Type race—for example, Fijian, Tongan, and so on. _____
_____
☐ Some other race. Type race. _____
_____

What is the other parent's ancestry or ethnic origin (for example: Italian, Jamaican, African American, Cambodian, Cape Verdean, Norwegian, Dominican, French Canadian, Haitian, Korean, Lebanese, Polish, Nigerian, Mexican, Taiwanese, Ukrainian, and so on)?

_____

On a scale from 0 to 5, how confident are you in these answers?

☐ 0 (not at all confident)
☐ 1
☐ 2
☐ 3
☐ 4
☐ 5 (completely confident)

Additional comments on confidence of answers:

_____
_____
_____

## Participant's Parents: Latino, Race, and Ancestry Information

We would like to know about your biological parents. We recognize that not everyone has full information about both parents. Please answer to the best of your ability and then tell us how confident you are about these answers.

Now some questions about your biological mother. Please answer all of these questions to the best of your ability, even if they seem repetitive or confusing. Thank you.

Is your biological mother of Hispanic, Latino, or Spanish origin? (*Note:* For this survey, Latino origins are not races.)

☐ No, not of Hispanic, Latino, or Spanish origin
☐ Yes, Mexican, Puerto Rican, Cuban, or another Spanish, Hispanic, or Latino origin

What is your biological mother's race? Select all that apply.

☐ White
☐ Black or African American
☐ American Indian or Alaska Native. Type name of enrolled or principal tribe. _____

_____

☐ Asian Indian
☐ Japanese
☐ Chinese
☐ Korean
☐ Filipino
☐ Vietnamese
☐ Other Asian. Type race—for example, Hmong, Laotian, Thai, Pakistani, Cambodian, and so on. _____

_____

☐ Native Hawaiian
☐ Guamanian or Chamorro
☐ Samoan
☐ Other Pacific Islander. Type race—for example, Fijian, Tongan, and so on. _____

_____

☐ Some other race. Type race. _____

What is your biological mother's ancestry or ethnic origin (for example: Italian, Jamaican, African American, Cambodian, Cape Verdean, Norwegian, Dominican, French Canadian, Haitian, Korean, Lebanese, Polish, Nigerian, Mexican, Taiwanese, Ukrainian, and so on)?

_____

On a scale from 0 to 5, how confident are you in these answers about your biological mother?

☐ 0 (not at all confident)
☐ 1
☐ 2

☐ 3
☐ 4
☐ 5 (completely confident)

Additional comments on confidence of answers:

_____

_____

_____

Now some questions about your biological father. Please answer all of these questions to the best of your ability, even if they seem repetitive or confusing. Thank you.

Is your biological father of Hispanic, Latino, or Spanish origin? (*Note:* For this survey, Latino origins are not races.)

☐ No, not of Hispanic, Latino, or Spanish origin
☐ Yes, Mexican, Puerto Rican, Cuban, or another Spanish, Hispanic, or Latino origin

What is your biological father's race? Select all that apply.

☐ White
☐ Black or African American
☐ American Indian or Alaska Native. Type name of enrolled or principal tribe. _____

_____

☐ Asian Indian
☐ Japanese
☐ Chinese
☐ Korean
☐ Filipino
☐ Vietnamese
☐ Other Asian. Type race—for example, Hmong, Laotian, Thai, Pakistani, Cambodian, and so on. _____

_____

☐ Native Hawaiian
☐ Guamanian or Chamorro

☐ Samoan

☐ Other Pacific Islander. Type race—for example, Fijian, Tongan, and so on. _____

_____

☐ Some other race. Type race. _____

What is your biological father's ancestry or ethnic origin (for example: Italian, Jamaican, African American, Cambodian, Cape Verdean, Norwegian, Dominican, French Canadian, Haitian, Korean, Lebanese, Polish, Nigerian, Mexican, Taiwanese, Ukrainian, and so on)?

_____

On a scale of 0 to 5, how confident are you in these answers about your biological father?

☐ 0 (not at all confident)

☐ 1

☐ 2

☐ 3

☐ 4

☐ 5 (completely confident)

Additional comments on confidence of answers:

_____
_____
_____

## Contact Information

We will get in touch with you to arrange a time and place for the in-person interview. Please provide your best contact information below.

*Contact information*

Name: _____

Town/city: _____

State: _____

Phone number: _____

Email: _____

*Preferred contact method*

☐ Phone
☐ Email
☐ Either

*Preferred time of day to call*

☐ Morning after 8:00 AM
☐ Afternoon
☐ Evening before 8:00 PM
☐ Fill in the best time _____

# INTERVIEW QUESTIONS

### How Do You Identify Racially?

- *(Remind participant of how she/he filled in race and ancestry questions on online survey.)* Can you say a bit about why you chose what you did? *(If there was a discrepancy between the race and ancestry responses, probe about why.)*
- How are you usually seen by others racially?
- Have you changed the way in which you racially identify at any point in your life—for example, at key junctures such as college, getting married, moving to a new city—and if so, what prompted the change?
- Is there any one race with which you most strongly identify?
- Which of these terms, if any, do you feel describes you: multiracial, mixed race, mixed heritage, mixed ancestry?
- Is there another word or phrase that you use to describe yourself?

### Your Upbringing

- Where have you lived throughout your life? *(Ask about birthplace, elementary school, high school, college, and so on.)*
- Was either parent an immigrant to the US or born here?
- How would you describe your upbringing, culturally and/or racially, and which parent did what? *(Probe about languages spoken in the home, cultural exposure to customs, foods, visits to parents' country of birth, if applicable.)*

- How much contact did you have with relatives on your mother's and father's sides, especially grandparents, aunts/uncles, cousins?
- Did you know other American Indian/Alaska Native, Asian, Black, or White families growing up?
- Did you know any other mixed-heritage people or mixed families growing up?
- Have you ever felt racially stigmatized or marginalized, and if so, in what circumstances and by whom?
- Is ethnic or racial stigma an ongoing concern for you now?

## How Did You Choose Your Spouse?

- How did you and your spouse meet?
- What was your dating history prior to your spouse?
- Was your spouse's racial or ethnic background of importance to you—and if so, how (or if not, why not)?
- What is your spouse's attitude toward your multiracial heritage?
- How does your family feel about your spouse, and how much interaction is there with either side of the family?

*(Probing may differ according to the nature of racial overlap between the participant and spouse and/or whether the spouse is White.)*

## How Do You Racially Identify Your Children?

- *(Remind participant of how she/he racially reported child(ren). Probe about why.)*
- Is this something you have discussed with your spouse?
- What is your child's appearance? How is she/he usually seen by others?
- Is racism a concern for you regarding your children?
- *(In the case of older children)* How do you think your children see themselves racially (*if at all*)?
- *(If applicable)* Do you identify your individual children differently?
- Is it important that your children identify in relation to their minority heritage?
- How would you describe the way in which you and your partner are raising your children? [Are any particular backgrounds or

practices emphasized? Do you and the other parent adopt similar or different approaches? For instance, one parent may speak in another language.]
· Do you have any views on the future partners of your children—especially in terms of their racial backgrounds?

## Context and Networks

· How ethnically diverse is your neighborhood [and wider region]?
· What is the racial atmosphere/environment of your workplace?
· What is your social network like? [Is it ethnically diverse? Do you know other mixed individuals and families?]

Thank you for your time. Do you know of any other possible participants?

APPENDIX D

# SUMMARY OF PARTICIPANT CHARACTERISTICS

Tables D.1 through D.3 provide a summary of the characteristics of the sixty-eight interview participants.

**Table D.1** *Characteristics of Asian-White Participants of Mixed Racial Heritage*

| Pseudonym | Age | Sex | Racial Identity | Spouse Race[a] | RESCI |
|-----------|-----|-----|-----------------|----------------|-------|
| Albert | 64 | M | White and Chinese | Chinese | 3 |
| Allison | 37 | F | White and Japanese | White | 2 |
| Andrew | 43 | M | White and Korean | White | 3 |
| Angela | 48 | F | White and Japanese | White | 3 |
| Annie | 29 | F | White and Chinese | White | 2 |
| Danny | 36 | M | White and Chinese | White | 3 |
| David | 35 | M | White and Chinese | Chinese | 3 |
| Donna | 48 | F | White and Japanese | White | 2 |
| Ellie | 39 | F | White and Japanese | White | 2 |
| Hilary | 42 | F | White and Asian Indian | White, Black, Chinese, Vietnamese | 3 |
| Jacqui | 39 | F | White and Korean | Puerto Rican and Colombian | 3 |
| Jane | 38 | F | White and Korean | White | 2 |
| Jonathan | 48 | M | White and Korean | Korean | 5 |
| Kari | 33 | F | White and Chinese | White | 3 |
| Lizzi | 38 | F | White and Chinese | White | 5 |
| Lori | 52 | F | White and Japanese | White | 3 |
| Makana | 42 | F | White, Japanese, Chinese | White | 2 |
| Maria | 59 | F | White and Filipina | White and Native | 3 |

*(continued)*

**Table D.1** *(continued)*

| Pseudonym | Age | Sex | Racial Identity | Spouse Race[a] | RESCI |
|---|---|---|---|---|---|
| Matthew | 50 | M | White and Korean | White | 3 |
| Mona | 63 | F | White and Japanese | White | 3 |
| Nani | 41 | F | White and Filipina | Chinese | 3 |
| Noelle | 38 | F | White and Chinese | White | 3 |
| Petra | 47 | F | White and Asian Indian | Asian Indian | 3 |
| Ray | 46 | M | White and Japanese | White | 3 |
| Sumi | 44 | F | White and Japanese | White | 1 |
| Victor | 45 | M | White and Chinese | White | 3 |
| Vincent | 32 | M | White and Filipino | Japanese | 3 |

*Source:* Authors' data from preinterview surveys and interviews.
[a]Native = American Indian/Alaska Native on the preinterview survey.

**Table D.2** *Characteristics of Black-White Participants of Mixed Racial Heritage*

| Pseudonym | Age | Sex | Racial Identity | Spouse Race | RESCI |
|---|---|---|---|---|---|
| Adriana | 37 | F | White and Black | Black | 3 |
| Andreas | 28 | M | White and Black | Black | 3 |
| Ariel | 30 | F | White and Black | Black | 3 |
| Blair | 46 | M | White and Black | White | 3 |
| Bradford | 36 | M | White and Black | White | 5 |
| Carl | 45 | M | White and Black | White | 2 |
| Corey | 28 | F | White and Black | White and Black | 3 |
| Darrell | 28 | M | White and Black | White and Black | 3 |
| Evan | 43 | M | White and Black | White | 3 |
| Helen | 42 | F | White and Black | Black | 2 |
| Jacob | 47 | M | White and Black | White | 3 |
| Jessica | 36 | F | White and Black | White | 3 |
| Katherine | 40 | F | White and Black | Black | 3 |
| Kendra | 30 | F | White and Black | Black | 1 |
| Mallory | 44 | F | White and Black | White | 3 |
| Max | 44 | M | White and Black | White | 3 |
| Saskia | 26 | F | White and Black | White | 3 |
| Vanessa | 38 | F | White and Black | Black and Puerto Rican | 1 |
| Wendy | 32 | F | White and Black | Black | 3 |
| Yetta | 60 | F | Black | Black | 2 |

*Source:* Authors' data from preinterview surveys and interviews.

**Table D.3** *Characteristics of Native-White Participants of Mixed Racial Heritage*

| Pseudonym | Age | Sex | Racial Identity[a] | Spouse Race[a] | RESCI |
|-----------|-----|-----|--------------------|----------------|-------|
| Aaron | 44 | M | White and Native | White | 3 |
| Alex | 38 | M | White and Native | Native | 4 |
| Benjamin | 60 | M | White and Native | White | 3 |
| Brendan | 64 | M | White and Native | White and Native | 2 |
| Cassidy | 43 | F | White and Native | Asian Indian | 3 |
| Cathy | 41 | F | White and Native | White and Native | 4 |
| Dawn | 40 | F | White | White | 3 |
| Devon | 43 | F | Native | White, Black, Native | 2 |
| Gabriella | 40 | F | White and Native | White | 2 |
| Jonas | 33 | M | White and Native | Black | 3 |
| Natalie | 40 | F | White and Native | White and Native | 3 |
| Nick | 34 | M | Native | White | 2 |
| Nina | 40 | F | White and Native | White | 3 |
| Ron | 47 | M | Native | White | 2 |
| Sam | 52 | M | Native | White | 2 |
| Sandy | 64 | F | White and Native | White | 2 |
| Sarah | 37 | F | White and Native | White and Native | 2 |
| Savannah | 34 | F | White and Native | Black | 3 |
| Skye | 37 | F | White and Native | White | 2 |
| Susie | 47 | F | Native | Native | 2 |
| Tara | 34 | F | White and Native | White | 3 |

*Source:* Authors' data from preinterview surveys and interviews.

[a]Native = American Indian/Alaska Native on the preinterview survey.

APPENDIX E

# RESCI

The Racial/Ethnic Spatial Context Indicator (RESCI) uses available quantitative measures to capture aspects of an area's history and contemporary characteristics that may impact the personal and family experiences of the people in this study. The measures cover aspects of US history and contemporary life related to all of the component race groups under study—Asian, Black, Native, and White.

Some researchers use simple measures—such as the contemporary racial composition of the area—to measure or account for context effects.[1] This focus on living individuals ignores place-specific histories, laws, and economics, as well as sociopolitical context. Simple measures can be particularly ineffective for studying Native people's context because they are a small minority group (particularly when including only single-race Native people). As our interviews show, proximity to tribally controlled lands and the history of reservations and dispossession can be important context for their experiences. In contrast, RESCI pulls from twenty-eight measures about each county in the United States in 1980, 1990, 2000, and 2010. Using principal components analysis and latent class analysis, each county-year was assigned one of the five RESCI categories.

We are grateful to Dr. Christopher Levesque for his work on developing the RESCI measure (funded in part by the Minnesota Population Center, NIH Award no. P2CHD041023).

# Twenty-Eight Measures of Counties Used to Create RESCI

## RACE-RELATED HISTORY OF THE PLACE

Of the seven measured aspects of the race-related history of each place, five focus on laws or treaties that covered the area (measures 1 to 5). The sixth measure—the incidence of race "riots"—gives an indication of historical racial tensions between Black and non-Black residents. This measure was developed by Seymour Spilerman.[2] The seventh measure, based on 1970 census data from ipums.org/usa, is meant to indicate whether the area was an early destination of Asian immigrants after the 1965 change in immigration law.[3]

1. Yes/No: Confederate slave state
2. Yes/No: Non-Confederate slave state
3. Yes/No: American Indian/Alaska Native reservation or trust land in 1875
4. Yes/No: American Indian/Alaska Native reservation or trust land in 1930
5. Yes/No: Was part of Mexico at some point
6. Number of race-related "riots" in the 1960s or 1970s
7. Yes/No: In 1970, there were at least twice the national average of Asian-born people

## RACE AND ETHNICITY OF THE CONTEMPORARY COUNTY POPULATION

The contemporary racial profile of the area is captured in five of these six measures (8 to 12); note that the percentage of the population identifying as multiple races in 2000 and 2010 is implicitly included because it is the remainder of the population after measures 8 to 12 are considered. These measures were drawn from the full-count decennial census data.[4] To develop measure 13 about interracial marriages, we used census microdata. A marriage was coded as interracial if the spouses' races did not exactly match.

8. Percentage of population single-race non-Latino White
9. Percentage of population single-race non-Latino Black
10. Percentage of population single-race non-Latino American Indian or Alaska Native

11. Percentage of population single-race non-Latino Asian or Pacific Islander
12. Percentage of population of Latino origins
13. Interracial marriages as a percentage of all marriages

### PERSONAL CONNECTIONS TO OTHER PLACES OR LANGUAGES

Three measures (14 to 16) focus on personal experiences with a non-English language or foreign places. When many people in an area have experiences like these, the area's racial regime may be more cosmopolitan or international. Native people speaking Indigenous languages (captured in measure 15) can strengthen commitment to Native identities.[5] These measures were drawn from the decennial census long-form data.

14. Percentage who speak Spanish language at home
15. Percentage who speak another non-English language at home
16. Percentage born outside the United States

### THE CONTEMPORARY SOCIOPOLITICAL CLIMATE

Two measures aim to capture the contemporary sociopolitical climate. Although hate groups, as defined and located by the Southern Poverty Law Center (measure 17), do not necessarily center on race/ethnicity, they nevertheless tend to increase insider/outsider politics and norms. A higher percentage of votes for a Democrat in US Senate races in an area may indicate relatively liberal or progressive local politics.

17. Number of "hate groups" according to the Southern Poverty Law Center
18. Percentage of votes that went to the Democrat in the US Senate race for that area (averaged across three election cycles in years ending in 4, 6, and 8)

### THE ECONOMIC SITUATION OF THE COUNTY POPULATION

Local socioeconomics can influence race relations. We include three household income-related measures (19 to 21), as well as a community-level indicator of blight, vacant homes (22). Our fifth economic measure, 23, focuses directly on racial income inequality. These measures are drawn from decennial census full-count and long-form data.

19. County poverty rate
20. Median per capita household income in 2010 dollars
21. Percentage who rent their home (versus owning)
22. Percentage of homes that are occupied (versus vacant)
23. Difference in the mean per capita household income between non-Latino White residents and all other county residents

## FAMILY COMPOSITION AND HOUSEHOLD STRUCTURE

Families and households come in many forms, which influences the experiences of their residents. When many children are living with a non-relative or a single mother, this can influence the way that families are talked about in schools and in the local society. Measures 24–26 focus on this topic. When there are relatively many elders in a community, as picked up by measure 27, local norms and values may reflect an earlier time when these elders were growing up.

24. Percentage of households that include a householder, a spouse, and a child
25. Percentage of children living with a nonrelative
26. Percentage of children living with a single mother
27. Percentage of householders age sixty-five and older

## DENSITY OF THE COUNTY

Our final measure (28) is a continuous variable indicating how urban the area is. The population density of urban areas might increase a person's freedom of identity expression, as well as their chances of interacting with someone in a particular race group.

28. Percentage of county tracts considered "urban" by the Census Bureau

## Working with RESCI and Public Use Microdata

The public use microdata does not reveal county information and instead uses county groups (in 1980) or public use microdata areas (PUMA starting in 1990). A PUMA is a contiguous area of at least one hundred thousand people. We used a county-to-PUMA crosswalk to create a PUMA version of RESCI for the analyses presented here.[6] The result was a list of all 1990–2010 PUMAs and 1980 county groups, each of which was assigned to one of the five RESCI areas. We merged this list with the individual-level census microdata to be able to characterize the locations of individuals and families in the census data. Throughout the book, we show results by RESCI area by pooling the census and ACS data (1980–2019) to gain sufficient sample size. Results by year generally showed few trends over time (besides the addition of the multiple-race option in 2000).

# NOTES

## Chapter 1: Identity, Spouse Choice, and Child-Rearing Among Mixed-Heritage Groups

1. Small and King-O'Riain 2014.
2. Alba 2020; Bonilla-Silva 2001; Davenport 2018; Parker and Song 2001; Solomos 2022.
3. Jones and Bullock 2012.
4. Lee and Bean 2004.
5. Jones et al. 2021; Marks and Rios-Vargas 2021. The 2020 census questionnaire, for the first time, allowed White and Black people to report detailed race information, and the Census Bureau also changed several procedures in the processing of race and Latino-origin data. One of these changes was to code based on information from both the race and Latino-origin response boxes simultaneously rather than coding them separately, as in the past. This change increased the number of people coded as multiple-race because, for example, a respondent who wrote, "Cuban, Thai, Filipino," would have been coded in 2010 as single-race "Asian" but in 2020 was coded as multiple-race "some other race" and Asian. The 2020 census procedure also provided two hundred characters for write-in responses, rather than thirty characters as in 2010, allowing more detail (and thus more multiple-race responses) to be captured (Marks and Vargas 2021). See Arias et al. 2025 and Starr and Pao 2024 for analyses of the impacts.
6. Morning and Saperstein 2018; Song 2021.
7. Gullickson and Morning 2011.
8. Parker et al. 2015.
9. Hout and Goldstein 1994; Morning and Saperstein 2018; Pilgrim 2021; Song 2017a; Waters 1990.
10. On racial identification stemming from linked fates, see Gonlin 2022. On connections through racially meaningful places, see Kana'iaupuni and Liebler 2005; Liebler 2001, 2010.

11. Harris and Sim 2002; Liebler et al. 2017; Rockquemore and Brunsma 2002; Song 2017b; Tashiro 2011.

12. Bonilla-Silva 2017; Hernández 2018; Treitler 2013.

13. Ifekwunigwe 2004.

14. Root 1996.

15. We would like to thank one of the anonymous reviewers of this manuscript for this observation.

16. Again, we would like to thank one of the reviewers for this insight.

17. Parker et al. 2015.

18. Aspinall and Song 2013; Davenport 2018; Lee and Bean 2007; Rockquemore and Brunsma 2002; Strmc-Pawl 2016.

19. See, for example, Gullickson and Morning 2011; Liebler and Zacher 2016.

20. Morning 2000; Song 2017a.

21. Morning and Saperstein 2018; Song 2017b; Xu et al. 2021.

22. Hackstaff 2010; Hout and Goldstein 1994; Waters 1990.

23. Murji and Solomos 2005; Morning 2018; Roth 2016.

24. Aspinall and Song 2013.

25. See Aspinall and Song 2013; Campion 2019; DaCosta 2007; Funderburg 1994; Harris and Sim 2002; Joseph-Salisbury 2019; Khanna 2004, 2011; King-O'Riain 2006; Mahtani et al. 2014; Paragg 2017; Rockquemore and Brunsma 2002; Root 1992, 1996; Song 2010; Spickard 1989; Tizard and Phoenix 1993.

26. Aspinall and Song 2013; Burke and Kao 2010; Harris and Sim 2002; Song 2003.

27. Campbell and Troyer 2007; Davenport 2016; Doyle and Kao 2007; Khanna 2004; Lee and Bean 2010; Liebler et al. 2016; Liebler et al. 2017; Renn 2000; Tashiro 2002.

28. Tashiro 2011.

29. Aspinall and Song 2013; Harris and Sim 2002; Kana'iaupuni and Liebler 2005; Liebler 2016; O'Connell et al. 2022. On the evolution of identifications, see Burke and Kao 2010; Song 2017b.

30. Porter et al. 2016.

31. Twine 2010.

32. Davenport 2018; Lopez 2003.

33. Hackstaff 2010.

34. See Aspinall and Song 2013; Khanna 2004; Rockquemore and Brunsma 2002.

35. Liebler et al. 2017.

36. Xu et al. 2021.

37. See, for example, Buggs 2017; Khanna 2004; Mahtani et al. 2014; Rockquemore and Brunsma 2002; Song 2017b.

38. For related research on this topic, see Sims and Joseph-Salisbury 2019.

39. Brubaker 2016.

40. Morning 2018. Spickard 2020. See also Roth 2018; Roth and Ivemark 2018.

41. Campion 2019; Khanna 2004; Paragg 2017; Song 2003; Song and Aspinall 2012; Waring 2022.

42. Heilman 2022.

43. Song 2003; Touré 2011. On the enlarged scope of identity options, see Brubaker 2016.
44. McKay 2021; Robertson 2013.
45. Gonlin 2022; Khanna 2010; Rondilla and Spickard 2007.
46. Aspinall and Song 2013; Davenport 2018; Song 2017b.
47. Davenport 2018, 90.
48. Dixon and Telles 2017.
49. Masuoka 2011.
50. Song 2020, 2021.
51. On perceptions of Black-White people, see Khanna 2010; Sims 2016. On perceptions of Asian-White people, see Aspinall and Song 2013; Khanna 2004; Song 2017b; Song 2020.
52. Garroutte 2001; McKay 2021.
53. Jacobs 2015.
54. Bean and Stevens 2003; Kalmijn 1998; Qian and Lichter 2007.
55. Irastorza 2016.
56. Song 2016; see also Osanami-Törngren, Irastorza, and Song 2016.
57. Wu et al. 2015, 735.
58. Qian and Lichter 2007.
59. Livingston and Brown 2017. Notably, there have recently been *declines* in intermarriage between Whites and other groups; Asians and Latinos are also increasingly marrying within their respective groups, but more often cross the US-born/foreign-born boundary (Lichter, Qian, and Tumen 2015). According to the Pew Research Center study, while Latino and Asian Americans are more likely than African Americans to intermarry, fewer Asian newlyweds were intermarried in 2015 (29 percent of US newlyweds) than in 1980 (33 percent) (Livingston and Brown 2017). The increase in unions between people from disparate Asian American ethnic groups has shown that the meanings of Asian ethnicity and race are still important for many Asian Americans (Chong 2020).
60. See Alba and Nee 2003; Gordon 1964.
61. Childs 2005; DaCosta 2007; Davenport 2018.
62. Song 2009.
63. DaCosta 2007.
64. See Childs 2005; Collet 2015; Rodríguez-García et al. 2015.
65. Rodríguez-García et al. 2015.
66. Vasquez 2014; Vasquez-Tokos 2017; see also Chong 2020; Osuji 2019; Song 2009.
67. Vasquez 2014, 403; see also Chong and Song 2022.
68. Prior studies of intermarriage in the United States have tended to contrast the lower incidence of Black people entering into interracial unions with Whites compared to Asians, Latinos, and, especially, American Indians, all of whom have very high rates of marriage with White people (Alba et al. 2017; Miyawaki 2015; Qian and Lichter 2007). But these findings do not translate

straightforwardly to the case of mixed-heritage Black-White, Asian-White, and Native-White people.

69. See Song 2015.
70. Bonam and Shih 2009.
71. Parker et al. 2015, 9.
72. Song 2015.
73. See, for example, Bratter 2007; Brunsma 2005; Kana'iaupuni and Liebler 2005; Lichter and Qian 2018; Liebler 2004, 2010, 2016; Qian 2004; Roth 2005; Saenz et al. 1995; Xie and Goyette 1997.
74. Aspinall and Song 2013.
75. On the raising of Black-White children, see Rockquemore and Laszloffy 2005; Twine 2010.
76. Song 2017b.
77. Song 2017b; Tashiro 2011; Vasquez-Tokos 2017.
78. Davenport 2018; Strmc-Pawl 2016. See also Lee and Bean 2007; Tashiro 2011.
79. Almaguer 1994/2009; Jung 2015; Omi and Winant 1994; Treitler 2013.
80. Omi and Winant 1994, 1. See also Alcoff 2003; Jung 2015.
81. Almaguer 1994/2009.
82. Almaguer 1994/2009, 7–8.
83. National Congress of American Indians 2020.
84. National Congress of American Indians 2020.
85. National Congress of American Indians 2020.
86. Ogbu 1990.
87. Li and Nicholson 2021.
88. Budiman and Ruiz 2021; Oh and Eguchi 2022; Wu 2015.
89. Li and Nicholson 2021; Okamoto 2014; Strmc-Pawl et al. 2022; Takaki 1989; Tsuda 2014.
90. Lee and Bean 2007; Qian 2004.
91. Alba 2020; Alba et al. 2017; Lee and Bean 2007, 2010.
92. Morning and Saperstein 2018; Song 2017b.
93. Xu et al. 2021; see also Gullickson and Morning 2011.
94. Xu et al. 2021, 1610.
95. Davenport 2018, 27.
96. Gullickson and Morning 2011; Xu et al. 2021.
97. Parker et al. 2015.
98. Iverson et al. 2022.
99. See Bratter 2007; Campbell and Troyer 2007; Gullickson and Morning 2011; Herman 2004; Korgen 1998; Pilgrim 2021; Rockquemore and Brunsma 2002; Roth 2005.
100. Kao et al. 2019, 2.
101. Alba 2020; Lee and Bean 2007; see also Gallagher 2004; Gans 2012; Twine and Gallagher 2008.
102. Lee and Bean 2007, 579.
103. See Gans 2012; Lee and Bean 2004; Rockquemore and Arend 2002; Twine and Gallagher 2008; Yancey 2006.

104. Bonam and Shih 2009; Masuoka 2008; Miyawaki 2015.
105. Alba 2020.
106. Song 2003; Waters 1990.
107. Alba 2020; Kauffman 2018.
108. Alba et al. 2017, 14–15.
109. Gans 2012 ("deracialized"); Strmc-Pawl 2016 ("White enough"); Alba 2020; Lee and Bean 2007; Strmc-Pawl 2016.
110. Bonilla-Silva 2004; Gallagher 2004; Lee and Bean 2007; Strmc-Pawl 2016; Yancey 2003.
111. Alba 2020, 213 (emphasis added).
112. Alba 2020.
113. Davenport 2018.
114. Davenport 2018, 49–50.
115. Gambol 2016; Livingston and Brown 2017.
116. Osanami-Törngren and Sato 2021.
117. Jiménez 2010; Song 2017b; Vasquez-Tokos 2017.
118. Holloway et al. 2012.
119. Song 2010, 2017b.
120. Aspinall and Song 2013; Chang 2016; Fulbeck 2006; Hunter 2007; King-O'Riain 2006; Murphy-Shigematsu 2012; Song 2019.
121. Alba 2020, 155.
122. Rondilla and Spickard 2007; Tharps 2016.
123. See, for example, Alba 2020.
124. Aspinall and Song 2013; Mok 2019.
125. Campbell 2007, 942.
126. Song 2017b, 2019.

## Chapter 2: Looking from Two Angles and Considering Context

1. Ruggles et al. 2019.
2. Porter et al. 2016.
3. Chun and Gan 2014.
4. Holloway et al. 2012, 76.
5. Liebler 2016; Roth 2005; Song 2017b.
6. In the 1980 data, the Census Bureau also included the most common three-answer responses, which were usually Native-White combinations.
7. Aspinall and Song 2013; Harris and Sim 2002; Liebler and Hou 2020; Liebler et al. 2017; Strmc-Pawl 2016.
8. The exact wording of the relationship question categories has changed over the years, making it possible to exclude stepchildren as of 1990 and exclude adopted children as of 2000. See the detailed codes at IPUMS USA, "Codes and Frequencies," https://usa.ipums.org/usa-action/variables/RELATE#codes_section.

9. See Qian and Shen 2020.

10. For simplicity, children's Latino status is not considered in these categories.

11. The 2020 census used a different race question format, but this format was not released until after our study was underway. As of this writing, detailed 2020 race data have not yet been released, nor have the 2020 census public-use microdata.

12. For an in-depth analysis of these results, see Song and Liebler 2022.

13. Fhagen-Smith 2010; Korgen 1998.

14. Campion 2019; Holloway et al. 2012; Kana'iaupuni and Liebler 2005; King-O'Riain et al. 2014; O'Connell et al. 2022.

15. Gullickson and Morning 2011; Iverson et al. 2022.

16. Massey and Denton 1993 (unemployment and poverty patterns); Welch et al. 2001 (attitudes toward public services); Lewis 2003 (educational outcomes).

17. Portes and Zhou 1993.

18. Jacobs 2015; Liebler 2010; Liebler and Zacher 2016.

19. Cooley et al. 2018; Light and Iceland 2016; Seaton et al. 2017.

20. On "seeing" race, see Porter et al. 2016; on potential marriage partners, see Blau et al. 1982; Bratter and O'Connell 2017; Vasquez-Tokos 2017.

21. Roth 2018; Xu et al. 2021.

## Chapter 3: How Do Mixed-Heritage People Identify Themselves?

1. Iverson and her colleagues (2022) argue that "co-descent"—mixed-heritage people identifying with multiple heritages—is especially applicable to mixed-heritage people who have no European ancestry and who have Asian and Latino heritage. This interpretation is consistent with the Asian-White census data.

2. Davis 1991; Spencer 2006.

3. Deloria 1969; Waters 1990.

4. On the "vanishing Indian," see Bross 2001; Dippie 1982.

5. Deloria 1969; Garroutte 2001; McKay 2021; Robertson 2013. On defining "American Indian/Alaska Native" as a race group, see Office of Management and Budget 1997.

6. Liebler 2001; McKay 2021.

7. Patterson 1982.

8. Takaki 1989; Tuan 1998.

9. Kim 1999; see also Tuan 1998.

10. Haney López 2006.

11. Davenport 2018, 42.

12. See Steinberg 1981; Wu 2015.

13. Malik 2021.

14. For more detail on our participants' responses to the ancestry question and their understanding of their ancestry, see Song and Liebler 2022.

15. Pratt 1892.

16. See Roth and Ivemark 2018; Song and Liebler 2022.
17. Liebler 2001; Phillips et al. 2007; Snipp 1997; Waters 1990.
18. Cornell and Hartmann 2007; Nagel 1995; Snipp 1997; Waters 1990.
19. Liebler 2010; Snipp 1989.
20. Liebler 2010; Liebler and Zacher 2016.
21. Robertson 2013.
22. Norris et al. 2012.
23. Liebler 2001.
24. McKay 2021; Phinney and Ong 2007.
25. Liebler 2001; McKay 2021; Montgomery 2017; Porter et al. 2016.
26. McKay 2021.
27. Liebler 2001.
28. Snipp 1997; Sturm 2011.
29. Roth and Ivemark 2018.
30. Davis 1991; Spencer 2006.
31. Williams 2020.
32. Williams 2006.
33. DaCosta 2007; Office of Management and Budget 1997.
34. Liebler 2016.
35. Roth 2005.
36. Bratter 2007; Roth 2005.
37. See, for example, Aspinall and Song 2013; Dalmage 2000; Joseph-Salisbury 2019; Khanna 2010; Rockquemore and Brunsma 2002; Sims and Njaka 2019.
38. Dyson 1994; Touré 2011.
39. See Twine 2010.
40. Aspinall and Song 2013; Twine 1996.
41. Waters 1999.
42. Dyson 1994; Touré 2011.
43. Campion 2019.
44. Tharps 2016.
45. Waters 1990.
46. Ogbu 1990.
47. Takaki 1989; Wu 2015; Zhou 2004.
48. Kibria 2002; Zhou 1997.
49. Kim 1999; King-O'Riain 2004; Okamoto 2014; Tuan 1998.
50. Okihiro 1994, 34.
51. Kim 2008.
52. The 2020 Census included, for the first time, fill-in-the-blank boxes for the "White" and "Black or African Am." categories. The instruction was changed to "Mark one or more boxes AND print origins."
53. Lee and Ramakrishnan 2020.
54. Chang 2016; Murphy-Shigematsu 2012.
55. Perhaps the recent anti-Asian violence prompted by the COVID crisis and the scapegoating of Asians as the originators of the virus will lead people with

Asian heritage to assertively declare their Asian-ness (Han et al. 2023; Strmc-Pawl et al. 2022).

56. Song 2003; Waters 1990.
57. Krogstad 2015; Spickard and Fong 1995. Although the Hawaiian term "Hapa," which means "part," refers to multiracial people of Asian and Pacific Islander descent and has been used on the US mainland (especially in California), some Hawaiians (and others) have objected to its use in relation to mixed people who do not have Hawaiian heritage.
58. Chang 2016.
59. Chang 2016; Fulbeck 2006; Rondilla and Spickard 2007; Song 2019.
60. See Alba 2020; Lee and Bean 2007; Strmc-Pawl 2016. On the range of racial appearances among Asian-White people, see Fulbeck 2006.
61. Song 2010.
62. Song and Aspinall 2012.
63. See Khanna 2004; Mengel 2001.
64. Kibria 2002; Kim 1999; Okamoto 2014; Tuan 1998.
65. Morning and Saperstein 2018.
66. Rondilla and Spickard 2007; Song 2010.
67. Cornell and Hartmann 2007.
68. On "spoiled" identities, see Goffman 1963.
69. Aspinall and Song 2013; Campion 2019; Khanna and Johnson 2010; Pilgrim 2021; Root 1996.
70. McKay 2021; Robertson 2013.
71. Liebler 2001.
72. Khanna and Johnson 2010; Touré 2011.
73. Song and Liebler 2022.
74. Aspinall and Song 2013; Rockquemore and Brunsma 2002.
75. Waters 1990.
76. Alba 1988.
77. Song 2003.
78. Thornton 1992.

## Chapter 4: Choosing a Spouse: The Implications of Racial Overlap

1. Miyawaki 2015.
2. Song 2015.
3. Spousal race similarity may be more pronounced if one spouse fills out the form for the family and reports for both spouses similarly. It could also result from the conscious or unconscious identity-related choices of the individuals or the couple.
4. Vasquez-Tokos 2017, 402; Vasquez 2014.
5. Song 2017b.
6. Luke and Luke 1998.

7. See the 2025 volume by Shivon Raghunandan, Roy Moodley, and Kelley Kenney, which addresses many factors shaping spousal choices.
8. Kao et al. 2019.
9. The partner may have reported one of these races, however, in combination with an additional race (for example, Asian-White). Most of the spouses in Hawaii and San Francisco (RESCI 5) who had no racial overlap with their partner reported Asian and/or Pacific Islander race.
10. Vasquez-Tokos 2017; see also Chong 2020 on Asian American marriages.
11. Chong and Song 2022; Song and Liebler 2022.
12. Chong 2013.
13. Chong 2020.
14. Tuan 1998.
15. Chong 2020; Kibria 2002; Livingston and Brown 2017.
16. Espiritu 1992; Okamoto 2014.
17. Campbell 2007.
18. O'Connell et al. 2022.
19. Tharps 2016.
20. Waring 2022.
21. Lacy 2007.
22. See Alba 2020; Strmc-Pawl 2016.
23. This statement pertains only to the groups studied in this research; other mixed-heritage groups may show a different pattern.
24. Song and Gutierrez 2015; Song 2017b.
25. Song 2015.

## Chapter 5: How Do Mixed-Heritage People Identify and Raise Their Children?

1. Bratter 2007; Brunsma 2005; Kana'iaupuni and Liebler 2005; Liebler 2004, 2010; Qian 2004; Saenz et al. 1995; Tafoya et al. 2004; Xie and Goyette 1997.
2. Campbell and Eggerling-Boeck 2006; Harris and Sim 2002.
3. Alba 2020; Lee and Bean 2007.
4. Song 2017b.
5. Bratter 2007.
6. Bratter 2010, 192.
7. Bratter 2010, 192.
8. See Song 2017b.
9. Song 2017b; Song and Gutierrez 2015.
10. While a significant proportion of participants across all three mixed-heritage groups had grown up in a household with a limited or even low income, many of these participants were now highly educated and comfortably middle-class and thus had certain options that their own parents had not enjoyed.
11. Le Gall and Meintel 2015; see also Caballero et al. 2008; Song 2017b.
12. Song and Liebler 2022.

13. Note that the Census Bureau provides only the first two ancestry responses in the data, but our participants usually wrote more than two for themselves and their children.
14. Bratter 2007.
15. See Fhagen-Smith 2010.
16. For a discussion, see Song 2017b.
17. On "thick" ties, see Cornell and Hartmann 2007; on "symbolic" ties, see Gans 1979.
18. Jiménez 2010.
19. Chong 2020.
20. Ifekwunigwe 1998; Song 2017b; Tharps 2016.
21. Bratter 2007.
22. Chong 2020; Kim 2008.
23. Campbell and Eggerling-Boeck 2006.
24. Bratter 2007.
25. See Bratter 2007; Khanna 2010; Roth 2005.
26. See Caballero et al. 2008; Song 2017b.
27. See also Song 2017b.
28. Song 2017b.
29. However, see Caballero et al. 2008; Song 2017b.
30. Bratter 2007.
31. Alba et al. 2017, 14–15.

## Chapter 6: Conclusions

1. We would like to thank one of the reviewers for this extremely insightful observation.
2. See Davenport 2018.
3. Roth and Ivemark 2018; Waters 1990.
4. See Parker et al. 2015.
5. See, for example, Liebler et al. 2017.
6. Alba 2020; Kaufmann 2018.
7. Alba 2020, 146.
8. Strmc-Pawl 2016.
9. Mok 2019.
10. Song 2017b.
11. Davenport 2018; see also Pilgrim 2021.
12. See Iverson et al. 2022.
13. Chong and Song 2022; Song 2019.
14. Jiménez 2010; Vasquez-Tokos 2017.
15. Park 1928; Stonequist 1935.
16. Alba 2020.
17. Jones et al. 2021.
18. Aspinall and Song 2013; DaCosta 2020; Parker and Song 2001; Root 1996.

19. DaCosta 2020, 340–41.
20. Morning and Saperstein 2018; Pilgrim 2021; Song 2021; Xu et al. 2021.
21. See also Iverson et al. 2022; Masuoka 2017; Song 2021.
22. Childs 2014; DaCosta 2020; Waring 2022; see also Song 2009.
23. Hernández 2018; Rich 2014.
24. Alba 2020.
25. Davenport 2018.
26. Campbell and Herman 2010; Davenport 2018; Hernández 2018.
27. Campbell and Herman 2010.
28. Rich 2014.
29. Johnston and Nadal 2010; Waring 2022.
30. Hernández 2018.
31. DaCosta 2020, 345–46; Hernández 2018.
32. See also Song 2021.
33. Song and Gutierrez 2015.
34. See Pilgrim 2021; Song 2017b, 2019.
35. See Roth 2018.
36. DaCosta 2020; Morning 2018.
37. Aspinall and Song 2013; Campion 2019; Liebler et al. 2017; Mahtani and Moreno 2001.
38. Fhagen-Smith 2010
39. Gullickson 2019.
40. Liebler 2016.

## Appendix A: Census Bureau Questions on Race and Ancestry

1. Gauthier 2002.
2. Office of Management and Budget 1997, 2024.
3. Office of Management and Budget 1997.
4. Office of Management and Budget 2024.
5. Gullickson and Morning 2011.
6. Office of Management and Budget 1997.
7. For example, Gullickson and Morning 2011; Liebler 2016.

## Appendix E: RESCI

1. See, for example, Roth 2005; Xie and Goyette 1997.
2. Spilerman 1970, 1971.
3. Ruggles et al. 2022.
4. Ruggles et al. 2022.
5. Liebler 2010.
6. Crosswalks were sourced from https://usa.ipums.org/usa/volii/pumas10.shtml and from Jonathan Schroeder (of IPUMS) at the University of Minnesota.

# REFERENCES

Alba, Richard. 1988. *Ethnic Identity: The Transformation of White America*. Yale University Press.

Alba, Richard. 2020. *The Great Demographic Illusion: Majority, Minority, and the Expanding American Mainstream*. Princeton University Press.

Alba, Richard, Brenden Beck, and Duygu Basaran Sahin. 2017. "The US Mainstream Expands—Again." *Journal of Ethnic and Migration Studies* 44(1): 99–117.

Alba, Richard, and Victor Nee. 2003. *Remaking the American Mainstream: Assimilation and Contemporary Immigration*. Harvard University Press.

Alcoff, Linda. 2003. "Latino/as, Asian Americans, and the Black-White Binary." *Journal of Ethics* 7(1): 5–27.

Almaguer, Tomás. 2009. *Racial Fault Lines: The Historical Origins of White Supremacy in California*. University of California Press. (Originally published in 1994.)

Arias, Elizabeth, Carolyn A. Liebler, Marc A. Garcia, and Rogelio Sáenz. 2025. "Data Impacts of Changes in U.S. Census Bureau Procedures for Race and Ethnicity Data." *SSM - Population Health* 29:101742.

Aspinall, Peter J., and Miri Song. 2013. *Mixed Race Identities*. Palgrave Macmillan.

Bean, Frank D., and Gillian Stevens. 2003. *America's Newcomers and the Dynamics of Diversity*. Russell Sage Foundation.

Blau, Peter M., Terry C. Blum, and Joseph E. Schwartz. 1982. "Heterogeneity and Intermarriage." *American Sociological Review* 47(1): 45–62.

Bonam, Courtney M., and Margaret Shih. 2009. "Exploring Multiracial Individuals' Comfort with Intimate Interracial Relationships." *Journal of Social Issues* 65(1): 87–103.

Bonilla-Silva. Eduardo. 2001. *White Supremacy and Racism in the Post–Civil Rights Era*. Lynne Rienner.

Bonilla-Silva, Eduardo. 2004. "From Bi-Racial to Tri-Racial: Towards a New System of Racial Stratification in the USA." *Ethnic and Racial Studies* 27(6): 931–50.

Bonilla-Silva, Eduardo. 2017. *Racism Without Racists: Color-Blind Racism and the Persistence of Racial Inequality in America*, 5th ed. Rowman and Littlefield.

Bratter, Jenifer. 2007. "Will 'Multiracial' Survive to the Next Generation? The Racial Classification of Children of Multiracial Parents." *Social Forces* 86(2): 821–49.

Bratter, Jenifer. 2010. "The 'One Drop' Rule Through a Multiracial Lens." In *Multiracial Americans and Social Class*, edited by Kathleen Odell Korgen. Routledge.

Bratter, Jenifer L., and Heather A. O'Connell. 2017. "Multiracial Identities, Single Race History: Contemporary Consequences of Historical Race and Marriage Laws for Racial Classification." *Social Science Research* 68: 102–16.

Bross, Kristina. 2001. "Dying Saints, Vanishing Savages: 'Dying Indian Speeches' in Colonial New England Literature." *Early American Literature* 36(3): 325–52.

Brubaker, Rogers. 2016. "The Dolezal Affair: Race, Gender, and the Micropolitics of Identity." *Ethnic and Racial Studies* 39(3): 414–48.

Brunsma, David. 2005. "Interracial Families and the Racial Identification of Mixed-Race Children: Evidence from the Early Child Longitudinal Study." *Social Forces* 84(2): 1131–57.

Budiman, Abby, and Neil G. Ruiz. 2021. "Key Facts About Asian Americans: A Diverse and Growing Population." Pew Research Center, April 29.

Buggs, Shantel. 2017. "Does (Mixed-) Race Matter? The Role of Race in Interracial Sex, Dating, and Marriage." *Sociology Compass* 11(11); e12531.

Burke, Ruth, and Grace Kao. 2010. "Stability and Change in the Racial Identities of Multiracial Adolescents." In *Multiracial Americans and Social Class: The Influence of Social Class on Racial Identity*, edited by Kathleen Odell Korgen. Routledge.

Caballero, Chamion, Rosalind Edwards, and Darren Smith. 2008. "Cultures of Mixing: Understanding Partnerships Across Ethnicity." *Twenty-First Century Society: Journal of the Academy of Social Sciences* 3(1): 49–63.

Campbell, Mary E. 2007. "Thinking Outside the (Black) Box: Measuring Black and Multiracial Identification on Surveys." *Social Science Research* 36(3): 921–44.

Campbell, Mary E., and Jennifer Eggerling-Boeck. 2006. "'What About the Children?' The Psychological and Social Well-Being of Multiracial Adolescents." *Sociological Quarterly* 47(1):147–73.

Campbell, Mary E., and Melissa R. Herman. 2010. "Politics and Policies: Attitudes Toward Multiracial Americans." *Ethnic and Racial Studies* 33(9): 1511–36.

Campbell, Mary E., and Lisa Troyer. 2007. "The Implications of Racial Misclassification by Observers." *American Sociological Review* 72(5): 750–65.

Campion, Karis. 2019. "'You Think You're Black?' Exploring Black Mixed-Race Experiences of Black Rejection." *Ethnic and Racial Studies* 42(16): 196–213.

Chang, Sharon. 2016. *Multiracial Asian Children in a Post-Racial World*. Routledge.

Childs, Erica Chito. 2005. *Navigating Interracial Borders: Black-White Couples and Their Social Worlds*. Rutgers University Press.

Childs, Erica Chito. 2014. "A Global Look at Mixing: Problems, Pitfalls, and Possibilities." *Journal of Intercultural Studies* 35(6): 677–88.

Chong, Kelly. 2013. "The Relevance of Race: Children and Shifting Racial/Ethnic Consciousness Among Interracially Married Asian Americans." *Journal for Asian American Studies* 16(2): 189–221.

Chong, Kelly. 2020. *Love Across Borders: Asian Americans, Race, and the Politics of Intermarriage and Family-Making.* Routledge.

Chong, Kelly and Miri Song. 2022. "Interrogating the 'White-Leaning' Thesis of White-Asian Multiracials." *Social Sciences* 11(3): 1–17.

Chun, Asaph Y., and Jessica Gan. 2014. "Analysis of the Source of Group Quarters Enumeration Data in the 2010 Census." Paper presented at the Joint Statistical Meetings of the American Statistical Association, "Survey Research Methods" session. Boston, August 2–7.

Collet, Beat. 2015. "From Intermarriage to Conjugal Mixedness." *Annals of the American Academy of Political and Social Sciences* 62(1): 129–47.

Cooley, Erin, Jazmin L. Brown-Iannuzzi, Darren Agboh, Brian Enjaian, Rachel Geyer, Nicole Lue, and Stephanie Wu. 2018. "The Fluid Perception of Racial Identity: The Role of Friendship Groups." *Social Psychological and Personality Science* 9(1): 32–39.

Cornell, Stephen, and Douglas Hartmann. 2007. *Ethnicity and Race: Making Identities in a Changing World*, 2nd ed. SAGE Publications.

DaCosta, Kimberly McClain. 2007. *Making Multiracials: State, Family, and Market in the Redrawing of the Color Line.* Stanford University Press.

DaCosta, Kimberly A. 2020. "Multiracial Categorization, Identity, and Policy in (Mixed) Racial Formations." *Annual Review of Sociology* 46(July): 335–53.

Dalmage, Heather M. 2000. *Tripping on the Color Line: Black-White Multiracial Families in a Racially Divided World.* Rutgers University Press.

Davenport, Lauren. 2016. "The Role of Gender, Class, and Religion in Biracial Americans' Racial Labeling Decisions." *American Sociological Review* 81(1): 57–84.

Davenport, Lauren. 2018. *Politics Beyond Black and White.* Cambridge University Press.

Davis, F. James. 1991. *Who Is Black? One Nation's Definition.* Pennsylvania State University Press.

Deloria, Vine, Jr. 1969. *Custer Died for Your Sins: An Indian Manifesto.* Macmillan.

Dippie, Brian W. 1982. *The Vanishing American: White Attitudes and US Indian Policy.* Wesleyan University Press.

Dixon, Angela, and Edward Telles. 2017. "Skin Color and Colorism: Global Research, Concepts, and Measurement." *Annual Review of Sociology* 43(1): 405–24.

Doyle, Jamie Mihoko, and Grace Kao. 2007. "Are Racial Identities of Multiracials Stable? Changing Self-Identification Among Single and Multiple Race Individuals." *Social Psychology Quarterly* 70(4): 405–23.

Dyson, Michael Eric. 1994. "Essentialism and the Complexities of Racial Identity." In *Multiculturalism: A Critical Reader*, edited by David Theo Goldberg. Wiley-Blackwell.

Espiritu, Yen Le. 1992. *Asian American Panethnicity: Bridging Institutions and Identities.* Temple University Press.

Fhagen-Smith, Peony. 2010. "Social Class, Racial/Ethnic Identity, and the Psychology of 'Choice.'" In *Multiracial Americans and Social Class: The Influence of Social Class on Racial Identity*, edited by Kathleen Odell Korgen. Routledge.

Fulbeck, Kip. 2006. *Part Asian, 100% Hapa.* Raincoat Books.

Funderburg, Lise. 1994. *Black, White, Other: Biracial Americans Talk About Race and Identity.* William Morrow.

Gallagher, Charles A. 2004. "Racial Redistricting: Expanding the Boundaries of Whiteness." In *The Politics of Multiracialism: Challenging Racial Thinking,* edited by Heather Dalmage. State University of New York Press.

Gambol, Brenda. 2016. "Changing Racial Boundaries and Mixed Unions: The Case of Second-Generation Filipino Americans." *Ethnic and Racial Studies* 39(14): 2621–40.

Gans, Herbert. 1979. "Symbolic Ethnicity: The Future of Ethnic Groups and Cultures in America." *Ethnic and Racial Studies* 2(1): 1–20.

Gans, Herbert. 2012. "'Whitening' and the Changing American Racial Hierarchy." *Du Bois Review* 9(2): 267–79.

Garroutte, Eva Marie. 2001. "The Racial Formation of American Indians: Negotiating Legitimate Identities Within Tribal and Federal Law." *American Indian Quarterly* 25(2): 224–39.

Gauthier, Jason G. 2002. *Measuring America: The Decennial Censuses from 1790 to 2000.* US Census Bureau.

Goffman, Erving. 1963. *Stigma: Notes on the Management of Spoiled Identity.* Simon & Schuster.

Gonlin, Vanessa. 2022. "Mixed-Race Ancestry ≠ Multiracial Identification: The Role Racial Discrimination, Linked Fate, and Skin Tone Have on the Racial Identification of People with Mixed-Race Ancestry." *Social Sciences* 11(4): 160.

Gordon, Milton. 1964. *Assimilation in American Life: The Role of Race, Religion, and National Origins.* Oxford University Press.

Gullickson, Aaron. 2019. "The Racial Identification of Young Adults in a Racially Complex Society." *Emerging Adulthood* 7(2): 150–61.

Gullickson, Aaron, and Ann Morning. 2011. "Choosing Race: Multiracial Ancestry and Identification." *Social Science Research* 40(2): 498–512.

Hackstaff, Karla. 2010. "Family Genealogy: A Sociological Imagination Reveals Intersectional Relations." *Sociology Compass* 4(8): 658–72.

Han, Sungil, Jordan R. Riddell, and Alex R. Piquero. 2023. "Anti–Asian American Hate Crimes Spike During the Early Stages of the COVID-19 Pandemic." *Journal of Interpersonal Violence* 38(3/4): 3513–33.

Haney López, Ian. 2006. *White by Law: The Legal Construction of Race.* New York University Press.

Harris, David R., and Jeremiah Joseph Sim. 2002. "Who Is Multiracial? Assessing the Complexity of Lived Race." *American Sociological Review* 67(4): 614–27.

Heilman, Monica. 2022. "The Racial Elevator Speech: How Multiracial Individuals Respond to Racial Identity Inquiries." *Sociology of Race and Ethnicity* 8(3): 370–85.

Herman, Melissa. 2004. "Forced to Choose: Some Determinants of Racial Identification in Multiracial Adolescents." *Child Development* 75(3): 730–48.

Hernández, Tanya Katerí. 2018. *Multiracials and Civil Rights: Mixed-Race Stories of Discrimination*. New York University Press.

Holloway, Steven, Richard Wright, and Mark Ellis. 2012. "Constructing Multiraciality in US Families and Neighborhoods." In *International Perspectives on Racial and Ethnic Mixedness and Mixing*, edited by Rosalind Edwards, Suki Ali, Chamion Caballero, and Miri Song. Routledge.

Hout, Michael, and Joshua Goldstein. 1994. "How 4.5 Million Irish Immigrants Became 40 Million Irish Americans: Demographic and Subjective Aspects of the Ethnic Composition of White Americans." *American Sociological Review* 59(1): 64–82.

Hunter, Margaret. 2007. "The Persistent Problem of Colorism." *Sociology Compass* 1(1): 237–54.

Ifekwunigwe, Jayne O. 1998. *Scattered Belongings: Cultural Paradoxes of Race, Nation, and Gender*. Routledge.

Ifekwunigwe, Jayne, ed. 2004. *"Mixed Race" Studies: A Reader*. Routledge.

Irastorza, Nahikari. 2016. "Sustainable Marriages? Divorce Patterns of Binational Couples in Europe Versus North America." *Ethnicities* 16(4): 649–83.

Iverson, Sarah, Ann Morning, Aliya Saperstein, and Janet Xu. 2022. "Regimes Beyond the One-Drop Rule: New Models of Multiracial Identity." *Genealogy* 6(2): 57.

Jacobs, Michelle R. 2015. "Urban American Indian Identity: Negotiating Indianness in Northeast Ohio." *Qualitative Sociology* 38(1): 79–98.

Jiménez, Tomàs. 2010. "Affiliative Ethnic Identity: A More Elastic Link Between Ethnic Ancestry and Culture." *Ethnic and Racial Studies* 33(10): 1756–75.

Johnston, Marc, and Kevin Nadal. 2010. "Multiracial Microaggressions: Exposing Monoracism in Everyday Life and Clinical Practice." *Microaggressions and Marginality: Manifestation, Dynamics and Impact*, edited by Derald Wing Sue. Wiley & Sons.

Jones, Nicholas A., and Jungmiwha J. Bullock. 2012. "The Two or More Races Population: 2010." *2010 Census Briefs* C2010BR-13. US Census Bureau, September.

Jones, Nicholas, Rachel Marks, Roberto Ramirez, and Merarys Ríos-Vargas. 2021. "2020 Census Illuminates Racial and Ethnic Composition of the Country." *Census Library Stories*. US Census Bureau, August 12.

Joseph-Salisbury, Remi. 2019. "Wrangling with the Black Monster: Young Black Mixed Race Men and Masculinities." *British Journal of Sociology* 70(5): 1754–73.

Jung, Moon-Kie. 2015. *Beneath the Surface of White Supremacy: Denaturalizing US Racisms Past and Present*. Stanford University Press.

Kalmijn, Matthijs. 1998. "Intermarriage and Homogamy: Causes, Patterns, Trends." *Annual Review of Sociology* 24(August): 395–421.

Kana'iaupuni, Shawn Malia, and Carolyn A. Liebler. 2005. "Pondering Poi Dog: Place and Racial Identification of Multiracial Native Hawaiians." *Ethnic and Racial Studies* 28(4): 687–721.

Kao, Grace, Kara Joyner, and Kelly Balistreri. 2019. *Interracial Friendships and Romantic Relationships from Adolescence to Adulthood.* Russell Sage Foundation.

Kauffman, Eric. 2018. *Whiteshift: Populism, Immigration, and the Future of White Majorities.* Penguin.

Khanna, Nikki. 2004. "The Role of Reflected Appraisals in Racial Identity: The Case of Multiracial Asians." *Social Psychology Quarterly* 67(2): 115–31.

Khanna, Nikki. 2010. "'If You're Half Black, You're Just Black': Reflected Appraisals and the Persistence of the One-Drop Rule." *Sociological Quarterly* 51(1): 96–121.

Khanna, Nikki. 2011. "Ethnicity and Race as 'Symbolic': The Use of Ethnic and Racial Symbols in Asserting a Biracial Identity." *Ethnic and Racial Studies* 34(6): 1049–67.

Khanna, Nikki, and Cathryn Johnson. 2010. "Passing as Black: Racial Identity Work Among Biracial Americans." *Social Psychology Quarterly* 73(4): 380–97.

Kibria, Nazli. 2002. *Becoming Asian American: Second-Generation Chinese and Korean American Identities.* Johns Hopkins University Press.

Kim, Claire Jean. 1999. "The Racial Triangulation of Asian Americans." *Politics and Society* 27(1): 105–38.

Kim, Nadia. 2008. *Imperial Citizens: Koreans and Race from Seoul to LA.* Stanford University Press.

King-O'Riain, Rebecca Chiyoko. 2004. "Model Majority? The Struggle for Identity Among Multiracial Japanese Americans." In *The Politics of Multiracialism: Challenging Racial Thinking*, edited by Heather Dalmage. State University of New York Press.

King-O'Riain, Rebecca Chiyoko. 2006. *Pure Beauty: Judging Race in Japanese American Beauty Pageants.* University of Minnesota Press.

King-O'Riain, Rebecca C., Stephen Small, Minelle Mahtani, Miri Song, and Paul Spickard, eds. 2014. *Global Mixed Race.* New York University Press.

Korgen, Kathleen Odell. 1998. *From Black to Biracial: Transforming Racial Identity Among Americans.* Praeger.

Krogstad, Jens Manuel. 2015. "Hawaii Is Home to the Nation's Largest Share of Multiracial Americans." Pew Research Center, June 17.

Lacy, Karyn. 2007. *Blue-Chip Black: Race, Class, and Status in the New Black Middle Class.* University of California Press.

Lee, Jennifer, and Frank D. Bean. 2004. "America's Changing Color Lines: Immigration, Race/Ethnicity, and Multiracial Identification." *Annual Review of Sociology* 30(August): 221–42.

Lee, Jennifer, and Frank D. Bean. 2007. "Reinventing the Color Line: Immigration and America's New Racial/Ethnic Divide." *Social Forces* 86(2): 561–86.

Lee, Jennifer, and Frank D. Bean. 2010. *The Diversity Paradox: Immigration and the Color Line in 21st Century America.* Russell Sage Foundation.

Lee, Jennifer, and Karthick Ramakrishnan. 2020. "Who Counts as Asian?" *Ethnic and Racial Studies* 43(10): 1733–56.

Le Gall, Josiane, and Deirdre Meintel. 2015. "Cultural and Identity Transmission in Mixed Couples in Quebec, Canada: Normalizing Plural Identities as a Path to Social Integration." *Annals of the American Academy of Political and Social Science* 662(1): 112–28.

Lewis, Amanda. 2003. *Race in the Schoolyard*. Rutgers University Press.

Li, Yao, and Harvey Nicholson. 2021. "When 'Model Minorities' Become 'Yellow Peril': Othering and the Racialization of Asian Americans in the COVID-19 Pandemic." *Sociology Compass* 15(2): 1–13.

Lichter, Daniel, and Zhenchao Qian. 2018. "Boundary Blurring? Racial Identification Among the Children of Interracial Couples." *Annals of the American Academy of Political and Social Science* 677(1): 81–94.

Lichter, Daniel, Zhenchao Qian, and Dmitry Tumen. 2015. "Whom Do Immigrants Marry? Emerging Patterns of Intermarriage and Integration in the United States." *Annals of the American Academy of Political and Social Sciences* 662(1). https://doi.org/10.1177/0002716215594614.

Liebler, Carolyn A. 2001. "Fringes of American Indian Identity." PhD diss., University of Wisconsin–Madison, Department of Sociology.

Liebler, Carolyn A. 2004. "Ties on the Fringes of Identity." *Social Science Research* 33(4): 702–23.

Liebler, Carolyn A. 2010. "Homelands and Indigenous Identities in a Multiracial Era." *Social Science Research* 39: 596–609.

Liebler, Carolyn A. 2016. "On the Boundaries of Race: Identification of Mixed-Heritage Children in the US, 1960 to 2010." *Sociology of Race and Ethnicity* 2(4): 548–68.

Liebler, Carolyn A. and Feng Hou. 2020. "Churning Races in Canada: Visible Minority Response Change Between 2006 and 2011." *Social Science Research* 86(February): 102388.

Liebler, Carolyn A., Renuka Bhaskar, and Sonya R. Porter. 2016. "Joining, Leaving, and Staying in the American Indian/Alaska Native Race Category Between 2000 and 2010." *Demography* 53(2): 507–40.

Liebler, Carolyn A., Sonya R. Porter, Leticia E. Fernández, James M. Noon, and Sharon R. Ennis. 2017. "America's Churning Races: Race and Ethnic Response Changes Between Census 2000 and the 2010 Census." *Demography* 54(1): 259–84.

Liebler, Carolyn A., and Meghan Zacher. 2016. "History, Place, and Racial Self-Representation in 21st Century America." *Social Science Research* 57(May): 211–32.

Light, Michael T., and John Iceland. 2016. "The Social Context of Racial Boundary Negotiations: Segregation, Hate Crime, and Hispanic Racial Identification in Metropolitan America." *Sociological Science* 3(4): 61–84.

Livingston, Gretchen, and Anna Brown. 2017. "Intermarriage in the US 50 Years After Loving v. Virginia." Pew Research Center, May 18.

Lopez, Alejandra. 2003. "Collecting and Tabulating Race/Ethnicity Data with Diverse and Mixed Heritage Populations." *Ethnic and Racial Studies* 26(5): 931–61.

Luke, Carmen, and Allan Luke. 1998. "Interracial Families: Difference Within Difference." *Ethnic and Racial Studies* 21(4): 728–54.

Mahtani, Minelle, Dani Kwan-Lafond, Leanne Taylor. 2014. "Exporting the Mixed-Race Nation: Mixed-Race Identities in the Canadian Context." In *Global Mixed Race*, edited by Rebecca King-O'Riain, Stephen Small, Minelle Mahtani, Miri Song, and Paul Spickard. New York University Press.

Mahtani, Minelle, and April Moreno. 2001. "Same Difference: Towards a More Unified Discourse in 'Mixed Race' Theory." In *Rethinking "Mixed Race*," edited by David Parker and Miri Song. Pluto.

Malik, Kenan. 2021. "Myths of Asian Privilege Fuel a Brutal and Cartoonish Bigotry." *The Guardian*, March 21.

Marks, Rachel, and Merarys Ríos-Vargas. 2021. "Improvements to the 2020 Census Race and Latino Origin Question Designs, Data Processing, and Coding Procedures." US Census Bureau, August 3.

Massey, Douglas S., and Nancy A. Denton. 1993. *American Apartheid: Segregation and the Making of the Underclass*. Harvard University Press.

Masuoka, Natalie. 2008. "Political Attitudes and Ideologies of Multiracial Americans." *Political Research Quarterly* 61(2): 253–67.

Masuoka, Natalie. 2011. "The 'Multiracial' Option: Social Group Identity and Changing Patterns of Racial Categorization." *American Politics Research* 39(1): 176–204.

Masuoka, Natalie. 2017. *Multiracial Identity and Racial Politics in the United States*. Oxford University Press.

McKay, Dwanna L. 2021. "Real Indians: Policing or Protecting Authentic Indigenous Identity?" *Sociology of Race and Ethnicity* 7(1): 12–25.

Mengel, Laurie. 2001. "Triples—The Social Evolution of a Multiracial Panethnicity." In *Rethinking "Mixed Race*," edited by David Parker and Miri Song. Pluto Press.

Miyawaki, Michael. 2015. "Expanding Boundaries of Whiteness? A Look at the Marital Patterns of Part-White Multiracial Groups." *Sociological Forum* 30(4): 995–1016.

Mok, Tze Ming. 2019. "Inside the Box: Ethnic Choice and Ethnic Change for Mixed People in the United Kingdom." PhD diss., London School of Economics, Department of Social Policy.

Montgomery, Michelle. 2017. *Identity Politics of Difference: The Mixed-Race American Indian Experience*. University Press of Colorado.

Morning, Ann. 2000. "Who Is Multiracial? Definitions and Decisions." *Sociological Imagination* 37(4): 209–29.

Morning, Ann. 2018. "Kaleidoscope: Contested Identities and New Forms of Race Membership." *Ethnic and Racial Studies* 41(6): 1055–73.

Morning, Ann, and Aliya Saperstein. 2018. "The Generational Locus of Multiraciality and Its Implications for Racial Self-Identification." *Annals of the American Academy of Political and Social Science* 677(1): 57–68.

Murji, Karim, and John Solomos, eds. 2005. *Racialisation: Studies in Theory and Practice*. Oxford University Press.

Murphy-Shigematsu, Stephen. 2012. *When Half Is Whole: Multiethnic Asian American Identities*. Stanford University Press.

Nagel, Joane. 1995. "American Indian Ethnic Renewal: Politics and the Resurgence of Identity." *American Sociological Review* 60(6): 947–65.

National Congress of American Indians. 2020. "Tribal Nations and the United States: An Introduction." January 15.

Norris, Tina, Paula L. Vines, and Elizabeth M. Hoeffel. 2012. "The American Indian and Alaska Native Population: 2010." Census Brief C2010BR-10. US Census Bureau, January.

O'Connell, Heather A., Jenifer L. Bratter, and Raul S. Casarez. 2022. "One Drop on the Move: Historical Legal Context, Racial Classification, and Migration." *Ethnic and Racial Studies* 45(5): 809–28.

Office of Management and Budget (OMB). 1997. "Revisions to the Standards for the Classification of Federal Data on Race and Ethnicity." *Federal Register* 52(210): 58782–90.

Office of Management and Budget (OMB). 2024. "Revisions to OMB's Statistical Policy Directive No. 15: Standards for Maintaining, Collecting, and Presenting Federal Data on Race and Ethnicity." *Federal Register* 89(62): 22182–96.

Ogbu, John U. 1990. "Minority Status and Literacy in Comparative Perspective." *Daedalus* 119(2): 141–68.

Oh, David, and Shinsuke Eguchi. 2022. "Racial Privilege as a Function of White Supremacy and Contextual Advantages for Asian Americans." *Communication, Culture, and Critique* 15(4): 471–78.

Okamoto, Dina G. 2014. *Redefining Race: Asian American Panethnicity and Shifting Ethnic Boundaries.* Russell Sage Foundation.

Okihiro, Gary. 1994. *Margins and Mainstreams: Asians in American History and Culture.* University of Washington Press.

Omi, Michael, and Howard Winant. 1994. *Racial Formation in the United States.* Routledge.

Osanami-Törngren, Sayaka, Nahikari Irastorza, and Miri Song. 2016. "Toward Building a Conceptual Framework on Intermarriage." *Ethnicities* 16(4). https://doi.org/10.1177/1468796816638402.

Osanami-Törngren, Sayaka, and Yuna Sato. 2021. "Beyond Being Either-Or: Identification of Multiracial and Multiethnic Japanese." *Journal of Ethnic and Migration Studies* 47(4): 802–20.

Osuji, Chinyere. 2019. *Boundaries of Love: Interracial Marriage and the Meaning of Race.* New York University Press.

Paragg, Jillian. 2017. "'What Are You?' Mixed Race Responses to the Racial Gaze." *Ethnicities* 17(3): 277–98.

Park, Robert. 1928. "Human Migration and the Marginal Man." *American Journal of Sociology* 33(6): 881–93.

Parker, David, and Miri Song, eds. 2001. *Rethinking "Mixed Race."* London: Pluto Press.

Parker, Kim, Juliana Menasce Horowitz, Rich Morin, and Mark Hugo Lopez. 2015. *Multiracial in America: Proud, Diverse, and Growing in Numbers.* Pew Research Center, June 11. https://www.pewresearch.org/social-trends/2015/06/11/multiracial-in-america.

Patterson, Orlando. 1982. *Slavery and Social Death: A Comparative Study.* Harvard University Press.

Phillips, Elizabeth M., Adebola O. Odunlami, and Vence L. Bonham. 2007. "Mixed Race: Understanding Difference in the Genome Era." *Social Forces* 86(2): 795–820.

Phinney, Jean, and Anthony Ong. 2007. "Conceptualization and Measurement of Ethnic Identity: Current Status and Future Directions." *Journal of Counseling Psychology* 54(3): 271–81. https://doi.org/10.1037/0022-0167.54.3.271.

Pilgrim, Haley. 2021. "'I Wish I Didn't Look So White': Examining Contested Racial Identities in Second-Generation Black-White Multiracials." *Ethnic and Racial Studies* 44(14): 2551–73.

Porter, Sonya R., Carolyn A. Liebler, and James M. Noon. 2016. "An Outside View: What Observers Say About Others' Races and Latino Origins." *American Behavioral Scientist* 60(4): 465–97.

Portes, Alejandro, and Min Zhou. 1993. "The New Second Generation: Segmented Assimilation and Its Variants." *Annals of the American Academy of Political and Social Science* 530(1): 74–96.

Pratt, Richard Henry. 1892. "The Advantages of Mingling Indians with Whites." National Conference of Charities and Correction, Denver, Colorado. June.

Qian, Zhenchao. 2004. "Options: Racial/Ethnic Identification of Children of Intermarried Couples." *Social Science Quarterly* 85(3): 746–66.

Qian, Zhenchao, and Daniel T. Lichter. 2007. "Social Boundaries and Marital Assimilation: Interpreting Trends in Racial and Ethnic Intermarriage." *American Sociological Review* 72(1): 68–94.

Qian, Zhenchao, and Yifan Shen. 2020. "Context of Interracial Childbearing in the United States." In *Analyzing Contemporary Fertility*, edited by Robert Schoen. Springer.

Raghunandan, Shivon, Roy Moodley, and Kelley Kenney, eds. 2025. *The Routledge International Handbook of Interracial and Intercultural Relationships and Mental Health.* Routledge.

Renn, Kristen A. 2000. "Patterns of Situational Identity Among Biracial and Multiracial College Students." *Review of Higher Education* 23(4): 399–420.

Rich, Camille Gear. 2014. "Elective Race: Identifying Race Discrimination in the Era of Racial Self-Definition." *Georgetown Law Journal* 102(5): 1501–72.

Robertson, Dwanna. 2013. "A Necessary Evil: Framing an American Indian Legal Identity." *American Indian Culture and Research Journal* 37(4): 115–40.

Rockquemore, Kerry Ann, and Patricia Arend. 2002. "Opting for White: Fluidity and Racial Identity Construction in Post–Civil Rights America." *Race and Society* 5(1): 49–64.

Rockquemore, Kerry Ann, and David Brunsma. 2002. *Beyond Black: Biracial Identity in America.* SAGE Publications.

Rockquemore, Kerry Ann, and Tracey Laszloffy. 2005. *Raising Biracial Children.* AltaMira Press.

Rodríguez-García, Dan, Miranda J. Lubbers, Miguel Solana, and Verónica de Miguel-Luken. 2015. "Contesting the Nexus Between Intermarriage and

Integration: Findings from a Multidimensional Study in Spain." *ANNALS of the American Academy of Political and Social Science* 662(1): 223–45.

Rondilla, Joanne, and Paul Spickard. 2007. *Is Lighter Better? Skin-Tone Discrimination Among Asian Americans.* Rowman and Littlefield.

Root, Maria P. P., ed. 1992. *Racially Mixed People in America.* SAGE Publications.

Root, Maria P. P., ed. 1996. *The Multiracial Experience: Racial Borders as the New Frontier.* SAGE Publications.

Roth, Wendy. 2005. "The End of the One-Drop Rule? Labeling of Multiracial Children in Black Intermarriages." *Sociological Forum* 20(1): 35–67.

Roth, Wendy. 2016. "The Multiple Dimensions of Race." *Ethnic and Racial Studies* 39(8): 1310–38.

Roth, Wendy. 2018. "Unsettled Identities Amidst Settled Classifications?" *Ethnic and Racial Studies* 41(6): 1093–1112.

Roth, Wendy, and Biorn Ivemark. 2018. "Genetic Options: The Impact of Genetic Ancestry Testing on Consumers' Racial and Ethnic Identities." *American Journal of Sociology* 124(1): 150–84.

Ruggles, Steven, Sarah Flood, Ronald Goeken, Josiah Grover, Erin Meyer, Jose Pacas, and Matthew Sobek. 2019. Integrated Public Use Microdata Series: Version 9.0 [dataset]. IPUMS, University of Minnesota.

Ruggles, Steven, Sarah Flood, Ronald Goeken, Megan Schouweiler, and Matthew Sobek. 2022. Integrated Public Use Microdata Series: Version 12.0 [dataset]. IPUMS, University of Minnesota.

Saenz, Rogelio, Sean-Shong Hwang, Benigno E. Aguirre, and Robert N. Anderson. 1995. "Persistence and Change in Asian Identity Among Children of Intermarried Couples." *Sociological Perspectives* 38(2): 175–94.

Seaton, Eleanor K., Stephen Quintana, Maykel Verkuyten, and Gilbert C. Gee. 2017. "Peers, Policies, and Place: The Relation Between Context and Ethnic/Racial Identity." *Child Development* 88(3): 683–92.

Sims, Jennifer. 2016. "Reevaluation of the Influence of Appearance and Reflected Appraisals for Mixed-Race Identity." *Sociology of Race and Ethnicity* 2(4): 569–83.

Sims, Jennifer, and Remi Joseph-Salisbury. 2019. "'We Were All Just the Black Kids': Black Mixed-Race Men and the Importance of Adolescent Peer Groups for Identity Development." *Social Currents* 6(1): 51–66.

Sims, Jennifer, and Chinelo Njaka. 2019. *Mixed-Race in the US and UK: Comparing the Past, Present, and Future.* Emerald.

Small, Stephen, and Rebecca King-O'Riain. 2014. "Global Mixed Race: An Introduction." In *Global Mixed Race*, edited by Rebecca King-O'Riain, Stephen Small, Minelle Mahtani, Miri Song, and Paul Spickard. New York University Press.

Snipp, C. Matthew. 1989. *American Indians: The First of This Land.* Russell Sage Foundation.

Snipp, C. Matthew. 1997. "Some Observations About Racial Boundaries and the Experiences of American Indians." *Ethnic and Racial Studies* 20(4): 668–89.

Solomos, John. 2022. *Race and Racism in Britain.* Springer Nature.

Song, Miri. 2003. *Choosing Ethnic Identity.* Polity Press.

Song, Miri. 2009. "Is Intermarriage a Good Indicator of Integration?" *Journal of Ethnic and Migration Studies* 35(2): 331–48.

Song, Miri. 2010. "Does 'Race' Matter? A Study of Mixed Race Siblings' Identifications." *Sociological Review* 58(2): 265–85.

Song, Miri. 2015. "What Constitutes Intermarriage for Multiracial People in Britain?" *Annals of the American Academy of Political and Social Sciences* 662(1): 94–111.

Song, Miri. 2016. "Multiracial People and Their Partners in Britain: Extending the Link Between Intermarriage and Integration?" *Ethnicities* 16(4): 631–48.

Song, Miri. 2017a. "Generational Change and How We Conceptualize and Measure Multiracial People and 'Mixture.'" *Ethnic and Racial Studies* 40(13): 2333–39.

Song, Miri. 2017b. *Multiracial Parents: Mixed Families, Generational Change, and the Future of Race.* New York University Press.

Song, Miri. 2019. "Is There Evidence of 'Whitening' for Asian/White Multiracial People in Britain?" *Journal of Ethnic and Migration Studies* 47(4): 934–50.

Song, Miri. 2020. "Rethinking Minority Status and 'Visibility.'" *Comparative Migration Studies* 8(5): 1–17.

Song, Miri. 2021. "Who Counts as Multiracial?" *Ethnic and Racial Studies* 44(8): 1296–1323.

Song, Miri, and Peter Aspinall. 2012. "Is Racial Mismatch a Problem for Young 'Mixed Race' People in Britain? The Findings of Qualitative Research." *Ethnicities* 12(6): 730–53.

Song, Miri, and Caitlin O. Gutierrez. 2015. "'Keeping the Story Alive': Is Ethnic and Racial Dilution Inevitable for Multiracial People and Their Children?" *Sociological Review* 63(3): 680–98.

Song, Miri, and Carolyn A. Liebler. 2022. "What Motivates Mixed Heritage People to Assert Their Ancestries?" *Genealogy* 6(3): 61.

Spencer, Rainier. 2006. "New Racial Identities, Old Arguments: Continuing Biological Reification." In *Mixed Messages: Multiracial Identities in the "Color-Blind" Era*, edited by David Brunsma. Lynne Rienner.

Spickard, Paul. 1989. *Mixed Blood: Ethnic Identity and Intermarriage in Twentieth-Century America.* University of Wisconsin Press.

Spickard, Paul. 2020. "Shape Shifting: Reflections on Racial Plasticity." In *Shape Shifters: Journeys Across Terrains of Race and Identity*, edited by Lily Anne Y. Welty, Ingrid Dineen-Wimberly, and Paul Spickard. University of Nebraska Press.

Spickard, Paul, and Rowena Fong. 1995. "Pacific Islander Americans and Multiethnicity." *Social Forces* 73(4): 1365–83.

Spilerman, Seymour. 1970. "The Causes of Racial Disturbances: A Comparison of Alternative Explanations." *American Sociological Review* 35: 627–49.

Spilerman, Seymour. 1971. "The Causes of Racial Disturbances: Tests of an Explanation." *American Sociological Review* 36: 427–42.

Starr, Paul, and Christina Pao. 2024. "The Multiracial Complication: The 2020 Census and the Fictitious Multiracial Boom." *Sociological Science* 11: 1107–23.

Steinberg, Stephen. 1981. *The Ethnic Myth: Race, Ethnicity, and Class in America.* Atheneum.

Stonequist, Everett. 1935. "The Problem of the Marginal Man." *American Journal of Sociology* 41(1): 1–12.

Strmc-Pawl, Hephzibah. 2016. *Multiracialism and Its Discontents: A Comparative Analysis of Asian-White and Black-White Multiracials.* Lexington Books.

Strmc-Pawl, Hephzibah, Erica Chito Childs, and Stephanie Laudone. 2022. "Asian-White Mixed Identity After COVID-19: Racist Racial Projects and the Effects on Asian Multiraciality." *Genealogy* 6(2): 53.

Sturm, Circe. 2011. *Becoming Indian: The Struggle over Cherokee Identity in the Twenty-First Century.* School for Advanced Research Press.

Tafoya, Sonya M., Hans Johnson, and Laura E. Hill. 2004. *Who Chooses to Choose Two?* Russell Sage Foundation and Population Reference Bureau.

Takaki, Ronald. 1989. *Strangers from a Different Shore: A History of Asian Americans.* Little, Brown.

Tashiro, Cathy. 2002. "Considering the Significance of Ancestry Through the Prism of Mixed-Race Identity." *Advances in Nursing Science* 25(2): 1–21.

Tashiro, Cathy J. 2011. *Standing on Both Feet: Voices of Older Mixed Race Americans.* Paradigm Publishers.

Tharps, Lori L. 2016. *Same Family, Different Colors: Confronting Colorism in America's Diverse Families.* Beacon Press.

Thornton, Michael. 1992. "Is Multiracial Status Unique? The Personal and Social Experience." In *Racially Mixed People in America*, edited by Maria P. P. Root. SAGE Publications.

Tizard, Barbara, and Ann Phoenix. 1993. *Black, White or Mixed Race? Race and Racism in the Lives of Young People of Mixed Parentage.* Routledge.

Touré. 2011. *Who's Afraid of Post-Blackness? What It Means to Be Black Now.* Free Press.

Treitler, Vilna Bashi. 2013. *The Ethnic Project: Transforming Racial Fiction into Ethnic Factions.* Stanford University Press.

Tsuda, Takeyuki. 2014. "'I'm American, not Japanese!': The Struggle for Racial Citizenship Among Later-Generation Japanese Americans." *Ethnic and Racial Studies* 37(3): 405–24.

Tuan, Mia. 1998. *Forever Foreigners or Honorary Whites? The Asian Ethnic Experience Today.* Rutgers University Press.

Twine, France Winddance. 1996. "Brown Skinned White Girls: Class, Culture and the Construction of White Identity in Suburban Communities." *Gender, Place & Culture* 3(2): 205–24.

Twine, France Winance. 2010. *A White Side of Black Britain: The Concept of Racial Literacy.* Duke University Press.

Twine, France Windance, and Charles Gallagher. 2008. "The Future of Whiteness: A Map of the Third Wave." *Ethnic and Racial Studies* 31(1): 4–24.

US Census Bureau. n.d. Booklet containing 2019 American Community Survey Questionnaire. https://www2.census.gov/programs-surveys/acs/methodology/questionnaires/2019/quest19.pdf.

Vasquez, Jessica M. 2014. "The Whitening Hypothesis Challenged: Biculturalism in Latino and Non-Latino White Intermarriage." *Sociological Forum* 29(2): 386–407.

Vasquez-Tokos, Jessica. 2017. *Marriage Vows and Racial Choices.* Russell Sage Foundation.

Waring, Chandra. 2022. "Appearance, Parentage, and Paradox: The White Privilege of Bi/Multiracial Americans with White Ancestry." *Sociology of Race and Ethnicity* 9(1): 56–71.

Waters, Mary C. 1990. *Ethnic Options: Choosing Identities in America.* University of California Press.

Waters. Mary. 1999. *Black Identities: West Indian Immigrant Dreams and American Realities.* Harvard University Press.

Welch, Susan, Lee Sigelman, Timothy Bledsoe, and Michael Combs. 2001. *Race and Place: Race Relations in an American City.* Cambridge University Press.

Williams, Caroline Randall. 2020. "You Want a Confederate Monument? My Body is a Confederate Monument." *New York Times,* June 26.

Williams, Kim M. 2006. *Mark One or More: Civil Rights in Multiracial America.* University of Michigan Press.

Wu, Ellen. 2015. *The Color of Success: Asian Americans and the Origins of the Model Minority.* Princeton University Press.

Wu, Zheng, Christoph M. Schimmele, and Feng Hou. 2015. "Group Differences in Intermarriage with Whites Between Asians, Blacks, and Hispanics." *Journal of Social Issues* 71(4): 733–54.

Xie, Yu, and Kimberly Goyette. 1997. "The Racial Identification of Biracial Children with One Asian Parent: Evidence from the 1990 Census." *Social Forces* 76(2): 547–70.

Xu, Janet, Aliya Saperstein, Ann Morning, and Sarah Iverson. 2021. "Gender, Generation, and Multiracial Identification in the United States." *Demography* 58(5): 1603–30.

Yancey, George. 2003. *Who Is White? Latinos, Asians, and the New Black/Nonblack Divide.* Lynne Rienner.

Yancey, George. 2006. "Racial Justice in a Black/Nonblack Society." In *Mixed Messages: Multiracial Identities in the Color-Blind Era,* edited by David Brunsma. Lynne Rienner.

Zhou, Min. 1997. "Growing Up American: The Challenge Confronting Immigrant Children and Children of Immigrants." *Annual Review of Sociology* 23: 63–95.

Zhou, Min. 2004. "Are Asian Americans Becoming White?" *Contexts* 3(1): 29–37.

# INDEX

Tables and figures are listed in **boldface**.